D0640544

THE INTELLIGENT WEB

WITHDRAWN

the Intelligent Web

Web

Search, Smart Algorithms, and Big Data

GAUTAM SHROFF

OXFORD
UNIVERSITY PRESS

OXFORD
UNIVERSITY PRESS

Great Clarendon Street, Oxford, OX2 6DP,
United Kingdom

Oxford University Press is a department of the University of Oxford.
It furthers the University's objective of excellence in research, scholarship,
and education by publishing worldwide. Oxford is a registered trade mark of
Oxford University Press in the UK and in certain other countries

© Gautam Shroff 2013

The moral rights of the author have been asserted

First Edition published in 2013

Impression: 1

Published in the United States of America by Oxford University Press
198 Madison Avenue, New York, NY 10016, United States of America

British Library Cataloguing in Publication Data

Data available

Library of Congress Control Number: 2013938816

ISBN 978-0-19-964671-5

Printed in Italy by
L.E.G.O. S.p.A.-Lavis TN

To my late father,
who I suspect would have enjoyed this book the most

ACKNOWLEDGEMENTS

Many people have contributed to my thinking and encouraged me while writing this book. But there are a few to whom I owe special thanks. First, to V. S. Subrahamanian, for reviewing the chapters as they came along and supporting my endeavour with encouraging words. I am also especially grateful to Patrick Winston and Pentti Kanerva for sparing the time to speak with me and share their thoughts on the evolution and future of AI.

Equally important has been the support of my family. My wife Brinda, daughter Selena, and son Ahan—many thanks for tolerating my preoccupation on numerous weekends and evenings that kept me away from you. I must also thank my mother for enthusiastically reading many of the chapters, which gave me some confidence that they were accessible to someone not at all familiar with computing.

Last but not least I would like to thank my editor Latha Menon, for her careful and exhaustive reviews, and for shepherding this book through the publication process.

CONTENTS

LIST OF FIGURES

Prologue

POTENTIAL

I grew up reading and being deeply influenced by the popular science books of George Gamow on physics and mathematics. This book is my attempt at explaining a few important and exciting advances in computer science and artificial intelligence (AI) in a manner accessible to all. The incredible growth of the internet in recent years, along with the vast volumes of 'big data' it holds, has also resulted in a rather significant confluence of ideas from diverse fields of computing and AI. This new 'science of *web intelligence*', arising from the marriage of many AI techniques applied together on 'big data', is the stage on which I hope to entertain and elucidate, in the spirit of Gamow, and to the best of my abilities.

* * *

The computer science community around the world recently celebrated the centenary of the birth of the British scientist Alan Turing, widely regarded as the father of computer science. During his rather brief life Turing made fundamental contributions in mathematics as well as some in biology, alongside crucial practical feats such as breaking secret German codes during the Second World War.

Turing was the first to examine very closely the meaning of what it means to 'compute', and thereby lay the foundations of computer science. Additionally, he was also the first to ask whether the capacity of intelligent thought could, in principle, be achieved by a machine that 'computed'. Thus, he is also regarded as the father of the field of enquiry now known as 'artificial intelligence'.

In fact, Turing begins his classic 1950 article[1] with, 'I propose to consider the question, "Can machines think?" ' He then goes on to describe the famous 'Turing Test', which he referred to as the 'imitation game', as a way to think about the problem of machines thinking. According to the Turing Test, if a computer can converse with any of us humans in so convincing a manner as to fool us into believing that it, too, is a human, then we should consider that machine to be 'intelligent' and able to 'think'.

Recently, in February 2011, IBM's Watson computer managed to beat champion human players in the popular TV show *Jeopardy!*. Watson was able to answer fairly complex queries such as 'Which New Yorker who fought at the Battle of Gettysburg was once considered the inventor of baseball?'. Figuring out that the answer is actually Abner Doubleday, and not Alexander Cartwright who actually wrote the rules of the game, certainly requires non-trivial natural language processing as well as probabilistic reasoning; Watson got it right, as well as many similar fairly difficult questions.

During this widely viewed *Jeopardy!* contest, Watson's place on stage was occupied by a computer panel while the human participants were visible in flesh and blood. However, imagine if instead the human participants were also hidden behind similar panels, and communicated via the same mechanized voice as Watson. Would we be able to tell them apart from the machine? Has the Turing Test then been 'passed', at least in this particular case?

There are more recent examples of apparently 'successful' displays of artificial intelligence: in 2007 Takeo Kanade, the well-known Japanese expert in computer vision, spoke about his early research in face recognition, another task normally associated with humans and at best a few higher-animals: 'it was with pride that I tested the program on 1000 faces, a rare case at the time when testing with 10 images was considered a "large-scale experiment".'[2] Today, both Facebook and Google's Picasa regularly recognize faces from among the hundreds of millions contained amongst the billions of images uploaded by users around the world.

Language is another arena where similar progress is visible for all to see and experience. In 1965 a committee of the US National Academy of Sciences concluded its review of the progress in automated translation between human natural languages with, 'there is no immediate or predicable prospect of useful machine translation'.[2] Today, web users around the world use Google's translation technology on a daily basis; even if the results are far from perfect, they are certainly good enough to be very useful.

Progress in spoken language, i.e., the ability to recognize speech, is also not far behind: Apple's Siri feature on the iPhone 4S brings usable and fairly powerful speech recognition to millions of cellphone users worldwide.

As succinctly put by one of the stalwarts of AI, Patrick Winston: 'AI is becoming more important while it becomes more inconspicuous', as 'AI technologies are becoming an integral part of mainstream computing'.[3]

* * *

What, if anything, has changed in the past decade that might have contributed to such significant progress in many traditionally 'hard' problems of artificial intelligence, be they machine translation, face recognition, natural language understanding, or speech recognition, all of which have been the focus of researchers for decades?

As I would like to convince you during the remainder of this book, many of the recent successes in each of these arenas have come through the deployment of many known but disparate techniques working together, and most importantly their deployment at *scale*, on large volumes of 'big data'; all of which has been made possible, and indeed driven, by the internet and the world wide web. In other words, rather than 'traditional' artificial intelligence, the successes we are witnessing are better described as those of *'web intelligence'* arising from 'big data'. Let us first consider what makes big data so 'big', i.e., its *scale*.

* * *

The web is believed to have well over a trillion web pages, of which at least 50 billion have been catalogued and *indexed* by search engines such as Google, making them searchable by all of us. This massive web content spans well over 100 million domains (i.e., locations where we point our browsers, such as <http://www.wikipedia.org>). These are themselves growing at a rate of more than 20,000 net domain additions daily. Facebook and Twitter each have over 900 million users, who between them generate over 300 million posts a day (roughly 250 million tweets and over 60 million Facebook updates). Added to this are the over 10,000 credit-card payments made per *second*,[*] the well-over 30 billion point-of-sale transactions per year (via dial-up POS devices[†]), and finally the over 6 billion mobile phones, of which almost 1 billion are smartphones, many of which are GPS-enabled, and which access the internet for e-commerce, tweets, and post updates on Facebook.[‡] Finally, and last but not least, there are the images and videos on YouTube and other sites, which by themselves outstrip all these put together in terms of the sheer volume of data they represent.

This deluge of data, along with emerging techniques and technologies used to handle it, is commonly referred to today as 'big data'. Such big data is both valuable and challenging, because of its sheer volume. So much so that the volume of data being created in the current five years from 2010 to 2015 will far exceed all the data generated in human history (which was estimated to be under 300 exabytes as of 2007[§]). The web, where all this data is being produced and resides, consists of millions of servers, with data storage soon to be measured in zetabytes.[¶]

---

[*] <http://www.creditcards.com>.
[†] <http://www.gaoresearch.com/POS/pos.php>.
[‡] <http://mobithinking.com/mobile-marketing-tools/latest-mobile-stats>.
[§] <http://www.bbc.co.uk/news/technology-12419672>.
[¶] petabyte = 1,000 GB, exabyte = 1,000 petabytes, and a zetabyte = 1,000 petabytes.

On the other hand, let us consider the volume of data an average human being is exposed to in a lifetime. Our sense of vision provides the most voluminous input, perhaps the equivalent of half a million hours of video or so, assuming a fairly a long lifespan. In sharp contrast, YouTube alone witnesses 15 million hours of *fresh* video uploaded every year.

Clearly, the volume of data available to the millions of machines that power the web far exceeds that available to any human. Further, as we shall argue later on, the millions of servers that power the web at least match if not exceed the raw computing capacity of the 100 billion or so neurons in a single human brain. Moreover, each of these servers are certainly much much faster at computing than neurons, which by comparison are really quite slow.

Lastly, the advancement of computing technology remains relentless: the well-known Moore's Law documents the fact that computing power per dollar appears to double every 18 months; the lesser known but equally important Kryder's Law states that storage capacity per dollar is growing even faster. So, for the first time in history, we have available to us both the computing power as well as the raw data that matches and shall very soon far exceed that available to the average human.

Thus, we have the *potential* to address Turing's question 'Can machines think?', at least from the perspective of raw computational power and data of the same order as that available to the human brain. How far have we come, why, and where are we headed? One of the contributing factors might be that, only recently after many years, does 'artificial intelligence' appear to be regaining a semblance of its initial ambition and unity.

* * *

In the early days of artificial intelligence research following Turing's seminal article, the diverse capabilities that might be construed to comprise intelligent behaviour, such as vision, language, or logical reasoning, were often discussed, debated, and shared at common forums. The goals exposed by the now famous Dartmouth conference of 1956, considered to be a landmark event in the history of AI, exemplified both a unified approach to all problems related to machine intelligence as well as a marked overconfidence:

> We propose that a 2 month, 10 man study of artificial intelligence be carried out during the summer of 1956 at Dartmouth College in Hanover, New Hampshire. The study is to proceed on the basis of the conjecture that every aspect of learning or any other feature of intelligence can in principle be so precisely described that a machine can be made to simulate it. An attempt will be made to find how to make machines use language, form abstractions and concepts, solve kinds of problems now reserved for humans, and improve themselves. We think that a significant advance can be made in one or more of these problems if a carefully selected group of scientists work on it together for a summer.[4]

These were clearly heady times, and such gatherings continued for some years. Soon the realization began to dawn that the 'problem of AI' had been grossly underestimated. Many sub-fields began to develop, both in reaction to the growing number of researchers trying their hand at these difficult challenges, and because of conflicting goals. The original aim of actually answering the question posed by Turing was soon found to be too challenging a task to tackle all at once, or, for that matter, attempt at all. The proponents of 'strong AI', i.e., those who felt that true 'thinking machines' were actually possible, with their pursuit being a worthy goal, began to dwindle. Instead, the practical applications of AI techniques, first developed as possible answers to the strong-AI puzzle, began to lead the discourse, and it was this 'weak AI' that eventually came to dominate the field.

Simultaneously, the field split into many sub-fields: image processing, computer vision, natural language processing, speech recognition, machine learning, data mining, computational reasoning, planning, etc. Each became a large area of research in its own right. And rightly so, as the practical applications of specific techniques necessarily appeared to lie within disparate areas: recognizing faces versus translating between two languages; answering questions in natural language versus recognizing spoken words; discovering knowledge from volumes of documents versus logical reasoning; and the list goes on. Each of these were so clearly separate application domains that it made eminent sense to study them separately and solve such obviously different practical problems in purpose-specific ways.

Over the years the AI research community became increasingly fragmented. Along the way, as Pat Winston recalled, one would hear comments such as 'what are all these vision people doing here'[3] at a conference dedicated to say, 'reasoning'. No one would say, 'well, because we think with our eyes',[3] i.e., our perceptual systems are intimately involved in thought. And so fewer and fewer opportunities came along to discuss and debate the 'big picture'.

* * *

Then the web began to change everything. Suddenly, the practical problem faced by the web companies became larger and more holistic: initially there were the search engines such as Google, and later came the social-networking platforms such as Facebook. The problem, however, remained the same: how to make more money from advertising?

The answer turned out to be surprisingly similar to the Turing Test: Instead of merely fooling us into believing it was human, the 'machine', i.e., the millions of servers powering the web, needed to *learn* about each of us, individually, just as we all learn about each other in casual conversation. Why? Just so that better, i.e., more closely targeted, advertisements could be shown to us, thereby leading to better 'bang for the buck' of every advertising dollar. This then became the holy grail: not intelligence per se, just doing better and better at this 'reverse' Turing Test, where instead of us being observer and 'judge', it is the machines in the web that observe and seek to 'understand' us better for their own selfish needs, if only to 'judge' whether or not we are likely buyers of some of the goods they are paid to advertise. As we shall see soon, even these more pedestrian goals required weak-AI techniques that could mimic many of *capabilities* required for intelligent thought.

Of course, it is also important to realize that none of these efforts made any strong-AI claims. The manner in which seemingly intelligent capabilities are computationally realized in the web does not, for the most part, even attempt to mirror the mechanisms nature has evolved to bring intelligence to life in real brains. Even so, the results are quite surprising indeed, as we shall see throughout the remainder of this book.

At the same time, this new holy grail could not be grasped with disparate weak-AI techniques operating in isolation: our queries as we searched the web or conversed with our friends were *words*; our actions as we surfed and navigated the web were *clicks*. Naturally we wanted to *speak* to our phones rather than type, and the videos that we uploaded and shared so freely were, well, videos.

Harnessing the vast trails of data that we leave behind during our web existences was essential, which required expertise from different fields of AI, be they language processing, learning, reasoning, or vision, to come together and connect the dots so as to even come close to understanding *us*.

First and foremost the web gave us a different way to *look* for information, i.e., web search. At the same time, the web itself would *listen* in, and *learn*, not only about us, but also from our collective knowledge that we have so well digitized and made available to all. As our actions are observed, the web-intelligence programs charged with pinpointing advertisements for us would need to *connect* all the dots and *predict* exactly which ones we should be most interested in.

Strangely, but perhaps not surprisingly, the very synthesis of techniques that the web-intelligence programs needed in order to connect the dots in their practical enterprise of online advertising appears, in many respects, similar to how we ourselves integrate our different perceptual and cognitive abilities. We consciously *look* around us to gather information about our environment as well as *listen* to the ambient sea of information continuously bombarding us all. Miraculously, we *learn* from our experiences, and *reason* in order to *connect* the dots and make sense of the world. All this so as to *predict* what is most likely to happen next, be it in the next instant, or eventually in the course of our lives. Finally, we *correct* our actions so as to better achieve our goals.

* * *

I hope to show how the cumulative use of artificial intelligence techniques at web scale, on hundreds of thousands or even millions of computers, can result in behaviour that exhibits a very basic feature of human intelligence, i.e., to colloquially speaking 'put two and two together' or 'connect the dots'. It is this ability that allows us to make sense of the world around us, make intelligent guesses about what is most likely to happen in the future, and plan our own actions accordingly.

Applying web-scale computing power on the vast volume of 'big data' now available because of the internet, offers the *potential* to create far more intelligent systems than ever before: this defines the new science of *web intelligence*, and forms the subject of this book.

At the same time, this remains primarily a book about weak AI: however powerful this web-based synthesis of multiple AI techniques might appear to be, we do not tread too deeply in the philosophical waters of strong-AI, i.e., whether or not machines can ever be 'truly intelligent', whether consciousness, thought, self, or even 'soul' have reductionist roots, or not. We shall neither speculate much on these matters nor attempt to describe the diverse philosophical debates and arguments on this subject. For those interested in a comprehensive history of the confluence of philosophy, psychology, neurology, and artificial intelligence often referred to as 'cognitive science', Margaret

Boden's recent volume *Mind as Machine: A History of Cognitive Science*[5] is an excellent reference.

Equally important are Turing's own views as elaborately explained in his seminal paper[1] describing the 'Turing test'. Even as he clearly makes his own philosophical position clear, he prefaces his own beliefs and arguments for them by first clarifying that 'the original question, "Can machines think?" I believe to be too meaningless to deserve discussion'.[1] He then rephrases his 'imitation game', i.e., the Turing Test that we are all familiar with, by a *statistical* variant: 'in about fifty years' time it will be possible to program computers ... so well that an average interrogator will not have more than 70 per cent chance of making the right identification after five minutes of questioning'.[1] Most modern-day machine-learning researchers might find this formulation quite familiar indeed. Turing goes on to speculate that 'at the end of the century the use of words and general educated opinion will have altered so much that one will be able to speak of machines thinking without expecting to be contradicted'.[1] It is the premise of this book that such a time has perhaps arrived.

As to the 'machines' for whom it might be colloquially acceptable to use the word 'thinking', we look to the web-based engines developed for entirely commercial pecuniary purposes, be they search, advertising, or social networking. We explore how the computer programs underlying these engines sift through and make sense of the vast volumes of 'big data' that we continuously produce during our online lives—our collective 'data exhaust', so to speak.

In this book we shall quite often use Google as an example and examine its innards in greater detail than others. However, when we speak of Google we are also using it as a metaphor: other search engines, such as Yahoo! and Bing, or even the social networking world of Facebook and Twitter, all share many of the same processes and purposes.

The purpose of all these web-intelligence programs is simple: 'all the better to understand us', paraphrasing Red Riding Hood's wolf in grandmother's clothing. Nevertheless, as we delve deeper into what these vast syntheses of weak-AI techniques manage to achieve in practice, we do find ourselves wondering whether these web-intelligence systems might end up serving us a dinner far closer to strong AI than we have ever imagined for decades.

That hope is, at least, one of the reasons for this book.

* * *

In the chapters that follow we dissect the ability to connect the dots, be it in the context of web-intelligence programs trying to understand us, or our own ability to understand and make sense of the world. In doing so we shall find some surprising parallels, even though the two contexts and purposes are so very different. It is these connections that offer the potential for increasingly capable web-intelligence systems in the future, as well as possibly deeper understanding and appreciation of our own remarkable abilities.

Connecting the dots requires us to *look* at and experience the world around us; similarly, a web-intelligence program looks at the data stored in or streaming across the internet. In each case information needs to be stored, as well as retrieved, be it in the form of memories and their recollection in the former, or our daily experience of web search in the latter.

Next comes the ability to *listen*, to focus on the important and discard the irrelevant. To recognize the familiar, discern between alternatives or identify similar things. Listening is also about 'sensing' a momentary experience, be it a personal feeling, individual decision, or the collective sentiment expressed by the online masses. Listening is followed eventually by deeper understanding: the ability to *learn* about the structure of the world, in terms of facts, rules, and relationships. Just as we learn common-sense knowledge about the world around us, web-intelligence systems learn about our preferences and behaviour. In each case the essential underlying processes appear quite similar: detecting the regularities and patterns that emerge from large volumes of data, whether derived from our personal experiences while growing up, or via the vast data trails left by our collective online activities.

Having learned something about the structure of the world, real or its online rendition, we are able to *connect* different facts and derive new conclusions giving rise to reasoning, logic, and the ability to deal with uncertainty. Reasoning is what we normally regard as unique to our species, distinguishing us from animals. Similar reasoning by machines, achieved through smart engineering as well as by crunching vast volumes of data, gives rise to surprising engineering successes such as Watson's victory at *Jeopardy!*.

Putting everything together leads to the ability to make *predictions* about the future, albeit tempered with different degrees of belief. Just as we predict and speculate on the course of our lives, both immediate and long-term, machines are able to predict as well—be it the supply and demand for products, or the possibility of crime in particular neighbourhoods. Of course, predictions are then put to good use for *correcting* and controlling our own actions, for supporting our own decisions in marketing or law enforcement, as well as controlling complex, autonomous web-intelligence systems such as self-driving cars.

In the process of describing each of the elements: *looking, listening, learning, connecting, predicting,* and *correcting,* I hope to lead you through the computer science of semantic search, natural language understanding, text mining, machine learning, reasoning and the semantic web, AI planning, and even swarm computing, among others. In each case we shall go through the principles involved virtually from scratch, and in the process cover rather vast tracts of computer science even if at a very basic level.

Along the way, we shall also take a closer look at many examples of web intelligence at work: AI-driven online advertising for sure, as well as many other applications such as tracking terrorists, detecting disease outbreaks, and self-driving cars. The promise of self-driving cars, as illustrated in Chapter 6, points to a future where the web will not only provide us with information and serve as a communication platform, but where the computers that power the web could also help us *control* our world through complex web-intelligence systems; another example of which promises to be the energy-efficient 'smart grid'.

* * *

By the end of our journey we shall begin to suspect that what began with the simple goal of optimizing advertising might soon evolve to serve other purposes, such as safe driving or clean energy. Therefore the book concludes with a note on *purpose*, speculating on the nature and evolution of large-scale web-intelligence systems in the future. By asking where goals come from, we are led to a conclusion that surprisingly runs contrary to the strong-AI thesis: instead of ever mimicking human intelligence, I shall argue that web-intelligence systems are more likely to evolve synergistically with our own evolving collective social intelligence, driven in turn by our use of the web itself.

In summary, this book is at one level an elucidation of artificial intelligence and related areas of computing, targeted for the lay but patient and diligent reader. At the same time, there remains a constant and not so hidden agenda: we shall mostly concern ourselves with exploring how today's web-intelligence applications are able to mimic some aspects of intelligent behaviour. Additionally however, we shall also compare and contrast these immense engineering feats to the wondrous complexities that the human brain is able to grasp with such surprising ease, enabling each of us to so effortlessly 'connect the dots' and make sense of the world every single day.

1

LOOK

In 'A Scandal in Bohemia'[6] the legendary fictional detective Sherlock Holmes deduces that his companion Watson had got very wet lately, as well as that he had 'a most clumsy and careless servant girl'. When Watson, in amazement, asks how Holmes knows this, Holmes answers:

> 'It is simplicity itself . . . My eyes tell me that on the inside of your left shoe, just where the firelight strikes it, the leather is scored by six almost parallel cuts. Obviously they have been caused by someone who has very carelessly scraped round the edges of the sole in order to remove crusted mud from it. Hence, you see, my double deduction that you had been out in vile weather, and that you had a particularly malignant boot-slitting specimen of the London slavery.'

Most of us do not share the inductive prowess of the legendary detective. Nevertheless, we all continuously *look* at the the world around us and, in our small way, draw inferences so as to make sense of what is going on. Even the simplest of observations, such as whether Watson's shoe is in fact dirty, requires us to first look at his shoe. Our skill and intent drive what we look at, and look *for*. Those of us that may share some of Holmes's skill look for far greater detail than the rest of us. Further, more information is better: 'Data! Data! Data! I can't make bricks without clay', says Holmes in another episode.[7] No inference is possible in the absence of input data, and, more importantly, the *right* data for the task at hand.

How does Holmes connect the observation of 'leather . . . scored by six almost parallel cuts' to the cause of 'someone . . . very carelessly scraped round the edges of the sole in order to remove crusted mud from it'? Perhaps, somewhere deep in the Holmesian brain lies a memory of a similar boot having been so damaged by another 'specimen of the London slavery'? Or, more likely, many different 'facts', such as the potential causes of damage to boots, including clumsy scraping; that scraping is often prompted by boots having been dirtied by mud; that cleaning boots is usually the job of a servant; as well as the knowledge that bad weather results in mud.

In later chapters we shall delve deeper into the process by which such 'logical inferences' might be automatically conducted by machines, as well as how such knowledge might be learned from experience. For now we focus on the fact that, in order to make his logical inferences, Holmes not only needs to look *at* data from the world without, but also needs to look *up* 'facts' learned from his past experiences. Each of us perform a myriad of such 'lookups' in our everyday lives, enabling us to recognize our friends, recall a name, or discern a car from a horse. Further, as some researchers have argued, our ability to converse, and the very foundations of all human language, are but an extension of the ability to correctly look up and classify past experiences from *memory*. 'Looking at' the world around us, relegating our experiences to memory, so as to later 'look them up' so effortlessly, are most certainly essential and fundamental elements of our ability to connect the dots and make sense of our surroundings.

The MEMEX Reloaded

Way back in 1945 Vannevar Bush, then the director of the US Office of Scientific Research and Development (OSRD), suggested that scientific effort should be directed towards emulating and augmenting human memory. He imagined the possibility of creating a 'MEMEX': a device

> which is a sort of mechanised private file and library . . . in which an individual stores all his books, records, and communications, and which is mechanised so that it may be consulted with exceeding speed and flexibility. It is an enlarged intimate supplement to his memory.[8]

A remarkably prescient thought indeed, considering the world wide web of today. In fact, Bush imagined that the MEMEX would be modelled on human memory, which

> operates by association. With one item in its grasp, it snaps instantly to the next that is suggested by the association of thoughts, in accordance with some intricate web of trails carried by the cells of the brain. It has other characteristics, of course; trails that are not frequently followed are prone to fade, items are not fully permanent, memory is transitory. Yet the speed of action, the intricacy of trails, the detail of mental pictures, is awe-inspiring beyond all else in nature.[8]

At the same time, Bush was equally aware that the wonders of human memory were far from easy to mimic: 'One cannot hope thus to equal the speed and flexibility with which the mind follows an associative trail, but it should be possible to beat the mind decisively in regard to the permanence and clarity of the items resurrected from storage.'[8]

Today's world wide web certainly does 'beat the mind' in at least these latter respects. As already recounted in the Prologue, the volume of information stored in the internet is vast indeed, leading to the coining of the phrase 'big data' to describe it. The seemingly intelligent 'web-intelligence' applications that form the subject of this book all exploit this big data, just as our own thought processes, including Holmes's inductive prowess, are reliant on the 'speed and flexibility' of human memory.

How is this big data stored in the web, so as to be so easily accessible to all of us as we surf the web every day? To what extent does it resemble, as well as differ from, how our own memories are stored and recalled? And last but not least, what does it portend as far as augmenting our own abilities, much as Vannevar Bush imagined over 50 years ago? These are the questions we now focus on as we examine what it means to remember and recall, i.e., to 'look up things', on the web, or in our minds.

* * *

When was the last time you were to meet someone you had never met before in person, even though the two of you may have corresponded earlier on email? How often have you been surprised that the person you saw looked different than what you had expected, perhaps older, younger, or built differently? This experience is becoming rarer by the day. Today you can Google persons you are about to meet and usually find half a dozen photos of them, in addition to much more, such as their Facebook page, publications or speaking appearances, and snippets of their employment history. In a certain sense, it appears that we can simply 'look up' the global, collective memory-bank of mankind, as collated and managed by Google, much as we internally look up our own personal memories as associated with a person's name.

Very recently Google introduced Google Glass, looking through which you merely need to look at a popular landmark, such as the Eiffel Tower in Paris, and instantly retrieve information about it, just as if you had typed in the query 'Eiffel Tower' in the Google search box. You can do this with books, restaurant frontages, and even paintings. In the latter case, you may not even know the name of the painting; still Glass will 'look it up', using the image itself to drive its search. We know for a fact that Google (and others, such as Facebook) are able to perform the same kind of 'image-based' lookup on human faces as well as images of inanimate objects. They too can 'recognize' people from their faces. Clearly, there is a scary side to such a capability being available in such tools: for example, it could be easily misused by stalkers, identity thieves, or extortionists. Google has deliberately not yet released a face recognition feature in Glass, and maintains that 'we will not add facial recognition to Glass unless we have strong privacy protections in place'.[9] Nevertheless, the ability to recognize faces is now within the power of technology, and we can experience it every day: for example, Facebook automatically matches similar faces in your photo album and attempts to name the people using whatever information it finds in its own copious memory-bank, while also tapping Google's when needed. The fact is that technology has now progressed to the point where we can, in principle, 'look up' the global collective memory of mankind, to recognize a face or a name, much as we recognize faces and names every day from our own personal memories.

* * *

Google handles over 4 billion search queries a day. How did I get that number? By issuing a few searches myself, of course; by the time you read this book the number would have gone up, and you can look it up yourself. Everybody who has access to the internet uses search, from office workers to college students to the youngest of children. If you have ever introduced a computer novice (albeit a rare commodity these days) to the internet, you might have witnessed the 'aha' experience: it appears that every piece of information known to mankind is at one's fingertips. It is truly difficult to remember the world before search, and realize that this was the world of merely a decade ago.

Ubiquitous search is, some believe, more than merely a useful tool. It may be changing the way we connect the dots and make sense of our world in fundamental ways. Most of us use Google search several times a day; after all, the entire collective memory-bank of mankind is just a click away. Thus, sometimes we no longer even bother to remember facts, such as when Napoleon was defeated at Waterloo, or when the East India Company established its reign in the Indian subcontinent. Even if we do remember our history lessons, our brains often compartmentalize the two events differently as both of them pertain to different geographies; so ask us which preceded the other, and we are usually stumped. Google comes to the rescue immediately, though, and we quickly learn that India was well under foreign rule when Napoleon met his nemesis in 1815, since the East India Company had been in charge since the Battle of Plassey in 1757. Connecting disparate facts so as to, in this instance, put them in chronological sequence, needs extra details that our brains do not automatically connect across compartments, such as European vs Indian history; however, within any one such context we are usually able to arrange events in historical sequence much more easily. In such cases the ubiquity of Google search provides instant satisfaction and serves to augment our cognitive abilities, even as it also reduces our need to memorize facts.

Recently some studies, as recounted in Nicholas Carr's *The Shallows: What the internet is Doing to Our Brains*,[10] have argued that the internet is 'changing the way we think' and, in particular, diminishing our capacity to read deeply and absorb content. The instant availability of hyperlinks on the web seduces us into 'a form of skimming activity, hopping from one source to another and rarely returning to any source we might have already visited'.[11] Consequently, it is argued, our motivation as well as ability to stay focused and absorb the thoughts of an author are gradually getting curtailed.

Be that as it may, I also suspect that there is perhaps another complementary capability that is probably being enhanced rather than diminished. We are, of course, talking about the ability to connect the dots and make sense of our world. Think about our individual memories: each of these is, as compared to the actual event, rather sparse in detail, at least at first glance. We usually remember only certain aspects of each experience. Nevertheless, when we need to connect the dots, such as recall where and when we might have met a stranger in the past, we seemingly need only 'skim through' our memories without delving into each in detail, so as to correlate some of them and use these to make deeper inferences. In much the same manner, searching and surfing the web while trying to connect the dots is probably a boon rather than a bane, at least for the purpose of correlating disparate pieces of information. The MEMEX imagined by Vannevar Bush is now with us, in the form of web search. Perhaps, more often than not, we regularly discover previously unknown connections between people, ideas, and events every time we indulge in the same 'skimming activity' of surfing that Carr argues is harmful in some ways. We have, in many ways, already created Vannevar Bush's MEMEX-powered world where

> the lawyer has at his touch the associated opinions and decisions of his whole experience, and of the experience of friends and authorities. The patent attorney has on call the millions of issued patents, with familiar trails to every point of his client's interest. The physician, puzzled by its patient's reactions, strikes the trail established in studying an earlier similar case, and runs rapidly through analogous case histories, with side references to the classics for the pertinent anatomy and histology. The chemist, struggling with the synthesis of an organic compound, has all the chemical literature before him in his laboratory, with trails following the analogies of compounds, and side trails to their physical and chemical behaviour. The historian, with a vast chronological account of a people, parallels it with a skip trail which stops only at the salient items, and can follow at any time contemporary trails which lead him all over civilisation at a particular epoch. There is a new profession of trail blazers, those who find delight in the task of establishing useful trails through the enormous mass of the common record. The inheritance from the master becomes, not only his additions to the world's record, but for his disciples the entire scaffolding by which they were erected.[8]

In many ways therefore, web search is in fact able to augment our own powers of recall in highly synergistic ways. Yes, along the way we do forget many things we earlier used to remember. But perhaps the things we forget are in fact irrelevant, given that we now have access to search? Taking this further, our brains are poor at indexing, so we search the web instead. Less often are we called upon to traverse our memory-to-memory links just to recall facts. We use those links only when making connections or correlations that augment mere search, such as while inferring patterns, making predictions, or hypothesizing conjectures, and we shall return to all these elements later in the book. So, even if by repeatedly choosing to use search engines over our own powers of recall, it is indeed the case that certain connections in our brains are in fact getting weaker, as submitted by Nicholas Carr.[11] At the same time, it might also be the case that many other connections, such as those used for deeper reasoning, may be getting strengthened.

Apart from being a tremendously useful tool, web search also appears to be important in a very fundamental sense. As related by Carr, the Google founder Larry Page is said to have remarked that 'The ultimate search engine is something as smart as people, or smarter...working on search is a way to work on artificial intelligence.'[11] In a 2004 interview with *Newsweek*, his co-founder Sergey Brin remarks, 'Certainly if you had all the world's information directly attached to your brain, or an artificial brain that was smarter than your brain, you would be better off.'

In particular, as I have already argued above, our ability to connect the dots may be significantly enhanced using web search. Even more interestingly, what happens when search and the collective memories of mankind are automatically tapped by computers, such as the millions that power Google? Could these computers themselves acquire the ability to 'connect the dots', like us, but at a far grander scale and infinitely faster? We shall return to this thought later and, indeed, throughout this book as we explore how today's machines are able to 'learn' millions of facts from even larger volumes of big data, as well as how such facts are already being used for automated 'reasoning'. For the moment, however, let us turn our attention to the computer science of web search, from the inside.

Inside a Search Engine

'Any sufficiently advanced technology is indistinguishable from magic'; this often-quoted 'law' penned by Arthur C. Clarke also applies to internet search. Powering the innocent 'Google search box' lies a vast network of over a million servers. By contrast, the largest banks in the world have at most 50,000 servers each, and often less. It is interesting to reflect on the fact that it is within the computers of these banks that your money, and for that matter most of the world's wealth, lies encoded as bits of ones and zeros. The magical Google-like search is made possible by a computing behemoth two orders of magnitude more powerful than the largest of banks. So, how does it all work?

Searching for data is probably the most fundamental exercise in computer science; the first data processing machines did exactly this, i.e., store data that could be searched and retrieved in the future. The basic idea is fairly simple: think about how you might want to search for a word, say the name 'Brin', in this very book. Naturally you would turn to the index pages towards the end of the book. The index entries are sorted in alphabetical order, so you know that 'Brin' should appear near the beginning of the index. In particular, searching the index for the word 'Brin' is clearly much easier than trawling through the entire book to figure out where the word 'Brin' appears. This simple observation forms the basis of the computer science of 'indexing', using which all computers, including the millions powering Google, perform their magical searches.

Google's million servers continuously crawl and index over 50 billion web pages, which is the estimated size of the *indexed** world wide web as of January 2011. Just as in the index of this book, against each word or phrase in the massive web index is recorded the web address (or URL†) of *all* the web pages that contain that word or phrase. For common words, such as 'the', this would probably be the entire English-language web. Just try it; searching for 'the' in Google yields

---

* Only a small fraction of the web is indexed by search engines such as Google; as we see later, the complete web is actually far larger.

† 'Universal record locater', or URL for short, is the technical term for a web address, such as <http://www.google.com>.

over 25 billion results, as of this writing. Assuming that about half of the 50 billion web pages are in English, the 50 billion estimate for the size of the *indexed* web certainly appears reasonable.

Each web page is regularly scanned by Google's millions of servers, and added as an entry in a huge web index. This web index is truly massive as compared to the few index pages of this book. Just imagine how big this web index is: it contains every word ever mentioned in any of the billions of web pages, in any possible language. The English language itself contains just over a million words. Other languages are smaller, as well as less prevalent on the web, but not by much. Additionally there are proper nouns, naming everything from people, both real (such as 'Brin') or imaginary ('Sherlock Holmes'), to places, companies, rivers, mountains, oceans, as well as every name ever given to a product, film, or book. Clearly there are many millions of words in the web index. Going further, common phrases and names, such as 'White House' or 'Sergey Brin' are also included as separate entries, so as to improve search results. An early (1998) paper[12] by Brin and Page, the now famous founders of Google, on the inner workings of their search engine, reported using a dictionary of 14 million unique words. Since then Google has expanded to cover many languages, as well as index common phrases in addition to individual words. Further, as the size of the web has grown, so have the number of unique proper nouns it contains. What is important to remember, therefore, is that today's web index probably contains hundreds of millions of entries, each a word, phrase, or proper noun, using which it indexes many billions of web pages.

What is involved in searching for a word, say 'Brin', in an index as large as the massive web index? In computer science terms, we need to explicitly define the steps required to 'search a sorted index', regardless of whether it is a small index for a book or the index of the entire web. Once we have such a prescription, which computer scientists call an 'algorithm', we can program an adequately powerful computer to search any index, even the web index. A very simple program might proceed by checking each word in the index one by one, starting from the beginning of the index and continuing to its end. Computers are fast, and it might seem that a reasonably powerful computer could perform such a procedure quickly enough. However, size is a funny thing; as soon as one starts adding a lot of zeros numbers can get very big very fast. Recall that unlike a book index, which may contain at most a few thousand words, the web index contains millions of words and hundreds of millions of phrases. So even a reasonably fast computer that might perform a million checks per second would still take many hours to search for just one word in this index. If our query had a few more words, we would need to let the program work for months before getting an answer.

Clearly this is not how web search works. If one thinks about it, neither is it how we ourselves search a book index. For starters, our very simple program completely ignores that fact that index words were already sorted in alphabetical order. Let's try to imagine how a smarter algorithm might search a sorted index faster than the naive one just described. We still have to assume that our computer itself is rather dumb, and, unlike us, it does *not* understand that since 'B' is the second letter in the alphabet, the entry for 'Brin' would lie roughly in the first tenth of all the index pages (there are 26 letters, so 'A' and 'B' together constitute just under a tenth of all letters). It is probably good to assume that our computer is ignorant about such things, because in case we need to search the web index, we have no idea how many unique letters the index entries begin with, or how they are ordered, since all languages are included, even words with Chinese and Indian characters.

Nevertheless, we do know that there is *some* ordering of letters that includes all languages, using which the index itself has been sorted. So, ignorant of anything but the size of the complete index, our smarter search program begins, not at the beginning, but at the very middle of the index. It checks, from left to right, letter by letter, whether the word listed there is alphabetically larger or smaller than the search query 'Brin'. (For example 'cat' is larger than 'Brin', whereas both 'atom' and 'bright' are smaller.) If the middle entry is larger than the query, our program forgets about the second half of the index and repeats the same procedure on the remaining first half. On the other hand, if the query word is larger, the program concentrates on the second half while discarding the first. Whichever half is selected, the program once more turns its attention to the middle entry of this half. Our program continues this process of repeated halving and checking until it finally finds the query word 'Brin', and fails only if the index does not contain this word.

Computer science is all about coming up with faster procedures, or algorithms, such as the smarter and supposedly faster one just described. It is also concerned with figuring out why, and by how much, one algorithm might be faster than another. For example, we saw that our very simple computer program, which checked each index entry sequentially from the beginning of the index, would need to perform a million checks if the index contained a million entries. In other words, the number of steps taken by this naive algorithm is exactly proportional to the size of the input; if the input size quadruples, so does the time taken by the computer. Computer scientists refer to such behaviour as *linear*, and often describe such an algorithm as being a linear one.

Let us now examine whether our smarter algorithm is indeed faster than the naive linear approach. Beginning with the first check it performs at the middle of the index, our smarter algorithm manages to discard half of the entries, leaving only the remaining half for it to deal with. With each subsequent check, the number of entries is further halved, until the procedure ends by either finding the query word or failing to do so. Suppose we used this smarter algorithm to search a small book index that had but a thousand entries. How many times could one possibly halve the number 1,000? Roughly ten, it turns out, because $2 \times 2 \times 2 \ldots \times 2$, ten times, i.e., 2^{10}, is exactly 1,024. If we now think about how our smarter algorithm works on a much larger index of, say, a million entries, we can see that it can take at most 20 steps. This is because a million, or 1,000,000, is just under $1,024 \times 1,024$. Writing each 1,024 as the product of ten 2's, we see that a million is just under $2 \times 2 \times \ldots 2$, 20 times, or 2^{20}. It is easy to see that even if the web index becomes much bigger, say a billion entries, our smarter algorithm would slow down only slightly, now taking 30 steps instead of 20. Computer scientists strive to come up with algorithms that exhibit such behaviour, where the number of steps taken by an algorithm grows much much slower than the size of the input, so that extremely large problems can be tackled almost as easily as small ones. Our smarter search algorithm, also known as 'binary search', is said to be a *logarithmic-time* algorithm, since the number of steps it takes, i.e., ten, 20, or 30, is proportional to the 'logarithm'* of the input size, namely 1,000, 1,000,000, or 1,000,000,000.

Whenever we type a search query, such as 'Obama, India', in the Google search box, one of Google's servers responsible for handling our query looks up the web index entries for 'Obama' and 'India', and returns the list of addresses of those web pages contained in both these entries. Looking up the sorted web index of about 3 billion entries takes no more than a few dozen or at most a hundred steps. We have seen how fast logarithmic-time algorithms work on even large inputs, so it is no problem at all for any one of Google's millions of servers to perform our search in a small fraction of a second. Of course, Google needs to handle billions of queries a second, so millions of servers are employed to handle this load. Further, many copies of the web index are kept on each of these servers to speed up processing. As a result,

---

* Log n, the 'base two *logarithm*' of n, merely means that $2 \times 2 \times 2 \ldots \times 2$, log n times, works out to n.

our search results often begin to appear even before we have finished typing our query.

We have seen how easy and fast the *sorted* web index can be searched using our smart 'binary-search' technique. But how does the huge index of 'all words and phrases' get sorted in the first place? Unlike looking up a sorted book index, few of us are faced with the task of having to sort a large list in everyday life. Whenever we are, though, we quickly find this task much harder. For example, it would be rather tedious to create an index for this book by hand; thankfully there are word-processing tools to assist in this task.

Actually there is much more involved in creating a book index than a web index; while the latter can be computed quite easily as will be shown, a book index needs to be more selective in which words to include, whereas the web index just includes all words. Moreover, a book index is hierarchical, where many entries have further sub-entries. Deciding how to do this involves 'meaning' rather than mere brute force; we shall return to how machines might possibly deal with the 'semantics' of language in later chapters. Even so, accurate, fully-automatic back-of-the-book indexing still remains an unsolved problem.[25]

For now, however, we focus on sorting a large list of words; let us see if our earlier trick of breaking the list of words into two halves works wonders again, as we found in the case of searching. Suppose we magically sort each half or our list. We then merge the two sorted half-lists by looking at words from each of the two lists, starting at the top, and inserting these one by one into the final sorted list. Each word, from either list, needs to be checked once during this merging procedure. Now, recall that each of the halves had to be sorted before we could merge, and so on. Just as in the case of binary search, there will be a *logarithmic* number of such halving steps. However, unlike earlier, whenever we combine pairs of halves at each step, we will need to check *all* words in the list during the merging exercises. As a result, sorting, unlike searching, is not that fast. For example, sorting a million words takes about 20 million steps, and sorting a billion words 30 billion steps. The algorithm slows down for larger inputs, and this slowdown is a shade worse than by how much the input grows. Thus, this time our algorithm behaves worse than linearly. But the nice part is that the amount by which the slowdown is worse than the growth in the input is nothing but the logarithm that we saw earlier (hence the 20 and 30 in the 20 million and 30 million steps). The sum and substance is that sorting a list twice as large takes very very slightly *more* than twice the time. In computer science terms, such behaviour is termed *super-linear*; a linear algorithm, on the other hand, would become exactly twice as slow on twice the amount of data.

So, now that we have understood sorting and searching, it looks like these techniques are just basic computer science, and one might rightly ask where exactly is the magic that makes web search so intuitively useful today? Many years ago I was speaking with a friend who works at Google. He said, 'almost everything we do here is pretty basic computer science; only the size of the problems we tackle have three or four extra zeros tagged on at the end, and then seemingly easy things become really hard'. It is important to realize that the web index is huge. For one, as we have seen, it includes hundreds of millions of entries, maybe even billions, each corresponding to a distinct word or phrase. But what does each entry contain? Just as an entry in a book index lists the pages where a particular word or phrase occurs, the web index entry for each word contains a list of all web addresses that contain that word. Now, a book index usually contains only the important words in the book. However, the web index contains *all* words and phrases found on the web. This includes commonly occurring words, such as 'the', which are contained in virtually all 25 billion English-language web pages. As a result, the index entry for 'the' will need to list almost half the entire collection of indexed web addresses. For other words fewer pages will need to be listed. Nevertheless many entries will need to list millions of web addresses. The sheer size of the web index is huge, and the storage taken by a complete (and uncompressed) web index runs into petabytes: a petabyte is approximately 1 with 15 zeros; equivalent to a thousand terabytes, and a million gigabytes. Most PCs, by comparison, have disk storage of a few hundred gigabytes.

Further, while many web pages are static, many others change all the time (think of news sites, or blogs). Additionally, new web pages are being created and crawled every second. Therefore, this large web index needs to be continuously updated. However, unlike looking up the index, computing the content of index entries themselves is in fact like sorting a very large list of words, and requires significant computing horsepower. How to do that efficiently is the subject of the more recent of Google's major innovations, called 'map-reduce', a new paradigm for using millions of computers together, in what is called 'parallel computing'. Google's millions of servers certainly do a lot of number crunching, and it is important to appreciate the amount of computing power coming to bear on each simple search query.

In fact the many such innovations in parallel computing on 'big data' by Google as well as other web companies, such as Yahoo!, Facebook, and Twitter in particular, have spawned a burgeoning revolution in the hitherto rather staid world of 'data management' technologies. Today many large organizations such as banks, retail stores, and even governments are rethinking the way they store and manage data, even though their data needs are but a small fraction in size as compared to the massive volumes of real 'big data' managed by web companies. However, all that is a separate subject in itself, i.e., 'big-data' technologies and how they are impacting traditional enterprise computing. We shall not stray further into data management *technology*, which while interesting and topical is nevertheless tangential to our main topic of *web-intelligence* applications that use big data to exhibit seemingly intelligent behaviour.

* * *

Impressive as its advances in parallel computing might be, Google's real secret sauces, at least with respect to search, lie elsewhere. Some of you might remember the world of search before Google. Yes, search engines such as Alta Vista and Lycos did indeed return results matching one's query; however, too many web pages usually contained all the words in one's query, and these were not the ones you wanted. For example, the query 'Obama, India' (or 'Clinton, India' at that time) may have returned a shop named Clinton that sold books on India as the topmost result, because the words 'Clinton' and 'India' were repeated very frequently inside this page. But you really were looking for reports on Bill Clinton's visit to India. Sometime in 1998, I, like many others, chanced upon the Google search box, and suddenly found that this engine *would* indeed return the desired news report amongst the top results. Why? What was Google's secret? The secret was revealed in a now classic research paper[12] by the Google founders Brin and Page, then still graduate students at Stanford.

Google's secret was 'PageRank', a method of calculating the relative *importance* of every web page on the internet, called its 'page rank'. As a result of being able to calculate the importance of each page in some fashion, in addition to matching the queried words, Google's results were also ordered by their relative importance, according to their page ranks, so that the most important pages showed up first. This appears a rather simple observation, though many things seem simple with the benefit of 20/20 hindsight. However, the consequent improvement in users' experience with Google search was dramatic, and led rapidly to Google's dominance in search, which continues to date.

The insight behind the PageRank algorithm is surprisingly simple, considering its eventual huge impact. In the early days of the web, the term 'surfing' the web began being used as people visited page after page, being led from one to the next by clicking on hyperlinks. In fact hyperlinks, which were invented by Tim Berners Lee in 1992,[13] came to define the web itself.

Usually people decide which links to follow depending on whether they expect them to contain material of interest. Brin and Page figured that the importance of a web page should be determined by how often it is likely to be visited during such surfing activity. Unfortunately, it was not possible to track who was clicking on which link, at least not at the time. So they imagined a dumb surfer, akin to the popular 'monkey on a typewriter' idiom, who would click links at *random*, and continue doing this forever. They reasoned that if a web page was visited more often, on the average, by such an imaginary random surfer, it should be considered more important than other, less visited pages.

Now, at first glance it may appear that the page rank of a page should be easy to determine by merely looking at the number of links that point to a page: one might expect such pages to be visited more often than others by Brin and Page's dumb surfer. Unfortunately, the story is not that simple. As is often the case in computer science, we need to think through things a little more carefully. Let us see why: our random surfer might leave a page only to return to it by following a sequence of links that cycle back to his starting point, thereby increasing the importance of the starting page indirectly, i.e., independently of the number of links coming into the page. On the other hand, there may be *no* such cycles if he chooses a different sequence of links.

Another way to think about this is that any particular web page is more important if other important pages point to it, as opposed to any other pages. Thus the importance of one page depends in turn on the importance of those pages that point to it, which in turn depend on the importance of pages many steps removed, and so on. As a result, the 'link structure' of other, unrelated pages indirectly affects the importance of each page, and needs to be taken into account while computing the page rank of each page. Since page rank is itself supposed to measure importance, this becomes a cyclic definition.

But that is not all; there are even further complications. For example, if some page contains thousands of outgoing links, such as a 'directory' of some kind, the chance of our dumb surfer choosing any one particular link from such a page is far less than if the page contained only a few links. Thus, the number of outgoing links also affects the importance of the pages that any page points to. If one thinks about it a bit, the page rank of each page appears to depends on the overall structure of the *entire* web, and cannot be determined simply by looking at the incoming or outgoing links to a single page in isolation. The PageRank calculation is therefore a 'global' rather than 'local' task, and requires a more sophisticated algorithm than merely counting links. Fortunately, as discovered by Brin and Page, computing the page rank of each and every page in the web, all together, turns out to be a fairly straightforward, albeit time-consuming, task.

Recall that each entry in the large web index contains a long list of web pages, which can often run into millions for each entry. Perhaps it may have occurred to you to ask in what order the page addresses are kept in these lists? By now the answer should be obvious: pages should be listed in order of their page ranks. This way the results of each search query will naturally show up with the most important pages first. As new pages get added to the web and existing ones get updated, possibly with new links, the link structure of the web is continuously changing, so Google's millions of servers continuously recalculate the page rank of each and every web page as fast as they possibly can manage. The sooner a page's importance is updated, the more likely it is that search results will be ordered better, and users will find what they want from their visit to Google. Page ranks also help Google store and search its huge search index faster. Since entries in the web index are stored in order of their page ranks, only a small number of these will usually be returned amongst the first few pages of any search result. And how often do you or I ever go beyond even the first page of results? So Google is able to get away by searching a much smaller index for the overwhelming majority of queries. By replicating copies of this index many times across its millions of servers, Google search becomes incredibly fast, almost instant, with results starting to appear even as a user is still typing her query.

Google and the Mind

We can now appreciate that Google does a lot of massive computing to maintain its huge index, and even more so to ensure that the page rank of each page is always accurate, which is the secret behind the quality of its search results. What does all this have to do with connecting the dots, making sense of the world, and intelligence? There are 50 billion or so indexed web pages, each possibly representing aspects of some human enterprise, person, or event. Almost anything one can think of is likely to have some presence on the web, in some form at least, however sparse or detailed. In many ways we can think of these 50 billion web pages as representing, in some sense, the collective experiences of a significant fraction of mankind—a global memory of sorts. Google's PageRank appears, magically, to be able to attach an importance to each page in a manner that we humans are able to relate to. The fact is that people find what they want faster because whatever PageRank throws up first often turns out to be what they were looking for. When it comes to 'looking up' our global collective memory as represented by the web, PageRank seems to work well for us, almost as well as if we were looking up the sought-after information from our own memories. So much so, as we have already mentioned, that we are gradually ceding the need to remember things in our own memories and instead relying on searching the global memory using web search.

So it makes sense to ask if the PageRank algorithm tells us anything about how we humans 'look up' our own internal memories. Does the way the web is structured, as pages linked to each other, have anything to do with how our brains store our own personal experiences? A particular form of scientific inquiry into the nature of human intelligence is that of seeking 'rational models'. A rational model of human cognition seeks to understand some aspect of how we humans think by comparing it to a computational technique, such as Page-Rank. We then try to see if the computational technique performs as well as humans do in actual experiments, such as those conducted by psychologists. Just such a study was performed a few years ago at Brown University to evaluate whether PageRank has anything to teach us about how human memory works.[14]

We don't, at least as of today, have any single scientific model of how human memory works. Nevertheless, it is clear enough that we don't store web pages like those that are on the internet. So we need some model of memory on which to try out the PageRank algorithm. Psychologists and cognitive scientists have used what is called a 'semantic model' where pairs of words are associated with each other in some way, such as being synonyms of each other, or one a generalization of the other. Some word associations arise out of experiments where human associates are presented with one word, and asked to name the first word that comes to mind. Words that are more frequently paired in such experiments also contribute to word associations in the semantic model. Just as the world wide web consists of web pages linked to each other by hyperlinks, such a semantic model consists of words linked to each other by word associations. Since word associations in a semantic model are backed by statistics on how people actually associate words, scientists consider such a model to be a reasonable 'working model' of some aspects of how humans store memories, even though it is very far from being anywhere near a complete or accurate model. However, such a model is at least suitable for testing other hypotheses, such as whether PageRank as a computational model might teach us something more about how human memory works.

PageRank is merely a computational technique for deciding the relative importance of a web page. Presumably we humans also assign importance to our own memories, and in particular to certain words over others. In the Brown University study,[14] a subject was presented with a letter, and each time asked to recall the first word that came to mind beginning with that letter. The aggregate results did indeed find that some words, such as 'apple' or 'dog', were chosen by most people. Next the researchers used a previously constructed semantic model of about 5,000 common words, i.e., a network of word-association pairs. They ran the PageRank algorithm, using the network of word associations in the semantic model rather than the network of web pages and hyperlinks, thereby producing a ranking of all the words by importance. Interestingly, the responses given by a majority of people (i.e., at least 50%) fell in the top 8% of the ranking given by PageRank. In other words, half the human responses fell in the top 40 words as ranked by PageRank, out of the total 5,000 words. They concluded that a PageRank-based ordering of 'words starting with the letter—' closely corresponds to the responses most often chosen by humans when presented with a letter and asked to state the first word it triggers.

Note that web pages link to other pages, while words in the semantic network link to other words; these two networks are completely unrelated to each other. What is being compared is the PageRank *algorithm's* ability to uncover a hidden property, rather close to what we understand as 'importance', for each node in two very different networks. Therefore, in this fairly limited sense it is reasonable to say that the PageRank algorithm, acting on a semantic word-association network, serves as a well-performing rational model of some aspects of human memory: PageRank gives us some insight into how a capability for ranking that possibly mimics how memories are assigned importance might be computationally implemented even in other situations, wherever rankings that mimic human memory are desirable.

Do our brains use PageRank? We have no idea. All we can say is that in the light of experiments such as the study at Brown University, PageRank has possibly given us some additional insight into how our brains work or, more aptly, how some of their abilities might be mimicked by a machine. More importantly, and this is the point I wish to emphasize, the success of PageRank in predicting human responses in the Brown University experiment gives greater reason to consider Google search as an example of a web-intelligence application that mimics some aspect of human abilities, while complementing the well-known evidence that we find Google's top search results to be highly relevant. Suppose, for argument's sake, human brains were to order web pages by importance; there is now even more reason to believe that such a human ordering, however impractical to actually perform, would closely match PageRank's.

Before we conclude this train of thought on Google and the Mind, should we not ask whether, just as the success of PageRank-based search seemingly impacts our minds, our own behaviour impacts. PageRank's effectiveness in any way? It seems rather far fetched, but it does. Google search is so good that we 'look up' things there instead of remembering them. Similarly, why follow hyperlinks on web pages when you can get more, and often better, information (in the sense of being more 'important', as per PageRank) by typing a short query into the Google search box atop one's browser window? In fact more and more people don't follow links. As a result, newer web pages have fewer links. Why bother to include links when the referenced pages can just as easily be searched for in Google? But PageRank is based on links, and relies on the fact that there are many links for its effectiveness. As fewer and new pages have as many links as earlier ones, PageRank's effectiveness decreases.

PageRank is so good that it is changing the way we navigate the web from surfing to searching, weakening the premise on which it itself is based. Of course, Google has many more tricks up its sleeve. For one, it can monitor your browsing history and use the links you actually click on to augment its decisions on which pages are important. Additionally, the terms that are more often queried by users may also be indirectly affecting the importance of web pages, with those dealing with more sought-after topics becoming more important over time. As the web, our use of it, and even our own memories evolve, so does search technology itself, each affecting the other far more closely than apparent at first glance.

* * *

It is important to note and remember that, in spite of the small insights that we may gain from experiments such as the one at Brown University, we really don't know how our brains 'look up' things. What causes Sherlock Holmes to link the visual image of scruffs on Watson's boot to their probable cause? Certainly more than a simple 'lookup'. What memory does the image trigger? How do our brains then crawl our internal memories during our reasoning process? Do we proceed link by link, following memories linked to each other by common words, concepts, or ideas, sort of like Serge and Brin's hypothetical random surfer hops from page to page? Or do we also use some kind of efficient indexing technique, like a search engine, so as to immediately recall all memories that share some features of a triggering thought or image? Many similar experiments have been conducted to study such matters, including those involving other rational models where, as before, computational techniques are compared with human behaviour. In the end, as of today we really don't have any deep understanding of how human memory works.

The brain's look up mechanisms are certainly more complex than the fairly simple look up that a search engine uses. For example, some people (including myself) report that they often fail to recognize a colleague from work when seeing them at, say, a wedding reception. The brain's face recognition process, for such people at least, appears to be context-dependent; a face that is instantly recognizable in the 'work' context is not at the top of the list in another, more 'social' context. Similarly, it is often easier to recall the name of a person when it is placed in a context, such as 'so-and-so whom you met at my last birthday party'. Another dimension that our memories seemingly encode is time. We find it easy to remember the first thing we did in the morning, a random incident from our first job, or a memory from a childhood birthday party. Along with each we may also recall other events from the same hour, year, or decade. So the window of time within which associated memories are retrieved depends on how far back we are searching. Other studies have shown that memories further back in time are more likely to be viewed in third-person, i.e., where one sees oneself. Much more has been studied about human memory; the book *Searching for Memory: The Brain, the Mind, and the Past*,[15] by Daniel Schacter is an excellent introduction.

The acts of remembering, knowing, and making connections are all intimately related. For now we are concerned with 'looking up', or remembering, and it seems clear from a lot of scientific as well as anecdotal evidence that not only are our memories more complex than looking up a huge index, but that we actually don't have any single huge index to look up. That is why we find it difficult to connect events from different mental compartments, such as the Battle of Plassey and Napoleon's defeat at Waterloo. At the same time, our memories, or experiences in fact, make us better at making connections between effects and causes: Holmes's memory of his boots being similarly damaged in the past leads him to the probable cause of Watson's similar fate.

Vannevar Bush also clearly recognized the differences between a mechanical index-based lookup that is 'able to key one sheet of a million before an operator in a second or two'[8] as 'might even be of use in libraries',[8] versus how human memory operates:

> The human mind does not work that way. It operates by association. With one item in its grasp, it snaps instantly to the next that is suggested by the association of thoughts, in accordance with some intricate web of trails carried by the cells of the brain. It has other characteristics, of course; trails that are not frequently followed are prone to fade, items are not fully permanent, memory is transitory. Yet the speed of action, the intricacy of trails, the detail of mental pictures, is awe-inspiring beyond all else in nature.[8]

So what, if anything, is missing from today's web-search engines when compared to human memory? First, the way documents are 'linked' to one another in the web, i.e., the hyperlinks that we might traverse while surfing the web, which are pretty much built in by the author of a web page. The connections between our experiences and concepts, our 'association of thoughts', are based far more on the similarities between different memories, and are built up over time rather than hard-wired like hyperlinks in a web page. (Even so, as we have hinted, Google already needs to exploit dynamic information such as browsing histories, in addition to hyperlinks, to compensate for fewer and fewer hyperlinks in new web pages.)

'Associative memories' are one class of computational models that attempt to mimic human memory's ability to dynamically form linkages based on similarities between experiences. We shall cover one such associative-memory model, called 'Sparse Distributed Memory' (SDM[16]), in Chapter 5, 'Predict'. Unlike web search that takes a query consisting of a few words as input, the SDM model assumes that the query is itself fairly large, i.e, a complete 'experience', with many details. This is like giving an entire document to a search engine as a query, rather than just a few words. Another possible difference between the way web search works has to do with how we perceive the results of a memory 'lookup'. Web search returns many, often thousands of, results, albeit ordered rather intuitively by PageRank. On the other hand, our own memory recall more often than not returns just one or at worst a small set of closely related concepts, ideas, or experiences, or even a curious mixture of these. Similarly, what an associative SDM recalls is in fact a combination of previously 'stored' experiences, rather than a list of search results—but more about SDM later in Chapter 5, 'Predict'.

In a similar vein, the web-search model is rather poor at handling duplicates, and especially near-duplicates. For example, every time we see an apple we certainly do not relegate this image to memory. However, when we interact with a new person, we do form some memory of their face, which gets strengthened further over subsequent meetings. On the other hand, a search engine's indexer tirelessly crawls every new document it can find on the web, largely oblivious of whether a nearly exactly similar document already exists. And because every document is so carefully indexed, it inexorably forms a part of the long list of search results for every query that includes any of the words it happens to contain; never mind that it is featured alongside hundreds of other nearly identical ones.

The most glaring instance of this particular aspect of web search can be experienced if one uses a 'desktop version' of web search, such as Google's freely downloadable desktop search tool that can be used to search for files on one's personal computer. In doing so one quickly learns two things. First, desktop search results are no longer 'intuitively' ordered with the most 'useful' ones magically appearing first. The secret-sauce of PageRank appears missing; but how could it not be? Since documents on one's PC rarely have hyperlinks to each other, there is no network on which PageRank might work. In fact, the desktop search tool does not even attempt to rank documents. Instead, search results are ordered merely by how closely they match one's query, much like the search engines of the pre-Google era.

The second important thing one notices with desktop search is that there are many near-duplicates in each list of search results. If you are a typical PC user, you would often keep multiple versions of every document you receive, edit, send out, receive further updates on, etc. Multiple versions of the 'same' document, differing from each other but still largely similar, are inevitable. And vanilla web-search cannot detect such near-duplicates. Apart from being annoying, this is also certainly quite different from how memory works. One sees one's own home every single day, and of course each time we experience it slightly differently: from different angles for sure, sometimes new furniture enters our lives, a new coat of paint, and so on. Yet the memory of 'our home' is a far more constant recollection, rather than a long list of search results.

How might a web-search engine also recognize and filter out near-duplicates? As we have seen, there are many billions of documents on the web. Even on one's personal desktop, we are likely to find many thousands of documents. How difficult would it be for computers, even the millions that power the web, to compare each pair of items to check whether or not they are so similar as to be potential 'near-duplicates'? To figure this out we need to know how many *pairs* of items can be formed, out of a few thousand, or, in the case of the web, many billions of individual items. Well, for n items there are exactly $\frac{n \times (n-1)}{2}$ pairs of items. If the number of items doubles, the number of pairs quadruples. A thousand items will have half a million pairs; a billion, well, half a billion trillion pairs. Such behaviour is called *quadratic*, and grows rapidly with n as compared to the more staid linear and mildly super-linear behaviours we have seen earlier. Clearly, finding all near-duplicates by brute force is unfeasible, at least for web documents. Even on a desktop with only tens of thousands of documents it could take many hours.

Quite surprisingly though, a new way to find near-duplicates in large collections *without* examining all pairs was invented as recently as the mid-1990s. This technique, called 'locality sensitive hashing' or (LSH[17]) has now found its way into different arenas of computing, including search and associative memories, as well as many other web-intelligence applications.

A simple way to understand the idea behind LSH is to imagine having to decide whether two books in your hand (i.e., physical volumes) are actually copies of the same book. Suppose you turned to a random page, say page 100, in each of the copies. With a quick glance you verify that they were the same; this would boost your confidence that the two were copies of the same book. Repeating this check for a few more random page choices would reinforce your confidence further. You would not need to verify whether each pair of pages were the same before being reasonably satisfied that the two volumes were indeed copies of the same book. LSH works in a similar manner, but on any collection of objects, not just documents, as we shall describe in Chapter 3, 'Learn'.

Towards the end of our journey, in Chapter 5, 'Predict', we shall also find that ideas such as LSH are not only making web-intelligence applications more efficient, but also underly the convergence of multiple disparate threads of AI research towards a better understanding of how computing machines might eventually mimic some of the brain's more surprising abilities, including memory.

Deeper and Darker

Stepping back a bit now, it may seem from our discussion so far that Google truly gives us instant access to 'all the world's information'. Clearly this is not the case. For one, as recounted earlier, our personal desktops are perhaps more difficult warehouses to search than the entire indexed web. But there is much more than the indexed web: for example, Google does not, as of now (thankfully), let anyone access my bank account number or, God forbid, my bank balance. Neither does it provide general access to my cellphone number or email address, and certainly not the contents of my emails—at least not yet. (Unfortunately, many people do make personal information public, often inadvertently, in which case Google's incessant crawlers do index that data and make it available to anyone who wants to look for it, and even others who happen to stumble upon it in passing.) All of this data is 'on the web' in the sense that users with the right privileges can access the data using, say, a password. Other information might well be public, such as the air fares published by different airlines between Chicago and New York, but is not available to Google's crawlers: such data needs specific input, such as the source, destination, and dates of travel, before it can be computed. Further, the ability to compute such data is spread across many different web-based booking services, from airlines to travel sites.

The information 'available' on the web that is actually indexed by search engines such as Google is called the 'surface web', and actually forms quite a small fraction of all the information on the web. In contrast, the 'deep web' consists of data hidden behind web-based services, within sites that allow users to look up travel prices, used cars, store locations, patents, recipes, and many more forms of information. The volume of data within the deep web is in theory huge, exponentially large in computer science terms. For example, we can imagine an unlimited number of combinations of many cities and travel fare enquiries for each. In practice of course, really useful information hidden in the deep web is most certainly finite, but still extremely large, and almost impossible to accurately estimate. It is certainly far larger than the indexed surface web of 50 billion or so web pages.

Each form can give rise to thousands, sometimes hundreds of thousands, of results, each of which qualify as a deep web page. Similarly, every Facebook or Twitter post, or every Facebook user's 'wall' might be considered a deep web page. Finally, if one considers all possible pages of search results, then the size of the deep web is potentially infinite. On the other hand, even if we omit such definitions that obviously bloat our estimates, we are still led to a fairly large figure: experiments published in 2007[18] reported that roughly 2.5% of a random sample of web pages were forms that should be considered part of the deep web. Even if we assume each form to produce at most a thousand possible results, we get a size of at least a trillion for the size of such a deep web.* If we increase our estimate of the number of distinct results the average form can potentially return, we get tens of trillions or even higher as an estimate for the size of the deep web. The point is that the Deeb web is huge, far larger than the the indexed web of 50 billion pages.

Search engines, including Google, are trying to index and search at least some of the more useful parts of the deep web. Google's approach[19] has been to automatically try out many possible inputs and input combinations for a deep web page and figure out those that appear to give the most results. These results are stored internally by Google and added to the Google index, thereby making them a part of the surface web. There have been other approaches as well, such as Kosmix,[20] which was acquired by Walmart in 2010. Kosmix's approach was to classify and categorize the most important and popular web-based services, using a combination of automated as well as human-assisted processes. In response to a specific query, Kosmix's engine would figure out a small number of the most promising web-services, issue queries to them on the fly, and then collate the results before presenting them back to the user. Searching the deep web is one of the more active areas of current research and innovation in search technology, and it is quite likely that many more promising start-ups would have emerged by the time this book goes to press.

* * *

The web has a lot of data for sure, but so do other databases that are not connected to the web, at least not too strongly, and in many cases for good reason. All the world's wealth resides in the computer systems of thousands of banks spread across hundreds of countries. Every day

---

* Two and a half per cent of 50 billion indexed web-pages times a thousand is 1.25 trillion.

billions of cellphones call each other, and records of 'who called whom when' are kept, albeit temporarily, in the systems of telecommunications companies. Every parking ticket, arrest, and arraignment is recorded in some computer or the other within most police or judicial systems. Each driving licence, passport, credit card, or identity card of any form is also stored in computers somewhere. Purchased travel of any kind, plane, rail, ship, or even rental car, is electronically recorded. And we can go on and on; our lives are being digitally recorded to an amazing degree, all the time. The question is, of course, who is looking?

Recently a Massachusetts resident got a letter informing him that his driving licence had been revoked. He could hardly recall the last time he had been cited for any traffic violations, so of course this was an unpleasant surprise.[21] It turned out that his licence was suspected of being fraudulent by a fraud detection tool developed by the Department of Homeland Security to check fraud and also assist in counter-terrorism. His only fault was that his face looked so similar to another driver that the software flagged the pair as a potential fraud. Clearly this is an example of a system failure; at some point human investigation should have taken place before taking the drastic action of licence cancellation. But the point is that someone, or some computer software, *is* looking at all our personal data, all the time, at least nowadays, and especially in some countries such as the US. Such intense surveillance by government agencies in the US is a recent phenomenon that has evolved after the 9/11 attacks. It is interesting to note that the success of Google and other web-intelligence applications has happened more or less in parallel with this evolution. At the same time, the ease with which disparate data from multiple sources can be accessed by such agencies, such as for correlating driving licence, phone, bank, and passport records, still has a long way to go, even though the situation is very different from where it was prior to 9/11.

Khalid Almihdhar was one of the nineteen terrorists involved in the 9/11 attacks. On 31 August 2001, Almihdhar was put on a national terrorist watchlist, based on the CIA's long-running investigation of him and other al-Qaeda terrorists that had thrown up enough evidence that he was in the US, and 'armed and dangerous'. That he should probably have been placed on the watchlist much earlier, as post-9/11 investigations have concluded, is another story. Nevertheless, the FBI began investigating Almihdhar's whereabouts and activities a few days later. Robert Fuller, the FBI investigator assigned to this task, claims to have searched a commercial database, called ChoicePoint, that even then maintained personal information on US residents, including their phone numbers and addresses. However, the ChoicePoint database did not reveal credit card transactions. As journalist Bob Woodward would later conclude, 'If the FBI had done a simple credit card check on the two 9/11 hijackers who had been identified in the United States before 9/11, Nawaf Alhazmi and Khalid Almihdhar, they would have found that the two men had bought 10 tickets for early morning flights for groups of other Middle Eastern men for September 11, 2001. That was knowledge that might conceivably have stopped the attacks'.[21] Whether or not such a search would have revealed this information in an obvious-enough way, or whether enough action would have ensued to actually stop the attacks, remains a matter of speculation. However, the point to note is that Robert Fuller could not just 'Google' Almihdhar in some manner. That was not because Google had yet to attain prominence, but because different databases, such as Choice-Point, credit card transaction records, and others were not crawled and indexed together in the manner that Google today crawls and indexes the entire web. Presumably, the situation is slightly different now, and law enforcement investigators have greater abilities to search multiple databases in a 'Google-like' fashion. We don't know the exact state of affairs in this regard in the US; the true picture is, for obvious reasons, closely guarded.

What we do know is that in 2002, immediately in the wake of 9/11, the US initiated a 'Total Information Awareness' (TIA) program that would make lapses such as that of Fuller a thing of the past. In addition, however, it would also be used to unearth suspicious behaviour using data from multiple databases, such as a person obtaining a passport in one name and a driving licence in another. The TIA program was shut down by the US Congress in 2003, after widespread media protests that it would lead to Orwellian mass surveillance of innocent citizens. At the same time, we also know that hundreds of terror attacks on the US and its allies have since been successfully thwarted.[22] The dismembering of a plot to bomb nine US airliners taking off from London in August 2006 could not have taken place without the use of advanced technology, including the ability to search disparate databases with at least some ease.

Whatever may be the state of affairs in the US, the situation elsewhere remains visibly lacking for sure. In the early hours of 27 November 2008, as the terrorist attacks on Mumbai were under way, neither Google or any other computer system was of any help. At that time no one realized that the terrorists holed up in the Taj Mahal and Trident hotels were in constant touch with their handlers in Pakistan. More importantly, no one knew if Mumbai was the only target: was another group planning to attack Delhi or another city the next day? The terrorists were not using some sophisticated satellite phones, but merely high-end mobile handsets, albeit routing their voice calls over the internet using VOIP.* Could intelligence agencies have come to know this somehow? Could they have used this knowledge to jam their communications? Could tracing their phones have helped guard against any accompanying imminent attacks in other cities? Could some form of very advanced 'Google-like' search actually

---

* 'Voice-over IP', a technique also used by the popular Skype program for internet telephony.

play a role even in such real-time, high-pressure counter-terrorism operations?

Every time a mobile phone makes a call, or, for that matter, a data connection, this fact is immediately registered in the mobile operator's information systems: a 'call data record', or CDR, is created. The CDR contains, among other things, the time of the call, the mobile numbers of the caller, and the person who was called, as well as the cellphone tower to which each mobile was connected at the time of the call. Even if, as in the case of the 26/11 terrorists, calls are made using VOIP, this information is noted in the CDR entries. The cellphone operator uses such CDRs in many ways, for example, to compute your monthly mobile bill.

While each mobile phone is connected to the nearest cellphone tower of the chosen network operator, its radio signal is also continuously received at nearby towers, including those of other operators. In normal circumstances these other towers largely ignore the signal; however, they do monitor it to a certain extent; when a cellphone user is travelling in a car, for example, the 'nearest' tower keeps changing, so the call is 'handed off' to the next tower as the location of the cell phone changes. In exceptional, emergency situations, it is possible to use the intensity of a cell phone's radio signal as measured at three nearby towers to accurately pin point the physical location of any particular cell phone. Police and other law-enforcement agencies sometimes call upon the cellular operators to collectively provide such 'triangulation-based' location information: naturally, such information is usually provided only in response to court orders. Similar regulations control the circumstances under which, and to whom, CDR data can be provided.

Nevertheless, for a moment let us consider what *could* have been possible if instant access to CDRs as well as triangulation-based location information could be searched, in a 'Google-like' fashion, by counter-terrorism forces battling the 26/11 terrorists in pitched gun-battles in the corridors of five-star hotels in Mumbai, India's financial capital, for over three days.

The CDR data, by itself, would provide cellphone details for all active instruments within and in the vicinity of the targeted hotels; this would probably have been many thousands—perhaps even hundreds of thousands—of cellphones. Triangulation would reveal the locations of each device, and those instruments operating only within the hotels would become apparent. Now, remember that no one knew that the terrorists were using data connections to make VOIP calls. However, having zeroed in on the phones operating inside the hotel, finding that a small number of devices were using data connections continually would have probably alerted the counter-terrorism forces to what was going on. After all, it is highly unlikely that a hostage or innocent guest hiding for their life in their rooms would be surfing the internet on their mobile phone. Going further, once the terrorists' cellphones were identified, they could have been tracked as they moved inside the hotel; alternatively, a tactical decision might have been taken to disconnect those phones to confuse the terrorists.

While this scenario may seem like a scene from the popular 2002 film *Minority Report*, its technological basis is sound. Consider, for the moment, what your reaction would have been to someone describing Google search, which we are all now used to, a mere fifteen or twenty years ago: perhaps it too would have appeared equally unbelievable. In such a futuristic scenario, Google-like search of CDR data could, in theory, be immensely valuable and provide in real-time information that could be of direct use to forces fighting on the ground.

Accepting that such a system may be a long way off, especially in India, even a rudimentary system such as one that could have helped Robert Fuller stumble upon Almihdhar's credit card purchases, would be of immense value in possibly preventing future terror attacks in the country. An investigator tracing a suspicious cellphone would greatly benefit from being able to instantly retrieve the most recent international calls made with the phone number, any bank accounts linked to it, any airline tickets booked using the number as reference along with the credit cards used in such transactions. All this without running around from pillar to post, as is the situation today, at least in most countries. Leave aside being able to search telecommunications and banking data together, as of today even CDR data from the same operator usually lies in isolated silos based on regions. Our web experience drives our expectations of technology in other domains, just as do films such as *Minority Report*. In the case of the web, however, we know that it really works, and ask why everything else can't be just as easy.

* * *

It is now known that the 26/11 Mumbai attacks were planned and executed by the Lashkar-e-Taiba, a terrorist group operating out of Pakistan. A recent book[23] by V. S. Subrahmanian and others from the University of Maryland, *Computational Analysis of Terrorist Groups: Lashkar-e-Taiba*, shows that many actions of such groups can possibly even be predicted, at least to a certain extent. All that is required is being able to collect, store, and analyse vast volumes of data using techniques similar to those we shall describe in later chapters. The shelved TIA program of the US had similar goals, and was perhaps merely ahead of its time in that the potential of big-data analytics was then relatively unknown and untested. After all, it was only in the remainder of the decade that the success of the web companies in harnessing the value of vast volumes of 'big data' became apparent for all to see.

In the days and months that followed the 26/11 attacks, a concerted nationwide exercise *was* initiated in India to develop a National Intelligence Grid, now called NATGRID,[24] that would connect many public databases in the country, with the aim of assisting intelligence and law enforcement activities in their counter-terrorism efforts. Informally, the expectation was and remains that of 'Google-like' searches across a variety of sources, be they well-structured data such as CDRs or bank transactions, or even unstructured public sources such as news, blogs, and social media.

Would the NATGRID system be required to replicate and store every piece of data in the country? We know from our deep dive into Google search that it would not; only the index would be required. But how much computing power would be needed? Would it need millions of servers like Google? An even bigger challenge was that data resides in disparate computer systems that are not, unlike web pages, all linked by the internet. Further, information is buried deep within disparate and largely disconnected software applications, rather than web pages using a common format. The situation is very much like the deep web, only deeper. Nevertheless, all these technical problems were found to be solvable, at least in principle. Cooperation across different organizations was more of a hurdle than technology. Additionally, there have been concerns about privacy, legality, and the dangers of misuse.[25] Would NATGRID be doomed to fail from the start, based on the sobering experience of the US with TIA? The jury is still open, but the program, which was initiated in mid-2009, has yet to begin implementation of any kind. As with TIA, there have been debates in the government and media, as well as turf wars between agencies, very similar to the situation in the US prior to the 9/11 attacks.[84]

* * *

'Looking' at things, and looking up facts, are part of our everyday thoughts and experience. In the past decade, we have also come to rely on Google search of our collective experiences as recorded in the massive volumes of 'big data' stored in the web's millions of servers. So much so that our dependence on search is also beginning to change the way we think; maybe for the worse in some respects, perhaps for the better in others. We have found that the same algorithms used on the web for determining importance, i.e., PageRank, can also closely predict the most important memories retrieved by humans, at least in some controlled experiments. Such observations lend credence to the suspicion that what we, in the guise of the smart engineers at Google and other search companies, are building into the web, is able to mimic, albeit in the weak-AI sense, some small element of our own intelligent abilities.

Aside from raising many philosophical and normative questions, web search is changing many other aspects of lives and society. Our experiences of instant gratification from web search are driving expectations in all quarters, including for access to our personal data by law enforcement agencies. It therefore seems inevitable that Google-like search of our personal data, however unpleasant, will only increase over time. As such systems get deployed, they will also appear to behave in increasingly intelligent ways, and often bordering on the spooky, such as the unfortunate driver whose licence was revoked out of the blue. Whether all this will lead to a safer world, or merely a more intrusive one, is yet to be seen.

We are all, it seems, looking at our world through new lenses; at the same time the lenses themselves are, in turn, looking back at us, and 'listening in', which is what we proceed to explore next.

2

LISTEN

As the scandal over Rupert Murdoch's News Corporation's illegal phone hacking activities broke to television audiences around the world, I could not help but wonder why?' And I am sure many others asked themselves the same question. What prompted Murdoch's executives to condone illegal activities aimed at listening into private conversations? Obvious, you might say: getting the latest scoop on a murder investigation, or the most salacious titbit about the royal family. But let us delve deeper and ask again, as a child might, why? So that more readers would read the *News of the World*, of course! Stupid question? What drove so many people, estimated at over 4 million, a significant fraction of Britain's population, to follow the tabloid press so avidly? The daily newspaper remains a primary source of news for the vast majority of the world's population. Of course, most people also read more serious papers than the *News of the World*. Still, what is it that drives some news items to become headlines rather than be relegated to the corner of an inside page?

Shannon and Advertising

The scientific answer is Information; capitalized here because there is more to the term than as understood in its colloquial usage. You may call it voyeurism in the case of *News of the World*, or the hunger to know what is happening around the world for, say, the *New York Times*. Both forms of enquiry suffer from the need to filter the vast numbers of everyday events that take place every second, so as to determine those that would most likely be of interest to readers. The concept of Information is best illustrated by comparing the possible headlines 'Dog Bites Man' and 'Man Bites Dog'. Clearly the latter, being a far rarer event, is more likely to prompt you to read the story than the former, more commonplace occurrence.

In 1948, Claude E. Shannon published a now classic paper entitled 'A Mathematical Theory of Communication'.[26] By then the telegraph, telephone, and radio had spawned a whole new communications industry with the AT&T company at its locus. Shannon, working at AT&T Bell Laboratories, was concerned with how fast one could communicate meaning, or information in its colloquial sense, over wires or even the wireless. In defining a new theory with which to solve such practical problems, he also arrived at a precise mathematical definition of Information. Shannon's Information measured the information (colloquial) content of a message in terms of the extent to which its being successfully transmitted reduced some degree of uncertainty on the part of the receiver. Thus, whether a telegraph operator transmitted 'the price of AT&T stock just rose by five cents', or 'ATT + 5c', the information content being transmitted was the same, at least to two equally intelligent receivers. Shannon quantified the amount of information in terms of the chance, or probability, of the event whose occurrences were being communicated. Thus, if it was quite normal for AT&T's stock to rise by 5 cents, the information content was lower than for a rarer event, say the stock suddenly falling by 5 dollars. Similarly, the story 'Man Bites Dog', being a rather rare event, has a far greater information content than 'Dog Bites Man'. The rarer the news, the more likely it is to catch our interest, and it therefore makes the headlines. Why? The paper wants you to buy a copy and read the story. In passing, you glance at the advertisements placed strategically close by, which is what an advertiser has paid good money for.

True, but what if some of us only read the sports pages?

Think of yourself at a party where you hear snippets of many conversations simultaneously, even as you focus on and participate in one particular interaction. Often you may pick up cues that divert your attention, nudging you to politely shift to another conversation circle. Interest is piqued by the promise both of an unlikely or original tale and one that is closely aligned with your own predilections, be they permanent or temporary. We all 'listen for' the unexpected, and even more so for some subjects as compared to the rest. The same thing is going on when we read a newspaper, or, for that matter, search, surf, or scan stories on the web. We usually know, at least instinctively or subconsciously, what should surprise or interest us. But the newspaper does not. Its only measure of success is circulation, which is also what advertisers have to rely on to decide how much space to book with the particular paper. Apart from this the only additional thing an advertiser can do is discover, *ex post facto*, whether or not their money was well spent. Did Christmas sales actually go up or not? If the latter, well, the damage has already been done. Moreover, which paper should they pull their ads from for the next season? No clue. In Shannon's language, the indirect message conveyed by a paper's circulation, or for that matter *ex post facto* aggregate sales, contains precious little Information, in terms of doing little to reduce the uncertainty of which pages we are actually reading and thereby which advertisements should be catching our eye.

Of course, it is well known that Google and the internet-based advertising industry it engendered have changed the rules of the game, as we shall describe in some detail very shortly. But it is interesting to view what they have actually achieved from the perspective of Shannon's information theory, which was itself concerned more with the transmission of signals over wires and the ether. In our case we should look instead at other kinds of signals, such a paper's circulation, or an advertiser's end-of-season sales figures. Think of these as being at the receiving end, again speaking in terms more familiar to Shannon's world. And then there is the actual signal that is transmitted by you and me, i.e., the stories we seek out and actually read. The transmission loss along this communication path, from actual reader behaviour to the 'lag' measures of circulation or sales, is huge, both in information content as well as delay. If such a loss were suffered in a telegraph network, it would be like getting the message 'AT&T goes out of business', a year after the transmission of the original signal, which might have reported a sudden dip in share price. No stock trader would go anywhere near such a medium!

Shannon was concerned both with precisely measuring the information content of a signal and with how efficiently and effectively information could be transmitted along a *channel*, such as a telephone wire. He defined the information content of any particular value of a signal as the probability of its occurrence. Thus, if the signal in question was the toss of a fair coin, then the information content of the signal 'heads' would be defined in terms of the probability of this value showing up, which is exactly 1/2. Provided of course that the coin was fair. A conman's coin that had two heads would of course yield no information when it inevitably landed on its head, with probability 1. Recall our discussion of logarithmic-time algorithms in Chapter 1, such as binary search. As it turns out, Shannon information is defined, surprising as it may seem, in terms of the *logarithm* of the inverse probability. Thus the information content conveyed by the fair coin toss is log 2, which is exactly 1, and that for the conman's coin is log 1, which, as expected, turns out to be 0.* Similarly, the roll of a fair six-sided dice

---

* Recall that we are using base-two logarithms; thus $\log 2 = 1$ because $2^1 = 2$; similarly 2^0, or 2 multiplied by itself zero times, is 1, so $\log 1 = 0$.

has an information content of log 6, which is about 2.58, and for the unusual case of an eight-sided dice, log 8 is exactly 3.

It turns out, as you might have suspected, that the logarithm crept into the formal definition of information for good reason. Recall once more how we searched for a word in a list using binary search in a logarithmic number of steps: by asking, at each step, which half of the list to look at; as if being guided through a maze, 'go left', then 'go right'. Now, once we are done, how should we convey our newly discovered knowledge, i.e., the place where our word actually occurs in the list? We might remember the sequence of decisions we made along the way and record the steps we took to navigate to our word of interest; these are, of course, logarithmic in number. So, recording the steps needed to reach one specific position out of n total possibilities requires us to record at most log n 'lefts' or 'rights', or equivalently, log n zeros and ones.

Say the discovered position was the eighth one, i.e., the last in our list of eight. To arrive at this position we would have had to make a 'right-wards' choice each time we split the list; we could record this sequence of decisions as 111. Other sequences of decisions would similarly have their rendition in terms of exactly three symbols, each one or zero: for example, 010 indicates that starting from the 'middle' of the list, say position 4,* we look leftward once to the middle of the first half of the list, which ends up being position 2.

Shannon, and earlier Hartley, called these zero–one symbols 'bits', heralding the information age of 'bits and bytes' (where a byte is just a sequence of eight bits). Three bits can be arranged in exactly eight distinct sequences, since $2 \times 2 \times 2 = 8$, which is why log 8 is 3. Another way of saying this is that because these three bits are sufficient to represent the reduction in uncertainty about which of the eight

---

* Since the list has an even number of items, we can choose to define 'middle' as either the 4th or 5th position; we choose the smaller option, consistently.

words is being chosen, so the information content in the message conveying the word position is 3. Rather long-winded? Why not merely convey the symbol '8'? Would this not be easier? Or were bits more efficient?

It makes no difference. The amount of information is the same whether conveyed by three bits or by one symbol chosen from eight possibilities. This was first shown by Shannon's senior at Bell Labs, Hartley, way back in 1928 well before Shannon's arrival there. What Shannon did was take this definition of information and use it to define, in precise mathematical terms, the *capacity* of any channel for communicating information. For Shannon, channels were wired or wireless means of communication, using the technologies of telegraph, telephone, and later radio. Today, Shannon's theory is used to model data communication on computer networks, including of course, the internet. But as we have suggested, the notion of a channel can be quite general, and his information theory has since been applied in areas as diverse as physics to linguistics, and of course web technology.

If the information content of a precise message was the degree to which it reduced uncertainty upon arrival, it was important, in order to define channel capacity, to know what the uncertainty was before the signal's value was known. As we have seen earlier, exactly one bit of information is received by either of the messages, 'heads' or 'tails', signalling the outcome of a fair coin toss. We have also seen that no information is conveyed for a two-headed coin, since it can only show one result. But what about a peculiar *coin that shows up heads a third of the time and tails otherwise?* The information conveyed by each signal, 'heads' or 'tails', is now different: each 'head', which turns up 1/3 of the time, conveys $\log 3$ bits of information, while 'tails' shows up with a probability 2/3 conveying $\log \frac{3}{2}$ bits. Shannon defined the term *entropy* to measure the *average* information conveyed over a large number of outcomes, which could be calculated precisely as the information conveyed by each outcome, weighted by the probability of that outcome. So the entropy of the fair coin signal is $1/2 \times 1 + 1/2 \times 1 = 1$, since each possible outcome conveys one bit, and moreover each outcome occurs half the time, on the average. Similarly, a sequence of tosses of the two-headed coin has zero entropy. However, for the loaded coin, the entropy becomes $\frac{1}{3} \log 3 + \frac{2}{3} \log \frac{3}{2}$, which works out to just under 0.7; a shade less than that of the fair coin.

Shannon was interested in a theory describing the transmission of information over *any* channel whatsoever. So he needed to figure out the relationship between the uncertainties in the two signals at each end of a communications channel, more precisely their entropies. He defined the idea of *mutual information* between the signal sent down a channel versus the one actually received. If the two signals corresponded closely to each other, with only occasional discrepancies, then the mutual information between them was high, otherwise it was lower. A simple way to understand mutual information is to imagine that you are the receiver of a signal, continuously getting messages over a communication channel such as a telegraph or radio. But you have no idea how closely the received messages match those that were sent. Now suppose you somehow got independent reports of what messages were actually sent, say by magic, or by a messenger on horseback who arrived days later. You could work out how often the channel misled you. The amount by which these reports would surprise you, such as how often there were transmission errors, would allow you to measure how good or bad the earlier transmissions were. As earlier with our coin tosses, the degree of surprise, on average, should be nothing but the entropy of these special reports, which Shannon called *conditional entropy*. If the conditional entropy was high, i.e., the reports often surprised you by pointing out errors in transmission, then the mutual information between the sent and received signals should be low. If the reports did not surprise you much, behaving almost like a loaded coin that always gave the same result as your observation of the received signal, then the conditional entropy was low and the mutual information high. Shannon defined the mutual information as the difference between the entropy of whatever was actually being transmitted and the conditional entropy.

For example, suppose that you are communicating the results of a fair coin toss over a communication channel that makes errors 1/3 of the time. The conditional entropy, measuring your surprise at these errors, is the same as for the loaded coin described earlier, i.e., close to 0.7.* The entropy of the transmitted signal, being a fair coin, is 1; it, and the mutual information, is the difference, or 0.3, indicating that the channel transmission does somewhat decrease your uncertainty about the source signal. On the other hand, if as many as half the transmissions were erroneous, then the conditional entropy would equal that of the fair coin, i.e., exactly 1, making the mutual information zero. In this case the channel transmission fails to convey anything about the coin tosses at the source.

Next Shannon defined the *capacity* of any communication channel as the maximum mutual information it could possibly exhibit as long as an appropriate signal was transmitted. Moreover, he showed how to actually calculate the capacity of a communication channel, without necessarily having to show which kind of signal had to be used to achieve this maximum value. This was a giant leap of progress, for it provided engineers with the precise knowledge of how much information they could actually transmit over a particular communication technology, such as a telegraph wire over a certain distance or a radio signal of a particular strength, and with what accuracy. At the same time it left them with the remaining task of actually trying to

---

* The calculations are actually more complicated, such as when the chances of error differ depending on what was transmitted, i.e., a head or a tail.

achieve that capacity in practice, by, for example, carefully encoding the messages to be transmitted.

Now, let us return to the world of advertising and the more abstract idea of treating paper circulation or sales figures as a signal about our own behaviour of seeking and reading. In terms of Shannon's information theory, the mutual information between reader behaviour and measures such as circulation or sales is quite low. Little can be achieved to link these since the channel itself, i.e., the connection between the act of buying a newspaper and aggregate circulation or product sales, is a very tenuous one.

The Penny Clicks

Enter online advertising on the internet. Early internet 'banner' advertisements, which continue to this day, merely translated the experience of traditional print advertising onto a web page. The more people viewed a page, the more one had to pay for advertising space. Instead of circulation, measurements of the total number of 'eyeballs' viewing a page could easily be derived from page hits and other network-traffic statistics. But the mutual information between eyeballs and outcomes remained as weak as for print media. How weak became evident from the dot.com bust of 2001. Internet companies had fuelled the preceding bubble by grossly overestimating the value of the eyeballs they were attracting. No one stopped to question whether the new medium was anything more than just that, i.e., a new way of selling traditional advertising. True, a new avenue for publishing justified some kind of valuation, but how much was never questioned. With 20/20 hindsight it is easy to say that someone should have questioned the fundamentals better. But hindsight always appears crystal clear. At the same time, history never fails to repeat itself.

As of this writing, a new bubble is looming in the world of social networking. Just possibly, a deeper analysis, based perhaps on the concept of mutual information, might reveal some new insight. Is the current enthusiasm for the potential profitability of 'new age' social networking sites justified? Only time will tell. In the meanwhile, recent events such as the relative lukewarm response to Facebook's initial public offering in mid-2012 do give us reason to pause and ponder. Perhaps some deeper analyses using mutual information might come in handy. To see how, let us first look at what the Google and other search engines did to change the mutual information equation between consumers and advertisers, thereby changing the fundamentals of online advertising and, for that matter, the entire media industry.

An ideal scenario from the point of view of an advertiser would be to have to pay only when a consumer actually buys their product. In such a model the mutual information between advertising and outcome would be very high indeed. Making such a connection is next to impossible in the print world. However, in the world of web pages and clicks, in principle this can be done by charging the advertiser only when an online purchase is made. Thus, instead of being merely a medium for attracting customer attention, such a website would instead become a sales channel for merchants. In fact Groupon* uses exactly such a model: Groupon sells discount coupons to intelligently selected prospects, while charging the merchants a commission if and only if its coupons are used for actual purchases.

In the case of a search engine, such as Yahoo! or Google, however, consumers may choose to browse a product but end up not buying it because the product is poor, for no fault of the search engine provided. So why should Google or Yahoo! waste their advertising space on such ads? Today online advertisers use a model called 'pay-per-click', or PPC, which is somewhere in between, where an advertiser pays only if a potential customer clicks their ad, regardless of whether that click gets converted to a sale. At the same time, the advertiser does not pay if a

---

* <http://www.groupon.com>.

customer merely looks at the ad, without clicking it. The PPC model was first invented by Bill Gross who started GoTo.com in 1998. But it was Google that made PPC really work by figuring out the best way to *charge* for ads in this model. In the PPC model, the mutual information between the potential buyer and the outcome is lower than for, say, a sales channel such as Groupon. More importantly, however, the mutual information is highly dependent on which ad the consumer sees. If the ad is close to the consumer's intent at the time she views it, there is a higher likelihood that she will click, thereby generating revenue for the search engine and a possible sale for the advertiser.

What better way to reduce uncertainty and increase the mutual information between a potential buyer's intent and an advertisement, than to allow advertisers to exploit the keywords being searched on? However, someone searching on 'dog' may be interested in dog food. On the other hand, they may be looking to adopt a puppy. The solution was to get out of the way and let the advertisers figure it out. Advertisers bid for keywords, and the highest bidder's ad gets placed first, followed by the next highest and so on. The 'keyword auction', called AdWords by Google, is a continuous global event, where all kinds of advertisers, from large companies to individuals, can bid for placements against the search results of billions of web users. This 'keyword auction' rivals the largest stock markets in volume, and is open to anyone who has a credit card with which to pay for ads!

Once more, as in the case of PPC, one should point out that the concept of a keyword auction was not actually Google's invention. GoTo.com, later acquired by Overture and then by Yahoo!, actually introduced keyword auctions. But there was a problem with their model. The PPC-auction model allowed advertisers to offer to pay only for those keywords that would, in their view, best increase the mutual information between a buyer's intent and the possible outcome of their viewing an ad. Still, the model would work only if the ads actually got displayed often enough. The problem was competition. Once Nike knew that Adidas ads were appearing first against some keywords, say 'running shoes', they would up their bid in an effort to displace their rival. Since the auction took place online and virtually instantaneously, Nike could easily figure out exactly what Adidas's bid was (and vice versa), and quickly learn that by bidding a mere cent higher they would achieve first placement. Since the cost of outplacing a rival was so low, i.e., a very small increment to one's current bid, Adidas would respond in turn, leading to a spiralling of costs. While this may have resulted in short-term gains for the search engine, in the long run advertisers did not take to this model due to its inherent instability.

Google first figured out how to improve the situation: instead of charging an advertiser the price they bid, Google charges a tiny increment over the next-highest bidder. Thus, Nike might bid 40 cents for 'running shoes', and Adidas 60 cents. But Adidas gets charged only 41 cents per click. Nike needs to increase its bid significantly in order to displace Adidas for the top placement, and Adidas can increase this gap without having to pay extra. The same reasoning works for each slot, not just the first one. As a result, the prices bid end up settling down into a stable configuration based on each bidder's comfort with the slot they get, versus the price they pay. Excessive competition is avoided by this 'second price' auction, and the result is a predictable and usable system. It wasn't too long before other search engines including Yahoo! also switched to this second-price auction model to ensure more 'stability' in the ad-market.

What does the second-price auction give an advertiser from the perspective of mutual information? By bidding on keywords, merchants can place their ads more intelligently, using keywords to gauge the intent of the searcher they want to target. Further, they pay for ads only when someone clicks on one. Both these factors, i.e., targeting ads to keywords and linking payment to clicks, increase the mutual information between each advertising dollar spent and an actual sale. In fact, the correlation between the advertising expense and hits on a merchant's website is perfect, i.e., the mutual information is exactly 1, since the merchant pays only if a user actually visits the merchant's site. The remaining uncertainty of whether such a visit actually translates to a sale is out of the hands of the search engine, and instead depends on how good a site and product the merchant can manage. Another way of looking at PPC is that the advertiser is paying to increase 'circulation' figures for his site, ensuring that eyeballs read the material he wants people to read, rather than merely hoping that they glance at his ad while searching for something else.

Statistics of Text

However effective search-engine advertising might be, nevertheless a bidder on Google's AdWords (or Yahoo!'s 'sponsored-search' equivalent) can only place advertisements on a search-results page, targeting only searchers who are looking for something. What about those reading material on the web after they have found what they wanted through search, or otherwise? They might be reading a travel site, blog, or magazine. How might such readers also be presented with ads sold through a keyword auction? Google's solution, called AdSense, did precisely this. Suppose you or I have published a web page on the internet. If we sign up for AdSense, Google allows us to include a few lines of computer code within our web page that displays *contextually* relevant ads right there, on our web page, just as if it were Google's own page. Google then shares the revenue it gets from clicks on these ads with us, the authors of the web page. A truly novel business model: suddenly large numbers of independent web-page publishers became Google's partners through whom it could syndicate ads sold through AdWords auctions.

Of course, as before in the case of the 'second-price auction' idea, other search engines including Yahoo! quickly followed Google's lead and developed AdSense clones. At the same time, they struggled to match Google's success in this business: Yahoo! shut down its AdSense clone called 'Publisher Network' in 2010, only to restart it again very recently in 2012, this time in partnership with Media.net, a company that now powers contextual search for both Yahoo! as well as Microsoft's Bing search engine.

So how does AdSense work? The AdWords ads are sold by keyword auction, so if Google could somehow figure out the most important keywords from within the contents of our web page, it could use these to position ads submitted to the AdWords auction in the same manner as done alongside Google search results. Now, we may think that since Google is really good at search, i.e., finding the right documents to match a set of keywords, it should be easy to perform the reverse, i.e., determine the best keywords for a particular document. Sounds simple, given Google's prowess in producing such great search results. But not quite. Remember that the high quality of Google search was due to PageRank, which orders *web pages* by importance, not words. It is quite likely that, as per PageRank, our web page is not highly ranked. Yet, because of our loyal readers, we do manage to get a reasonable number of visitors to our page, enough to be a worthwhile audience for advertisers: at least we think so, which is why we might sign up for AdSense. 'Inverting' search sounds easy, but actually needs much more work.

The keywords chosen for a particular web page should really represent the content of the page. In the language of information theory, the technique for choosing keywords should make sure that the mutual information between web pages and the keywords chosen for them should be as high as possible. As it turns out, there is such a technique, invented as long ago as 1972,[27] called TF-IDF, which stands for 'term frequency times inverse document frequency'. The core idea here is the concept of inverse document frequency, or IDF, of a word (also called 'term'). The idea behind IDF is that a word that occurs in many documents, such as the word 'the', is far less useful for searching for content than one that is rare, such as 'intelligence'. All of us intuitively use this concept while searching for documents on the web; rarely do we use very common words. Rather, we try our best to choose words that are likely to be highly selective, occurring more often in the documents we seek, and thereby give us better results. The IDF of a word is computed from a ratio—the total number of web pages divided by the number of pages that contain a particular word. In fact the IDF that seemed to work best in practice was, interestingly enough, the *logarithm* of this ratio.* Rare words have a high IDF, and are therefore better choices as keywords.

The term frequency, or TF, on the other hand, is merely the number of times the word occurs in some document. Multiplying TF and IDF therefore favours generally rare words that nevertheless occur often in our web page. Thus, out of two equally rare words, if one occurs more often in our web page, we would consider that a better candidate to be a keyword, representative of our content.

TF-IDF was invented as a heuristic, based only on intuition, and without any reference to information theory. Nevertheless, you might well suspect such a relationship. The presence of a rare word might be viewed as conveying more information than that of more common ones, just as does a message informing us that some unexpected event has nevertheless occurred. Similarly the use of the logarithm, introduced in the TF-IDF formula due to its practical utility, points to a connection with Shannon's theory that also uses logarithms to define information content. Our intuition is not too far off; recent research has indeed shown that the TF-IDF formulation appears quite naturally when calculating the mutual information between 'all words' and 'all pages'. More precisely, it has been shown that the mutual information between words and pages is proportional to the sum, over all words, of

---

* The IDF of a word w is defined to be $\log \frac{N}{N_w}$; N being the total number of pages, of which N_w contain the word w.

the TF-IDFs of each word taken in isolation.[28] Thus, it appears that by choosing, as keywords, those words in the page that have the highest TF-IDF, we are also increasing the mutual information and thereby reducing the uncertainty regarding the intent of the reader.

Is keyword guessing enough? What if an article mentions words such as 'race', 'marathon', and 'trophy', but omits a mention of 'running' or 'shoes'. Should an AdWords bidder, such as Nike or Adidas, be forced to imagine all possible search words against which their ads might be profitably placed? Is it even wise to do so? Perhaps so, if the article in question was indeed about running marathon races. On the other hand, an article with exactly these keywords might instead be discussing a national election, using the words 'race', 'marathon', and 'trophy' in a totally different context. How could any keyword-guessing algorithm based on TF-IDF possibly distinguish between these situations? Surely it is asking too much for a computer algorithm to understand the *meaning* of the article in order to place it in the appropriate context. Surprisingly though, it turns out that even such seemingly intelligent tasks can be tackled using information-theoretic ideas like TF-IDF.

Just as TF-IDF measures the relative frequency of a word in a page weighted by its relative rarity overall, we can also consider pairs of words occurring together. For example, the words 'marathon' and the terms '42 kilometres' or '26 miles' are likely to occur together in at least some articles dealing with actual running. On the other hand, words such as 'election', 'voters', or 'ballot' are likely to occur together in news about campaigning and politics. Can a computer algorithm figure out such relationships by itself, without actually 'understanding' the content, whatever that means? The frequency with which each pair of words occur together, averaged over all pages, can certainly be calculated. Essentially we need to count co-occurrences of words, i.e., the number of times words occur together. But, just as in the case of individual words, it is also a good idea to weight each such co-occurrence by the IDF of both words in the pair. By doing this, the co-occurrence of a word with a very common word, such as 'the', is not counted, since its IDF will be almost zero.* In other words we take a pair of words and multiply their TF-IDF scores in *every* document, and then add up all these products. The result is a measure of the correlation of the two words as inferred from their co-occurrences in whatever very large set of documents is available, such as *all* web pages. Of course, this is done for every possible pair of words as well. No wonder Google needs millions of servers.

Exploiting such word–word correlations based on co-occurrences of words in documents is the basis of 'Latent Semantic Analysis', which involves significantly more complex mathematics than the procedure just outlined.[29] Surprisingly, it turns out that Latent Semantic Analysis (or LSA) can perform tasks that appear to involve 'real understanding', such as resolving ambiguities due to the phenomenon of *polysemy*, where the same word, such as 'run', has different meanings in different contexts. LSA-based algorithms can also figure out the many millions of different *topics* that are discussed, in billions of pages, such as 'having to do with elections' versus 'having to do with running', and also automatically determine which topic, or topics, each page is most likely about.

Sounds incredible? Maybe a simple example can throw some light on how such *topic analysis* takes place. For the computer, a topic is merely a bunch of words; computer scientists call this the 'bag of words' model. For good measure, each word in a topic also has its TF-IDF score, measuring its importance in the topic weighted by its overall rarity across all topics. A bag of words, such as 'election', 'running', and 'campaign', could form a topic associated with documents having to do with elections. At the same time, a word such as 'running'

---

* 'The' occurs in almost all documents, so the ratio $\frac{N}{N_w}$ is close to 1, and log 1 is 0.

might find a place in many topics, whereas one such as 'election' might span fewer topics.

Such topics can form the basis for disambiguating a web page on running marathons from a political one. All that is needed is a similarity score, again using TF-IDF values, between the page and each topic: for each word we multiply its TF-IDF in the page in question with the TF-IDF of the same word in a particular topic, and sum up all these products. In this manner we obtain scores that measure the relative contribution of a particular topic to the content of the page. Thus, using such a procedure, Google's computers can determine that an article we may be reading is 90% about running marathons and therefore place Nike's advertisement for us to see, while correctly omitting this ad when we read a page regarding elections. So, not only does Google watch what we read, it also tries to 'understand' the content, albeit 'merely' by using number crunching and statistics such as TF-IDF.

It is important to note that while the computer might place many words such as 'election', 'running', and 'campaign', in a topic that we easily recognize as 'dealing with elections', it usually cannot come up with a meaningful title for this topic. For it, a topic is a bag of words, and just that, without any other 'meaning'. The problem of finding 'good' labels for such automatically detected topics remains difficult for computers to do. Topic labelling is also closely related to the problem of automatically creating a 'back of the book' index, which was briefly mentioned in Chapter 1. As in the case of topic titles, entries in a back-of-the-book index need to be succinct and informative, summarizing the most important concepts being discussed. Bags of words will not do. Accurate automatic back-of-the-book indexing is still an open problem, as discussed in a recent paper by András Csomai and Rada Mihalcea: 'Although there is a certain degree of computer assistance, consisting of tools that help the professional indexer to organize and edit the index, there are however no methods that would allow for a complete or nearly-complete automation'.[30]

* * *

It seems that Google is always listening to us: what we search for, what we read, even what we write in our emails. Increasingly sophisticated techniques are used, such as TF-IDF, LSA, and topic analysis, to bring this process of listening closer and closer to 'understanding'—at least enough to place ads intelligently so as to make more profits.

Therein lies the rub. Is Google really understanding what we say? How hard does it need to try? Are TF-IDF-based techniques enough, or is more needed? Very early on after Google launched AdSense, people tried, not surprisingly, to fool the system. They would publish web pages full of terms such as 'running shoes', 'buying', and 'price', without any coherent order. The goal was to ensure that their pages were returned in response to genuine search queries. When visitors opened such a page they would realize that it contained junk. But it was hoped that even such visitors might, just maybe, click on an advertisement placed there by AdSense, thereby making money for the publisher of the junk page. Google needed to do more than rely only on the bag-of-words model. It needed to extract deeper understanding to combat such scams, as well as much more. Thus, inadvertently driven by the motive of profitable online advertising, web companies such as Google quite naturally strayed into areas of research having to deal with language, meaning, and understanding. The pressure of business was high. They also had the innocence of not necessarily wanting to solve the 'real' problem of language or understanding—just good enough would do—and so they also made a lot of progress.

Turing in Reverse

Let us now return to the 'Turing Test', with which we began this book. You may recall that the Turing Test was proposed in 1950 by Alan

Turing[1] as a way to evaluate progress towards the emulation of intelligent behaviour by a computer. The 'standard' Turing Test is most often stated as follows: there are two players, a computer A and a human B, each of whom communicate with a human interrogator C. The job of C is to determine which of the two players is a computer, and which is human. If a computer could be so designed as to fool the interrogator often enough, it may as well, as Turing argued, be considered 'intelligent'. Turing was after the core essence of intelligence, in an abstract form, divorced of the obvious physical aspects of being human, such as having a body or a voice. Therefore, he suggested, 'In order that tones of voice may not help the interrogator the answers should be written, or better still, typewritten. The ideal arrangement is to have a teleprinter communicating between the two rooms'. In other words, the interrogator could only listen to his subjects via text, much as, for example, Google or Facebook do with our emails, queries, posts, friend-requests, and other web writings or activities. Only in this case Google and Facebook are machines.

Over the years, many variations of the Turing Test have been proposed, each for a different purpose. The term 'reverse Turing Test' is most often used for the case where the interrogator is also a computer, such as a website's software, whose purpose is to determine whether it is communicating with a human or another computer. The use of image-based 'CAPTCHAs',* where alphabets are rendered in the form of distorted images that need to be identified, is a practical application that can be viewed as a reverse Turing Test: CAPTCHAs are used to prevent automated attacks on e-commerce sites. Here the interrogator is the website software that uses the CAPTCHA image to ensure that only genuine humans access the site's services.

(As an aside, you may well wonder how correct answers for so many different CAPTCHA problems are generated in the first place: services

---

* **C**ompletely **A**utomated **P**ublic **T**uring Test to Tell **C**omputers and **H**umans **A**part.

such as recaptcha.net automate this step as well, using *machine learning* techniques, as we shall describe in Chapter 3. Moreover, these services provide an interesting side-benefit: contributing to efforts to digitize printed as well as handwritten text.)

As described in Turing's original article, he derived his test from an imaginary 'imitation game', in which the participants are all human. Player A is a man and player B a woman. Player A tries to fool player C that he is in fact a woman, whereas the woman attempts to convey the truth. Player C wins if he successfully guesses who is who. In Turing's Test, player C is a human, whereas in 'reverse' variations of the Turing Test C is a computer, such as a server providing the CAPTCHA service, or even a collection of millions of servers such as those powering Google or Facebook.

As we have seen earlier, all web-based services that depend on online advertising revenue need to extract deeper understanding about consumers visiting the web, so as to better target ads to them. Mutual information needs to be maximized to attract advertisers. I would argue that there is yet another variation of the reverse Turing Test at play here, closer, in fact, to Turing's initial imitation game. Players A and B are merely humans conversing with each other on the web, say via email, or publishing and reading content on websites or blogs. The interrogators are Google, Yahoo!, or Bing in the guise of AdSense or any of its clones, as well as other web services such as Facebook, Twitter, and their ilk. Their goal is to determine as much as possible about A and B, and all others using the web. This could just as well include whether A or B is male or female. They are also interested in figuring out who is old or young, happy or sad, affluent or poor..., a list that can go on forever. This 'generalized reverse Turing Test' is the lifeblood of online advertising. The better Google and others are at guessing our attributes, the more targeted their ads can be, and the higher the likelihood that we will click such ads. As a result the mutual information between what advertisers spend and what they receive is increased. 'Intelligent' behaviour is merely a side effect required to achieve this aim. Perhaps that is why web companies have been somewhat successful, bothered as they are only with very practical results, rather than with more lofty goals such as truly understanding intelligence.

Can the 'web-intelligence engines' built by Google, Facebook, and others really guess who is male or female, old or young, happy or angry? Or whether a web page is targeted at the very affluent or not, to a wide section of society or a niche? Most important from their perspective is to determine the *intent* of the web user: is she interested in buying something or not? Even more simply, does a web page convey any meaning to a human reader, or is it merely junk being used to spam a contextual engine such as AdSense? What we might well suspect is that in order to answer such questions with any hope of success, the techniques used need to go beyond the bag-of-words model described earlier. After all, if someone writes 'my new . . . phone is not terribly bad, compared to my old one . . .', are they making a positive or negative comment? The bag-of-words model would see a bunch of negative words and wrongly conclude that the comment is negative. Just perhaps, some deeper analysis is required. Maybe our usage of language needs to be deconstructed? It certainly appears that the machine needs to listen to us much more carefully, at least for some purposes.

Language and Statistics

The web is largely about text, or the written word. Search, surfing, and advertising are all based on the premise that users of the web *read*. Of course, there is also ample video and music content available on the web today. Still, even though some new services such as Google Glass allow us to search using images, for the most part our interaction with even video and audio material remains largely through words:

we search for, write about, and share videos and music through social networks, blogs, and email—all based on text. Today there is a lot of speculation about the so-far-elusive 'spoken web', using which we might search using voice, and listen to web content, using technologies for speech recognition and speech-to-text conversion.[31] Even if this comes about, the 'word' and its usage via human language remains central.

Language is, as far as we know, a uniquely human mechanism. Even though many animals communicate with each other, and some might even use a form of code that could be construed as language, the sophistication and depth of human language is certainly missing in the wider natural world. The study of language is vast, even bordering on the philosophical in many instances. We shall not endeavour to delve too deep in these waters, at least for now. Instead we shall focus only on a few ideas that are relevant for the purpose at hand, namely, how might Google, or 'the web' in general, get better at our 'generalized' reverse Turing Test described earlier.

If there are just two important attributes about human language that a machine facing the reverse Turing Test would need to deal with, these are probably *redundancy* on the one hand, and *ambiguity* on the other. Human language is highly redundant. (Even the previous few paragraphs might convince you of this.) In order to convey an idea with clarity, we often repeat the same message in different ways. From the perspective of Shannon's information theory, the redundancy of language might well be understood as an elaborate coding scheme so construed as to compensate for any 'loss of information' during 'transmission' from one person's mind to another. In fact, Shannon studied the inherent redundancy of the English language in detail, but from a purely information-theoretic viewpoint. As per Shannnon's estimate, English is 75% redundant, by which he meant that of all the possible sentences that could be formed using a fixed number of letters and spaces, only 25% of these convey new information. Shannon tested this hypothesis by asking a human subject, his wife in fact, to guess the next letter in some text chosen at random.[32] In the beginning, she obviously guessed wrong; but as more and more text was revealed, for example 'the lamp was on the d——', she was accurately able to guess the next three letters. Often even more could be guessed accurately, by taking into account relationships across sentences and the story as a whole. Clearly, Shannon's wife was using her *experience* to guess the word 'desk' as being more likely than, say, 'drape'. Similarly, given only the partial sentence 'the lamp was on——', she might well have guessed 'the' to be the next word. After all, what else could it be, if the sentence did not end at that point?

What constitutes the 'experience' that we bring to bear in a task such as 'predicting the next letter'? Many things: our experience of the usage of language, as well as 'common-sense knowledge' about the world, and much more. Each of these forms of experience has been studied closely by linguists and philosophers as well as computer scientists. Might this simple task be worthy of a *rational model*, as we have seen earlier in the case of memory, which could shed some light on how we convey and understand meaning through language? One way of modelling 'experience' is mere statistics. A machine that has access to vast amounts of written text should be able to calculate, merely by brute force counting, that *most* of the time, across *all* the text available to it, 'the' follows 'the lamp was on——', or that 'desk' is the most likely completion for 'the lamp was on the d——'. Google certainly has such a vast corpus, namely, the entire web. Such a statistical approach might not seem very 'intelligent', but might it perhaps be effective enough for a limited-purpose reverse Turing Test?

But the web is public, and its pages are available to us all. Let us for the moment imagine that we use the statistics of language as inferred by brute force using the entire web, to *generate* letters and spaces with the same frequencies. Using such a procedure, most of the time we would produce valid words in the language. By further using statistics to generate the most likely pairs of words, one after another in sequence, what kind of text would result? In fact Shannon did exactly this, using a far smaller corpus of English text of course. Even using statistics from such a small base, he was able to generate text such as 'THE HEAD AND IN FRONTAL ATTACK ON AN ENGLISH WRITER THAT THE CHARACTER OF THIS POINT'.[32] Clearly gibberish, conveying no meaning. Now suppose we used exactly such a procedure to produce junk web pages appropriately peppered, in statistically likely places, with selected words so as to attract contextual online ads. Statistically speaking, a contextual ad-placement engine such as Google's AdSense would be unable to distinguish our junk from real text, even though our text would be immediately flagged as meaningless by a human reader. Thus, at least the particular reverse Turing Test of disambiguating junk pages from meaningful ones does not appear to have a purely statistical solution. Does the statistical approach to language have inherent limitations? What more is required?

Imagine another limited reverse Turing Test, this time to judge the *intent* of a human posting a query on Twitter, Facebook, or just email: the post 'looking to use an American flight to London next week' should probably be accompanied by an airline advertisement. But is it better to choose a discount offer to London being offered by American Airlines, or should AdSense find the highest bid amongst advertisements across *all* carriers of US origin that fly to London, rather than only the airline named 'American'? Would the answer differ if it was known that the author was writing from Paris rather than somewhere in the US? (American Airlines presumably does not fly across the English channel.) What if the sentence was 'got into London on American, loved their service, what's happening here?' Clearly the latter post does not indicate any imminent travel planning; instead the person has already arrived in London, appears to be on holiday, and might be more interested in ads from restaurants or theatres than airlines. Further, it is quite likely that she already has a return flight on the same airline whose service she was already happy with; why waste an airline ad on her?

You may well be thinking that this new reverse Turing Test is too challenging for a machine. Humans, on the other hand, would often make the right decision. What is the problem? Human language is, unfortunately for the machine, quite full of ambiguities. Ambiguity lends efficiency in the sense that we can use the same word, 'American', in a variety of contexts. However, only our shared experience with other humans, together with knowledge grounded in the real world, such as the location of the author, and what routes American Airlines services, allows us to disambiguate such sentences with high accuracy. It is also precisely *because* of the ambiguity of language that we so liberally employ redundancy in its usage.

Recent research has revealed deep connections between redundancy in language, or rather our use of language, and the ambiguities inherent in the medium itself as well as the world it seeks to describe. For example, it has been shown through experiments that when we speak we also tend to introduce redundancy in exactly those portions that convey larger amounts of information (in the Shannon sense of the word). Spoken language appears to exhibit a 'uniform information density'.[33] It is precisely when we are making a specific point, conveying a remarkable insight, or describing an unusual event, that we somehow increase the redundancy in our usage of words, say the same thing in different ways, and, while speaking at least, 'hum and haw' a bit, introducing pauses in speech filled with utterances such as 'um', 'uh', and 'you know'.

It has also been recently argued that ambiguity, or more precisely *vagueness*, is often used purposefully. Not deliberately to confuse, but rather to convey *more* meaning, and not less.[34] 'I am looking for a large car', might mean different things to me, who might be used to driving a compact car, versus someone who regularly drives a minivan. Yet, the speaker may not be unwilling to consider the latest discounted rental price for an SUV. Vagueness has purpose, and precisely because our use of language is often more than, or in fact not even, to convey a message as clearly as possible. We expect a reply; communication is a two-way street. The sum and substance is that language is not easy to 'process'. It's a wonder how we all manage nevertheless, almost intuitively.

Language and Meaning

Probably the most fundamental advance in the study of language, at least from the perspective of computer-based processing of natural languages, is due to Noam Chomsky. Chomsky's now famous 1957 treatise *Syntactic Structures*[35] was the first to introduce the idea of a formal grammar. We all know language is governed by grammatical rules; some sentences are obviously 'wrong', not because they convey an untruth, but because they don't follow the rules of the language. The example used by Chomsky to demonstrate this distinction between syntactic correctness and meaning, or semantics, is also now well known: the sentence 'Colourless green ideas sleep furiously', follows the rules of language but means nothing, since ideas cannot be green. Chomsky invented the theory of 'phrase structure grammars' to pre-cisely define what it meant for a sentence to be grammatically correct. A phrase-structure 'parse' of a sentence would group words together; for example [[Colourless [green [ideas]]][sleep [furiously]]]. The parse indicates that 'Colourless' and 'green' are adjectives in a compound noun phrase, and each modify the noun 'ideas'. The adverb 'furiously' modifies the verb 'sleep' in the second grouping, which is a verb phrase. The sentence as a whole follows a 'subject-verb' pattern, with the iden-tified noun phrase and verb phrase playing the roles of subject and verb respectively.

According to Chomsky's theory, sentences that can be successfully 'parsed' are syntactically correct. Syntax certainly provides a clue to meaning, if it is there, but by itself does not reveal or indicate meaning. Syntactical analysis of a sentence can be at many levels. In simple 'part-of-speech tagging', we merely identify which words are nouns, verbs, adjectives, etc. More careful analysis yields what is called shallow parsing, where words are grouped together into phrases, such as noun phrases and verb phrases. The next level is to produce a parse tree, or nested grouping of phrases, such as depicted in the previous paragraph. The parse tree throws some light on the relationship between the constituent phrases of the sentence. However, deeper analysis is required to accurately establish the semantic, i.e., meaningful, roles played by each word. A statement such as 'the reporter attacked the senator' might be parsed as [[the [reporter]][attacked [the [senator]]]]. Here the parse-tree appears to clearly identify who attacked whom. On the other hand, a slightly modified statement, 'the reporter who the senator attacked' would be syntactically parsed as [[the [reporter]][who [[the [senator]] attacked]]]. Now the scenario being talked about is not as clearly visible as earlier. 'Dependency parsers' and 'semantic role labelling' techniques seek to bring more clarity to such situations and clearly identify what is happening, e.g., who is playing the role of an attacker, and who is the victim attacked. Humans perform such semantic role labelling with ease. Machines find it much harder. Nevertheless, much progress has been made in the processing of natural language by machines. Generating parse trees is now easily automated. Dependencies and semantic roles have also been tackled, to a certain extent, but only recently in the past decade.

Most surprisingly though, most of the recent advances in natural language processing (NLP) have been made using statistical techniques, which, as you may recall, we had earlier thought were not good enough for such purposes. On the contrary, Chomsky's philosophy of language was founded on a deep distrust of statistical explanations for human language. Chomsky himself elucidated his position explicitly in his 1957 paper by comparing the two sentences (1) 'colourless green ideas sleep furiously' and (2) 'furiously sleep ideas green colourless'. To quote Chomsky

> It is fair to assume that neither the sentence (1) nor (2) (nor indeed any part of these sentences) has ever occurred in English discourse. Hence, in any statistical model for grammaticalness, these sentences will be ruled out on identical grounds as equally 'remote' from English. Yet (1), though nonsensical, is grammatical, while (2) is not.[35]

Chomsky used this and similar examples to argue that the human ability for communicating via language is inborn and innate, built into our brains, rather than something that we learn from experience as we grow up.

We shall not dwell on such philosophical matters here. The fact is that it is through statistical models, similar in spirit to Shannon's calculations of word-pair frequencies, that computer scientists have been able to build highly accurate algorithms for shallow parsing, computing parse trees, as well as unearthing dependencies and semantic roles. NLP remains a vibrant area of research where progress is being made every day. At the same time, it is important to realize that the statistical approach relies heavily on the availability of large corpora of text. Unlike Shannon's task of computing pair-wise frequencies, statistical NLP techniques need far richer data. The corpus needs to have been 'marked up', to indicate the parts of speech a word can take, its grouping with other words in a phrase, the relative structure of phrases in a parse tree, dependencies of words and their semantic roles.

As one might imagine, producing such a corpus of marked-up text requires tedious manual labelling of large volumes of text. Many such corpora have been created, at least in English and a few other languages (such as German and French). In comparison there is a marked paucity of labelled corpora for many other languages. The availability of large, accurately labelled corpora is the single limiting factor determining the rate of progress in statistical NLP research in any language.

So while earlier approaches to NLP that used human-defined linguistic rules have come nowhere close to the success achieved using purely statistical tools, manually coded rules are still used for languages where large labelled corpora are missing. Nevertheless, we can safely say that statistics has won, at least in practice: Google's web-based machine-translation service uses statistical NLP, and is surprisingly effective, at least when dealing with some of the more popular languages.

* * *

How are NLP techniques used by search engines and other web services for their own selfish purposes? A few years ago in 2006–7, a start-up company called Powerset set out to improve basic web search using deep NLP. Powerset wanted to be able to answer pointed queries with accurate results, rather than a list of results as thrown up by most search engines, including Google. Yes, Powerset attempted to take on Google, using NLP. Thus, in response to a query such as 'which American flight leaves Chicago for Paris late Sunday night?', Powerset would attempt to find the exact flights. Surely, it would need to resolve ambiguities such as those we have already discussed, i.e., whether 'American' is the airline or the nationality of the carrier. Deep NLP technology was supposed to be the answer, which, by the way, Powerset had licensed from Xerox's R&D labs. Did it work? Unfortunately we don't quite know yet. Powerset was acquired by Microsoft in mid-2008. Natural language search has yet to appear on Microsoft's search engine Bing. So the jury is still out on the merits of 'natural language search' versus the 'plain old' keyword-based approach.

What seems to be the problem? Should we not be running to use a service that allows us to type our queries in natural language, rather than dream up a likely combination of keywords that represents our intent, and to which a search engine might best respond? Recently *The Atlantic* conducted a survey on how people used web search, i.e., what they would type into a search box in order to answer a set of questions posed by the magazine.[36] For example, one of the questions posed was 'You want to know how many people have fast internet connections in Brazil, where you're going to study abroad for a year'. The responses ranged from the simple 'Brazil internet stats' to the more sophisticated 'UN data + Brazil + internet connections'. *Not a single* answer was posed in grammatically correct language, such as 'How many people have fast internet connections in Brazil?'. Over 600 responses were collected, for this and four other similar questions. Again, *none* of the responses were in 'natural language'. Now, this behaviour might merely be a reflection of the fact that people know that search responds to keywords, and not natural language queries. At the same time, the fact that we have got so used to keyword searches might itself work against the case for natural language search. Unless the results are dramatically better, we won't switch (moreover, keywords queries are faster to type).

Just as Google's PageRank-based search demonstrated a marked improvement over the early search engines, natural language search now needs to cross a much higher bar than perhaps a decade ago. If a Powerset-like engine had come out in the year 2000, rather than in 2007, who knows what course search technology might have taken? Natural language queries, suitably 'understood' through automatically derived semantics, would certainly have given search engines a far greater handle on the intent of the searcher. The quest for high mutual information between the searcher's intent and an advertiser's ads might have been somewhat easier.

* * *

But even more hurdles face the use of NLP in the web. In the early days most web content consisted of fairly structured, grammatically correct prose, much like print media. In recent years however, the democratization of web-based publishing through wikis, blogs, and most recently Facebook and Twitter, is beginning to change this balance. The majority of Twitter posts are certainly not grammatically correct.

A sizeable fraction of Facebook posts and blogs also display incorrect grammar, at least partially. Not only is grammar a casualty, the sanctity of words themselves no longer hold true. The use of abbreviations, such as 'gr8' for 'great', and 'BTW' for 'by the way', are commonplace even on the web, even though these have emerged from the world of mobile-phone text messages. Nevertheless, we certainly manage to convey meaning effectively in spite of our lack of respect for grammar and spelling.

In fact, the study of how we read and derive meaning from the written word has itself become a rich area of research: 'Aoccdrnig to a rscheearch at Cmabrigde Uinervtisy, it deosn't mttaer in waht oredr the ltteers in a wrod are, the olny iprmoetnt tihng is taht the frist and lsat ltteer be at the rghit pclae'. Such popularly shared examples (*not* actually studied at Cambridge University, in fact) have demonstrated that often, though certainly not always, 'it doesn't matter in what order the letters in a word are, the only important thing is that the first and last letter be at the right place'.[37] So, where does meaning reside in language? If the information being transmitted is so poorly related to grammar and even spelling, what does this mean for the NLP approach to understanding how we use language? What exactly is the role of grammar and how does it relate to meaning? And finally, what does this say about the utility of NLP in efforts to understand *us*, via the generalized reverse Turing Test. Can any of our deeper intentions, opinions, or predilections be derived from our conversations on the web?

Recall that for Chomsky, grammar was central to the understanding of language. Human beings could converse because of an innate grammatical ability, using which they could express themselves and understand others. Imagine a machine that could determine with accuracy whether or not a given sentence was grammatically correct or not, and if so what its constituent parts and their relationships were. From the Chomskian viewpoint, such a machine would be a perfectly adequate rational model, shedding adequate light on what it means to 'understand language'. Any meaning beyond this was not of great concern to Chomsky. If you had grammar, meaning would come, somehow.

Richard Montague, a contemporary of Chomsky in the mid-20th century, thought differently. For him, meaning was central. Montague imagined another machine, quite different from a Chomskian one. Montague's machine would be able to distinguish 'true' statements from 'false', rather than merely opine on grammatical correctness.[34] Montague imagined that a sentence's 'meaning' could be computed, in some manner, from the meanings of its constituent parts. Grammar, which would serve to decompose a sentence into parts, was thus merely a means to the end goal.

Montague's grand vision of being able to automatically 'discern truth from falsehood' is probably too simplistic. After all, the well-known paradoxical statement 'this sentence is false' highlights the dangers that lurk in the world of truth and falsehood. As we shall see in Chapter 4, even the very logical and precise world of mathematical formulae has been shown to inevitably contain statements that are *provably* neither true nor false. Nevertheless, Montague's imaginary machine is perhaps closer to the quest for solutions to our 'generalized reverse Turing Test', aimed at deciphering some 'truths' about the authors of web pages, emails, blogs, or posts.

The sentences 'I only eat Kellogg cornflakes' and 'Only I eat Kellogg cornflakes' are both grammatically correct, but certainly convey different meanings. The amount of information each of these sentences convey about the author's family is also very different. The latter sentence pretty much brands her family members as people who avoid Kellogg cornflakes, whereas the first sentence says nothing about anyone but the author. From the perspective of a tool such as AdSense, this could mean the difference between deciding to present an ad for Kellogg or for another cereal. Such distinctions might appear needlessly petty and microcosmic. But they are the lifeblood of online advertising, which in turn, powers the free economy of the web that we all take for granted.

So can NLP help to target ads better? The jury is still out on this. Web companies are all working on technologies for 'reading' our posts, emails, and blogs with every greater sophistication. NLP techniques still continue to offer hope, especially as in other arenas—albeit slightly removed from online advertising, for example, mining sentiment and intent—such techniques have already shown remarkable progress.

Sentiment and Intent

In mid-2011, one man, a relatively unknown activist called Anna Hazare, began a small anti-corruption movement in India that rapidly caught the imagination of the middle class, fuelled in no small measure by social media, i.e., Facebook and Twitter. Mr Hazare's initial rallies drew million-strong crowds in some cities, and ever since then Mr Hazare and his associates have been in the news on an almost daily basis.

A similar and probably more well-known phenomenon has been the 'Arab Spring': the spate of social unrest beginning with Egypt, moving on to Libya, and then Syria. Dictators have been overthrown, put in jail, or even executed, transforming the polities of entire nations. Here too, the mobilization of large numbers of citizens via social media has played a crucial role.

In times of social unease, or even unrest, everyone wants to know 'what is the country thinking, really?' The news media cover some views; but the volume they can cover is limited by time and space. The crowds are there for everyone to see on TV. But what are other people thinking, those that do not have the time or courage to come out on the streets, either out of fear in some instances, or only because of the hot and humid weather during other, gentler movements? Social media, in particular Twitter, comes to the rescue, as a means for people both to air their views as well as get a feel for what others are thinking, and engage in animated debate. Still, how many tweets can one read? Could we instead get an aggregate view of how people are feeling about a social movement, at least on Twitter—positive, negative, or neutral?

In the midst of the initial excitement over Mr Hazare's rallies, I turned to Feeltiptop,[38] a start-up company based far away in Silicon Valley. Feeltiptop analyses the global *sentiment* about any topic of your choice, in the aggregate. I entered 'Anna Hazare' into Feeltiptop's search box. A few moments later a pie chart came up—28% positive, 28% negative, and the rest neutral, based on 80 recent tweets. A few days later, the ratios changed to 54% positive. I could also look at the tweets automatically classified by Feeltiptop as positive or negative. The obvious ones 'I support Anna Hazare', or 'Anna Hazare is wrong' were classified correctly. But so were more difficult ones: 'the whole country and all patriotic Indians are with him', is identified as positive, whereas 'Anna Hazare: the divisive face of a new India', comes up in the negative column. At the same time, there are many errors as well: 'Support Anna Hazare against corruption' is misclassified as negative, and 'all the talk about no corruption is just talk' as positive. Nevertheless, in the aggregate, a quick browse convinces me that the noise is probably 10% or so, and evenly distributed. I began trusting the figures, and monitored them periodically. In fact, I found that it was also possible to view the variation of sentiment over time as it swung from one side to the other.

Suddenly it appears that one can, in fact, 'listen' to the 'voice of the country', in the aggregate, or at least its vocal minority who use Twitter. Citizens have another channel to tune to, in addition to established media. Consider the potential of such a tool: for example, which politician would not benefit from such information? Similarly, businesses can listen to the 'voice of their customers', gauge reactions to their advertising campaigns, and monitor how well their products or brands are faring vis-à-vis their competition. Feeltiptop also allows you to filter sentiments by city. So, for example, I could see at a glance that the numbers in support of Mr Hazare's movement were more volatile in Delhi than in, say, Mumbai or Calcutta. This made me wonder why— something I would not have even thought about otherwise. It also makes one wonder how Feeltiptop manages to 'listen' to sentiments, 'mined', so to speak, from the vast stream of hundreds of millions of tweets a day.

Sentiment mining seeks to extract opinions from human-generated text, such as tweets on Twitter, articles in the media, blogs, emails, or posts on Facebook. In recent years sentiment mining has become one of the most talked-about topics in the NLP and text-mining research communities. But extracting sentiment from 'noisy' text, such as tweets, with any degree of accuracy is not easy. First of all, tweets are far from being grammatically correct. It is virtually impossible to determine a complete phrase-tree parse from most tweets. A shallow parse, revealing only the parts of speech with at most nearby words grouped into phrases, is all that one can expect using basic NLP.

Now, certain words are known to be 'opinion' words, such as 'like' or 'hate'. Others might be qualifying words that contribute towards positivity or otherwise; e.g., 'good', 'bad', 'nice', 'poor'. Negations, at least within the same phrase, can change the polarity: so, 'don't like', or 'not good', are obviously negative rather than positive. Next, we tabulate features of each sentence, such as how close other words are to each other, and to opinion words and qualifiers. All this is done for a reasonably large number of actual samples of text culled from Twitter, or whatever medium is being investigated. Such samples are then *manually* tagged as being positive or negative. Then, just as in the case of NLP parsing itself, statistics is applied once more to determine the chance of a sentence being positive or negative, based on its constituent 'features'. This, and the use of statistics for NLP, are examples of *machine learning*, a topic which we shall return to in more detail in

Chapter 3. Such statistical methods are, naturally, error-prone. At the same time, they get better and better with the amount of manually tagged text one uses to 'train' the system. Further, depending on the appropriateness of the features that one can extract and the accuracy of manual tagging, the machine can even surprise us: thus, the tweet 'I am beginning to look fat because so many people are fasting' is classified as negative. So, have we somehow taught the machine to understand sarcasm? (Probably not, but it certainly makes one wonder.)

* * *

Feeltiptop and other similar sentiment-mining engines are getting quite good at figuring out what 'we' feel about virtually any topic, brand, product, or person—at least as represented by some of us who use social media. But, what *are* the topics we are all most concerned about? Feeltiptop's home page presents us with something close: a list of keywords that are, at that moment, the most frequent amongst recent tweets. But topics are not keywords themselves, but groups of words, as we have noted earlier, and we can do better. Using topic analysis it is possible to discover, automatically, which groups of words occur together, most often. Further, topics evolve over time; seemingly different topics merge and others split into new groupings. Completely new topics emerge. Topic analysis of discussions on social media, across Twitter, Facebook, blogs, as well as in good old news, is a burgeoning area of current research. As we all increasingly share our thoughts on the web, we too are able to tap the resulting global 'collective stream of consciousness', and figure out what we are 'all' talking about. Some topics resonate around the world, such as the Arab Spring. Some emerge suddenly in specific countries, such as Anna Hazare's protests in India, but also find prominence in other parts of the world, such as the US and the UK, due to the large Indian diaspora settled there.

What about topics that have not yet reached the stage of discourse and discussion in social media, or for that matter any media? 'That's impossible', you might well say. Not quite. Let us step back a bit to where we began, *search*. Our searches reveal our intentions, which is why Google and others are so interested in understanding them. Search keywords, viewed in the aggregate, reveal our collective curiosity at any point in time. Google Trends is a freely available service using which we can see what keywords are being searched for the most; right now, or at any point of time in the past. Truly a 'database of intentions', the phrase with which John Battelle begins his book about Google, '*The Search*'.[39] Using query trends, we can see at a glance exactly when interest in Anna Hazare's movement suddenly increased, not surprisingly coinciding with his illegal arrest and subsequent release on 16 August 2011. We also can look back in time at another geography to 'recollect', in the aggregate, what topics the British populace was worried about during the week of the London riots in mid-2011. Further, we might also come to notice that, at exactly the same time, the US was more worried about its looming debt crisis, so 'federal reserve' was the most popular search term, globally, rather than 'riot'.

It is not only our intentions that are being filed away in the data stores of the search engines of today. Other entities, mostly unheard-of by most of us, are tracking our *actions* as well. We have come across ChoicePoint earlier in Chapter 1: ChoicePoint was used by the FBI agent Robert Fuller while following up on the soon-to-be 9/11 terrorist Khalid Almihdhar. Database aggregators such as ChoicePoint and its competitor Acxiom track a large fraction of our credit-card purchases, motor-vehicle records, property transactions, births, marriages, divorces, and deaths. Axciom maintains information on nearly every household in the United States. Both ChoicePoint and Acxiom are giants, not as large or as well known as Google, but certainly as powerful when it comes to the information they have. As in the case of Google, each data item they keep track of is public, at least in theory, and therefore legal for them to store. However, such data becomes especially powerful when fused together to 'connect the dots', as we shall examine more closely in later chapters. For the moment we need only be aware that many others apart from the web companies such as Google and Facebook are listening to us, tracking not only our thoughts, but also our actions.

It is as if we are at a global party, able to hear all the conversations that are taking place across the world. Some are louder than others; some are hotly debated while we seem to have similar feelings about others. And we can Listen to all of these, in the aggregate. We can also look over each other's 'collective shoulders' at the topics we together search for and consume. Our collective past intentions are also available to browse and reflect on, again in the aggregate as measured by our most frequent searches. Finally, we also cannot leave the party: our lives are embedded here; our every digital action is also being noticed and filed away, at least by some machine somewhere.

* * *

We live in a sea of ambient information, from the conversations in our daily lives to the newspapers we read, and, increasingly, the web content that we search for and surf. Each of us needs to 'listen' carefully enough to not miss what is important, while also avoiding being inundated. At the same time, the web-based tools that we have wrought are listening to us. While listening we seek to extract what is relevant from all that we hear, maximizing the Information we receive: from the perspective of Shannon's information theory, optimal communication increases mutual information, be it between sender and receiver, or even speakers and an eavesdropper.

And the web is indeed an eavesdropper, listening to our intentions, conversations, and reading habits, as well as many of our increasingly digital actions. Just as Alan Turing's 'test for intelligence' defines how a machine might seek to imitate a human, our 'generalized reverse Turing Test' models a machine eavesdropper, seeking to extract information as it listens in. The eavesdropper's purpose is far more prosaic than Turing's lofty goal of imitating human intelligence: online advertising, the lifeblood of the 'free internet economy', is what motivates and drives it. Our intentions are laid bare from our searches, the subjects of our thoughts from the topics we read, and our sentiments from how we react to content, events, and each other. To reach its mundane goals, the web harnesses the power of information theory, statistical inference, and natural language processing. In doing so, has it succeeded in at least pretending to understand, if not actually understanding, us? At the very least, the web serves as a powerful rational model that has furthered our own understanding of language, its relationship to information and entropy, as well as the still elusive concept of 'meaning'.

Many years ago, as far back as 1965 and long before the internet, the Canadian philosopher Marshall McLuhan wrote:

> we have extended our central nervous systems in a global embrace, abolishing both space and time as far as our planet is concerned. Rapidly we approach the final phase of the extensions of man—the technological simulation of consciousness, when the creative process of knowing will be collectively and corporately extended to the whole of human society.[40]

McLuhan was talking about the onset of the age of global communication, with the telephone, radio, and television being his focus. But his insight appears remarkably prescient today. It certainly appears that we can indeed 'listen to the world'. Moreover, the machines which we have built, for purely 'corporate' purposes, to aid us in this task, are the ones listening. So far, at least, they only serve as our intermediaries. For how long? *Listening* is the precursor to *learning*, after all. How much can the machine learn from this vast storehouse of information? Knowledge about us, much of it new knowledge, much of it that we are ourselves unaware of. A brave new world, for sure.

3

LEARN

In February 2011, IBM's Watson computer entered the championship round of the popular TV quiz show *Jeopardy!*, going on to beat Brad Rutter and Ken Jennings, each long-time champions of the game. Fourteen years earlier, in 1997, IBM's Deep Blue computer had beaten world chess champion Garry Kasparov. At that time no one ascribed any aspects of human 'intelligence' to Deep Blue, even though playing chess well is often considered an indicator of human intelligence. Deep Blue's feat, while remarkable, relied on using vast amounts of computing power to look ahead and search through many millions of possible move sequences. 'Brute force, not "intelligence",' we all said. Watson's success certainly appeared similar. Looking at Watson one saw dozens of servers and many terabytes of memory, packed into 'the equivalent of eight refrigerators', to quote Dave Ferrucci, the architect of Watson.* Why should Watson be a surprise?

Consider one of the easier questions that Watson answered during *Jeopardy!*: 'Which New Yorker who fought at the Battle of Gettysburg was once considered the inventor of baseball?' A quick Google search

---

* Watson had 90 IBM Power 750 servers comprised of a total of 2,880 'cores' and 15 terabytes of *memory*, as related in a TED talk, and documented in a paper.[41]

might reveal that Alexander Cartwright wrote the rules of the game; further, he also lived in Manhattan. But what about having fought at Gettysburg? Adding 'civil war' or even 'Gettysburg' to the query brings us to a Wikipedia page for Abner Doubleday where we find that he 'is often mistakenly credited with having invented baseball'. 'Abner Doubleday' is indeed the right answer, which Watson guessed correctly. However, if Watson was following these sequence of steps, just as you or I might, how advanced would its abilities to understand natural language have to be? Notice that it would have had to parse the sentence 'is often mistakenly credited with . . .' and 'understand' it to a sufficient degree and recognize it as providing sufficient evidence to conclude that Abner Doubleday was 'once considered the inventor of baseball'. Of course, the questions can be tougher: 'B.I.D. means you take and Rx this many times a day'—what's your guess? How is Watson supposed to 'know' that 'B.I.D.' stands for the Latin *bis in die*, meaning twice a day, and not for 'B.I.D. Canada Ltd.', a manufacturer and installer of bulk handling equipment, or even BidRx, an internet website? How does it decide that Rx is also a medical abbreviation? If it had to figure all this out from Wikipedia and other public resources it would certainly need far more sophisticated techniques for processing language than we have seen in Chapter 2.

Does Watson actually do all this? Perhaps it finds the right answer more directly, not by reading publicly available material, but by merely looking up a massive table of facts that its inventors have somehow created. *Jeopardy!* questions can come from any subject whatsoever, such as '17th-century artists' or 'TV shows by character'. However, often the characterizations of the topic are themselves vague as in 'around the world', which could mean, well . . . what? To manually extract all possible facts covering the breadth of human experience and knowledge is certainly impossible. But IBM has many computers, surely, and could have used thousands or even millions to pre-compute such a table automatically. But from what sources? The web, Wikipedia, the *Encyclopaedia Brittanica*? More importantly, how?

Suppose the following sentence occurs somewhere in a book or letter: 'One day, from among his city views of Ülm, Otto chose a water-colour to send to Albert Einstein as a remembrance of Einstein's birth-place.' We might correctly infer from this statement that Einstein was born in Ülm. But could a computer? It would need to figure out that the proper noun Ülm was a city, while Einstein referred to a person; that the sentence referred to Ülm as the 'birthplace of Einstein', and that persons are 'born' at their 'birthplace', which could be country, province, or, as in this case, a city: quite a lot of work for a machine! Now suppose the sentence instead read '. . . a remembrance of *his* birth-place', i.e., slightly ambiguous, as much usage of language tends to be. Shouldn't the machine be less confident about Einstein's birthplace from this sentence as compared to the former? Even more work for the poor machine.

The fact is that in building Watson, the computer, or rather a very large number of computers, did indeed process many millions of such documents to 'learn' many hundreds of thousands of 'facts', each with an appropriate level of 'confidence'. Even so, all these were still not enough, and had to be augmented and combined, on the fly as the machine played, by searching and processing an even larger corpus of pages extracted from the web.* So, whichever way one looks at it, Wat-son's feat certainly indicates a significant advance in natural language understanding by computers, be they those inside Watson's cabinets, or those used to populate Watson's copious memory banks. Moreover, Watson (and here we include the machines used to program it) not only 'processed' language surprisingly well, but was also able to learn in the process, and managed to convert raw text into knowledge that could be reused far more easily. Further, Watson was able use this vast

---

* Watson had all the information it needed in its memory, both pre-learned facts as well as a large volume of raw text; i.e., it did not access the web directly during play.

and, as in the example of Einstein's birthplace, imprecise knowledge base, to reason as it explored alternative possibilities to answer a question correctly. But we are getting ahead of ourselves; we shall come to reasoning in Chapter 4. For now, let us take a step back to see what it means to 'learn', and in particular what it might mean for a computer to learn.

Learning to Label

Our learning begins from birth, when a baby learns to recognize its mother. The first acts of learning are primarily to recognize. Many experiences of, say, seeing a cat or a dog, along with an adult voicing their names, i.e., 'cat' and 'dog', eventually result in a toddler learning to accurately label cats and dogs, and distinguish between them. How does the child's mind learn to name the objects it perceives? Presumably via some distinguishing features, such as their size, shape, and sounds. Other features of cats and dogs, such as the fact that they both have four legs, are less useful to distinguish between them. Nevertheless such features are also important, since they differentiate cats and dogs from, say, humans and birds.

Of course, the curious reader might spot a potentially infinite regress: how are the features themselves recognized as such, even if not explicitly labelled? How does the child classify the size, shape, and sound of an animal, or identify features such as legs and their number? No one is explicitly explaining these features and giving them names. At least not in the preschooling, early stage of the child's life. Yet the features must be recognized, at least unconsciously, if indeed they are used to learn the explicit labels 'cat' and 'dog'. Further, once the child has somehow learned to recognize and label cats, we might also say that the child has learned the rudimentary *concept* of a cat.

In the language of machine learning, or the computer science of learning, the first case is one of *supervised* learning, where the child is *trained* to recognize concepts, by being provided with labels for each experienced instance of the two concepts cat and dog. Learning the features themselves, however, is an example of *unsupervised* learning, in which lower-level features are automatically grouped, or 'clustered', based on how similar they are across many observed instances. For example, the lowest-level visual features are the sensory perceptions recorded by our retinas. In computing terms, we would call these images, i.e., collections of pixels. As a child sees many many images of dogs or, say, cats, those pixels that form legs are automatically grouped or clustered together. We could then say that the child has learned the *concept* of a 'leg', without explicit supervision, even if it does not know the actual name 'leg'. Next, the 'leg' concept becomes a feature at the next, higher level of learning, i.e., labelling cats and dogs. It is important to note that exactly how the process of going from perception to features takes place in humans is not known. For instance, 'leg' is most likely also to be a higher-level concept, learned from yet other lower-level features.

Note though that the perception problem, i.e., learning features automatically from sensory inputs, is thankfully absent at least in the case of machines learning from textual examples. The lowest-level features that a computer needs to deal with are characters, which we further explicitly group into words. In other words, the machine's sensory input is 'hard-coded', and there is no perception 'problem' to explain or resolve. We almost always resort to at least some form of hard-coding for extracting the lowest-level features when dealing with other kinds of input, such as images or a video stream from a camera, or for that matter, voice input for the purposes of speech recognition. This is but natural, when the purpose is a particular application, rather than mimicking human perception and cognition. Towards the end of this chapter we shall revisit the 'problem of perception' once more, and see how it has been philosophically debated, as well as computationally modelled, if only partially.

Theories of learning in humans abound, spanning philosophy, psychology, and cognitive science. Many of these have also influenced certain sub-areas of computer science such as vision and image processing, and rightly so. Nevertheless, we quickly find that learning, at least in humans, is a deep and troublesome subject about which much has been studied but little is known for sure. So we shall concentrate instead on asking what it means for a machine to learn.

We have already seen many instances of learning in Chapter 2: learning how to parse sentences, learning to recognize whether a tweet is positive or negative, learning the topic a particular web page is talking about, or discovering the topics that are being discussed in a corpus of text. In most cases, the machine needs to be trained using data labelled by humans, such as for parsing or sentiment mining; these are thus examples of *supervised* learning. On the other hand, 'topic discovery' is an example of *unsupervised* learning, where there is no pre-existing knowledge being provided by outside human intervention.

* * *

Let us try to see how we might program a computer to learn the difference between two concepts, say 'cat' and 'dog'. The computer has available to it many 'instances' of highly idealized 'cats' and 'dogs'. Each such instance is merely a list of features, such as size, head shape, sound, and, for good measure, number of legs. Thus one instance might be [size:large, head shape:long, sound:bark, legs:4, animal:dog], and another [size:medium, head shape:round, sound:meow, legs:4, animal:cat]. Many combinations are possible, including, for example [size:small, head shape:square, sound:squeak, legs:3, animal:cat], which might well occur, as well as some that are highly unlikely to occur, such as [size:large, head shape:long, sound:meow, legs:4, animal:dog]. There may also be some such as [size:large, head shape:square, sound:roar, legs:4, animal:lion], which are perhaps slightly more problematic; but we shall ignore such complications for the moment, i.e., the distinction between the animal 'cat' and the animal family by the same name.

Our computer observes a number of such instances, say a thousand or so. Its task is to learn the concepts 'dog' and 'cat' from this *training set*, so as to be able to recognize future instances that are not already labelled with their animal name. Hopefully the machine will learn these concepts well enough to correctly distinguish between dogs and cats. Even though this might appear to be a rather unrealistic example from the perspective of intelligent web applications, or even Watson, we shall soon see that we can just as easily replace the features 'size', 'shape', etc., with words that occur in sentences. Instead of 'dog' and 'cat, we could label sentences as 'positive' or 'negative', and we would have replicated the sentiment-mining scenario addressed by services such as Feeltiptop.* Further, focusing on the cat-versus-dog classification problem might just reveal a useful rational model that aids our understanding of human learning, if only a little.

A simplistic computer program for the cat-dog example might choose to store all the observed instances, much as Google stores web pages, perhaps even creating an index of features just as Google indexes documents using the words they contain. Then when presented with a new instance, our program merely looks up its past experience very fast, using binary search as we saw Chapter 1. In case an exact match is found, the new observation is given the same animal label as the old one it matches with. If not, we might use the closest match, in terms of the number of features that match exactly, or use a small number of close matches and choose the label that occurs most often amongst these. This rather simple algorithm is called a *k-nearest-neighbour* (or KNN) 'classifier' (since it classifies the instances given to it), and is often actually used in practice.

* See Chapter 2.

However, the simple KNN approach does pose some problems. For one, in case the number of past observations is very large, the classification process can be slow, especially if it needs to be done continuously. We are all constantly observing objects and subconsciously labelling them based on our past experience. Similarly, sites such as Feeltiptop are continuously assigning sentiment labels to hundreds of millions of tweets arriving each day. The KNN classifier is like doing arithmetic by counting on one's fingers. It gets tedious to do repeatedly, so better means are needed; the computer needs to 'learn its multiplication tables'.

The easy case just discussed was where we could find an exact match from our past experience. However, what if we found many exact matches, and they did not all have the same animal label? Chihuahuas could be a reason why; after all, apart from being small and having rounder heads than other dogs, many of them do come fairly close to meowing. Well, we might decide to choose the majority label again, just as in the case of KNN. What we are doing here, albeit indirectly, is calculating the *probability* of a cat given a particular set of features, by looking at the fraction of instances having a particular combination of features that are cats, as opposed to dogs.

Perhaps we could compute such 'posterior' probabilities in advance for every combination of features? After all, how many combinations are there? Even if each of the four features, 'size', 'head shape', 'sound', and 'legs' can take, say, five possible values, the number of possible combinations is only 5^4, or 625. Once more there are problems. As before, it may well turn out that in spite of having observed hundreds of animals, we still might not have observed every possible combination: suppose we had never seen a 'very large' dog that also had a 'rectangular' head shape, such as a Great Dane, ever. How would we ascribe probabilities to such combinations?

* * *

Coming to our aid is a rather famous observation made by the 18th-century mathematician and pastor Thomas Bayes. 'Bayes' Rule' is now included in advanced high-school and college mathematics. It turns out that this simple rule can be used by a machine to 'learn'.

Just as we attempted to compute the 'posterior' probabilities, i.e., the probability that a particular, newly observed, set of features represents a dog (or a cat), we could alternatively choose to compute the 'likelihood' that a dog has some particular feature, such as being 'very large'. It is reasonable to hope that we would find at least some of our past observations that were 'very large', even if their head shapes were not 'rectangular', such as a St Bernard, mastiff, and many others. For example, suppose out of our thousand past observations, there are 600 dogs, but only 90 are 'very large' dogs. The likelihood of a dog being very large is simply $\frac{90}{600}$. Likelihoods are about individual features, whereas posterior probabilities are about the classes or concepts the machine is trying to learn.

Likelihoods are far more easy to compute using past data, since all we ask is that each possible value of a feature has been observed earlier. This is much more reasonable than the more stringent need of 'posterior' calculations, i.e., of having witnessed each combination of feature values. Further, computing likelihoods is also computationally easier. For instance we only need $2 \times 5 \times 4$, or 40 likelihoods, i.e., two for each of the five values of each of the four features. For example, for the feature 'size', we would compute the likelihoods of 'very large', 'large', 'medium', 'small', and 'tiny', using only 'dog' instances from past data, and four similar likelihoods for 'cat' instances. We would do this for each of the four features, resulting in a total of 40 likelihood numbers.

Continuing with our example now, we focus only on very large dogs. Of our 1,000 past observations, suppose we find that 100 are 'very large' animals, of which 90 are very large dogs. The fraction of observations that are very large dogs is $\frac{90}{1000}$; which is also an estimate of the 'true probability' of observing a very large dog. Now comes the crucial trick that leads to Bayes' Rule. We write this fraction as:

$$\frac{90}{1000} = \frac{90}{100} \times \frac{100}{1000}$$

Notice that all we have done is multiply and divide by the number 100, writing $\frac{90}{1000}$ as the product of two other fractions. Now we observe that the first term $\frac{90}{100}$ is nothing but the posterior probability of a dog, for all instances that are very large. The second term, $\frac{100}{1000}$ is just the probability of the feature itself, i.e., the fraction of instances that are very large.

Bayes' very simple observation was that we could just as well write the same fraction of very large dogs, i.e., $\frac{90}{1000}$ as a different product, this time multiplying and dividing by 600 instead of 100:

$$\frac{90}{1000} = \frac{90}{600} \times \frac{600}{1000}$$

This time, the first term $\frac{90}{600}$ is the *likelihood* of a dog being very large, and the second term $\frac{600}{1000}$ is just the overall probability of dogs in the observed population. Bayes' Rule is merely a consequence of this obvious arithmetic, and is obtained by equating the two different ways of expanding the fraction $\frac{90}{1000}$ of very large dogs:

$$\frac{90}{100} \times \frac{100}{1000} = \frac{90}{600} \times \frac{600}{1000}$$

Replacing each fraction by its interpretation we get Bayes' Rule for our example of very large dogs: the posterior probability of a large animal being a dog ($\frac{90}{100}$), times the probability of 'very largeness' ($\frac{100}{1000}$), equals the likelihood of a dog being large ($\frac{90}{600}$) times the probability of dogs in general ($\frac{600}{1000}$):

$$P(\text{dog}|\text{very large}) \times P(\text{very large}) = P(\text{very large}|\text{dog}) \times P(\text{dog})$$

Bayes' Rule is often stated as 'the posterior probability $P(\text{dog}|$ very large), is proportional to the likelihood of a feature, $P(\text{very large})$ times the "prior", $P(\text{dog})$'. The the ratio of proportionality is just $\frac{1}{P(\text{very large})}$, the probability of the 'evidence', i.e., the chance of observing any 'very large' animal.

Quite surprisingly, this simple and, as we have seen, easily derived rule has historically been the subject of much heated debate in the world of statistics. The source of the controversy is actually rather subtle and philosophical, having to do with different definitions of the concept of 'probability' itself and how the results of applying Bayes' Rule should be interpreted. The battle between Bayesian versus 'frequentist' statistics over the years has been entertainingly described in a recent book by Sharon McGrayne entitled *The Theory That Would Not Die*.[42] Be that as it may, the field of modern machine learning relies heavily on Bayesian reasoning, so this philosophical debate is now largely ignored by computing practitioners.

* * *

What Bayes' Rule does is tell us how to arrive at the required 'posterior' probabilities from the 'likelihoods'. In our calculation we used only one feature, 'size'. In reality we would observe all five features together. The next step is a simple but important assumption, i.e., that all the features are *conditionally independent*. What this means is that the chance of a dog (or for that matter, a cat) being very large is independent of, say, its head shape, as well as all other features. Most importantly, it turns out that independence implies that the fraction of dogs with a feature combination 'very large' and 'square head', i.e., the likelihood of such a combination, can be obtained by multiplying the fraction of very large dogs (i.e., the likelihood of 'very large' dogs) with the likelihood of square-headed ones. While such an assumption seems reasonable at first glance, a closer look might lead us to suspect that size and sound may not be that independent after all; how many very large dogs meow? However, we ignore such subtleties and go ahead assuming all features are *conditionally* independent. The caveat 'conditionally' is used because the likelihoods in the statements made earlier were for all the *dogs* we had observed, rather than for all animals. A similar statement could be made using the condition that only cats be considered while computing likelihoods.

Given a new observation with a particular combination of feature values, we use Bayes' Rule to conclude that 'the posterior probability of a dog is proportional to the likelihood of that particular combination, amongst all dogs'. But because of independence, the likelihood of the combination of features is just the product of the individual likelihoods. In other words, Bayes' Rule for conditionally independent features tells us how to compute the posterior probability that an animal is a dog based on any number of features (say n) that we might observe about it. The exact formula, assuming we observe a very large, long animal with a square head that barks, becomes:

$$P(\text{dog} \mid \text{the observed features}) = P(\text{very large}|\text{for all dogs})$$
$$\times\ P(\text{long shape}|\text{for all dogs})$$
$$\times\ P(\text{square head}|\text{for all dogs})$$
$$\times\ P(\text{four legs}|\text{for all dogs})$$
$$\times\ P(\text{barks}|\text{for all dogs})$$
$$\times\ \frac{P(\text{an animal being a dog})}{P(\text{the observed features})}$$

The terms like $P(\text{very large}|\text{for all dogs})$ are merely the likelihoods we computed earlier, i.e., the fraction of all dogs with a particular feature. The last term has two pieces—the numerator, $P(\text{an animal being a dog})$, is the just 'prior' probability of all dogs, i.e., the ratio of dogs in all our observations. The denominator, on the other hand, is the likelihood of this particular combination of features being observed in dogs. As we already saw, the number of such combinations can be large; luckily however, as we shall see soon, we actually do not need to ever calculate these denominators in practice.

So once we have computed all our 40 likelihoods and 2 priors (i.e., the fraction of dogs and cats respectively among all our observations), we can forget about our past experiences. Faced with a new animal, we observe the values that each of its features take, and multiply the respective likelihoods of these values, once using the likelihoods given a 'dog', and once more using likelihoods given a 'cat'; in each case also multiplying by the 'prior' probability of a dog or cat respectively. The posterior probabilities, i.e., the chances of a particular instance being a dog, or a cat, respectively, are, due to Bayes' Rule, proportional to these two computed 'products of likelihood' (and prior). Further, the ratio of proportionality, i.e., the probability of the observed 'evidence', is the same in each case, so we just choose the label for which the computed product of likelihoods and prior is larger.

This well-known technique for programming a computer to learn using Bayes' Rule is called the 'naive Bayes classifier' (NBC). What is so 'naive' about it, one may well ask. The word 'naive' is used because we have ignored any dependencies between features—a subtle but often important point.

In what way, one might well ask, has NBC 'learned' anything about the concept 'dog' or 'cat'? Well, instead of having to search all one's memories of past experience, in the form of stored observations, the computer is able to classify new instances as dogs or cats by merely using the 42 ratios (40 likelihoods and 2 prior probabilities) that it computes from past data, once.

Further, as new observations arrive, and if its decisions are checked and corrected by some appropriate 'trainer', the computer can quite easily recompute these ratios from time to time, and in the process get better at the task of classifying. In this sense, the machine has learned from past data, and can continue to learn in the future. Apart from NBC, there are many many more complex classifiers, such as 'neural networks' and 'support vector machines'. Using any of these it is possible for a machine to be trained and to learn from labelled observations.

At the same time, it is important to observe that the learned concepts, 'dog' and 'cat' in our example, are merely, and nothing but, the trained classifiers themselves. In the case of NBC, these are comprised of 42 ratios for our example, which constitute the sum and substance of the machine's 'understanding' of the concepts 'dog' and 'cat'. Not very satisfying, perhaps, as far as understanding what it 'means to learn'; but quite useful in practice, as we shall soon see.

* * *

Google, Feeltiptop, and many other web-intelligence applications regularly use classifiers, often NBC itself, to filter spam, learn user preferences for particular topics, or classify tweets as positive or negative. Machine learning using classifiers is also at the heart of natural language processing, wherein the computer is trained to parse sentences from large corpora of human-parsed text, as we mentioned in Chapter 2. Automated translation between different languages, to the extent achievable today in tools such as Google Translate, also makes heavy use of machine learning. In such scenarios the labelling is complex, as are the features, and many classifiers are used to learn different aspects of parsing or translation. I will refrain from going into the gory details of how features are defined for complex machine-learning tasks such as parsing or translation. Instead, let us see how we might use NBC to train a machine to 'understand' sentiment, as Feeltiptop appears to.

In our previous example we were observing animals; now our observations are sentences. The goal is to determine whether a new sentence is expressing positive or negative opinion, and to learn how to do so from past observations of sentences that have somehow been labelled correctly (by a human). Instead of size and sound, now our features are the occurrences of words in sentences. The sentence 'I love this phone, it's really great' has the features 'phone', 'love', 'really', 'great'. Note that 'stop words', such as prepositions and articles, have been omitted, which is easily done by looking up a dictionary. We might, for the purpose of sentiment alone, have wished to remove nouns as well, but that would have required more work. So we leave them be. Thus there are millions of features, even though only a very small fraction occur in each sentence. To handle negation of positive words, such as 'this film was not great', we group negation words, such as 'not', with the nearest following word; thus the features for 'this film was not great' would be 'film', 'was', and 'not great'.

Now we can see the power of Bayes' Rule: it would have been impossible to calculate the posterior probability of a positive opinion for every possible combination of words. In theory, there are infinite such combinations, or at least a very very large number: allowing sentences of at most ten words, and conservatively assuming there are 10 million possible words,* there would be $10^{10,000,000}$ combinations; infinite enough, for all practical purposes (in comparison, the number of atoms in the observable universe is a mere 10^{80}).

However, using Bayes' Rule, we can get away with computing the likelihood of a sentence being positive or negative for each of the 10 million words. For example, suppose we have 3,000 labelled sentences, of which 1,000 are labelled positive, and the rest negative. Of the 1,000 positive sentences, say 110 contain the word 'good', while only 40 of the negative sentences have 'good' in them. Then the likelihood of a positive sentence containing 'good' is $\frac{110}{1000}$. Similarly, the likelihood of finding 'good' amongst the 2,000 negative sentences is simply $\frac{40}{2000}$. We can do similar calculations for every word that we find. Of course, there will always be words that are missing from our training set; for these we have no likelihoods, so they are simply ignored.† NBC does what it can with what it has. Surprising as it may seem at first glance, NBC does quite well indeed at classifying simple sentences based merely on word occurrence. Of course, it goes terribly wrong in the face of sarcasm, such as 'what a lovely experience, waiting for two hours to get a table!'

---

* In Chapter 2 we had mentioned Google's estimate as being 14 million.
† In practice, a technique called *Laplacian smoothing* is used to avoid zero likelihoods: a word is assumed to occur at least once.

When Google records the web pages we view, scans the queries we use to search, or even 'reads' our emails, it does so with the intent to somehow label us. It might choose to discover if we are, at that point of time, interested in buying something or not. This is clearly an important thing for Google to accurately guess, so that it can avoid placing online ads alongside its results when not required. Machine learning might well be used for this purpose, very similar to the binary classification of tweets into those espousing positive versus negative sentiments. All Google would need is a moderately large corpus of pages and emails, hand-labelled as 'buying-oriented' or not. There is reasonable evidence that Google actually does this: try searching for 'wedding bouquet'; at least I don't see any ads. Now change your query to 'cheap wedding bouquet', and a host of ads appear to the right of the screen. Thus Google might well be using machine learning to learn a classifier, such as NBC, to distinguish between buyers and browsers.

So, machines can be trained and thereby learn, which is merely to say that given enough labelled examples, machines can learn to discern between these labels. The web-based systems we have built, as well as projects such as Watson, use such machine learning all the time to label what they observe about us or the world. Thereafter these labels are used for their own purposes, such as answering quiz questions in Watson's case. Of course, in the case of most web-based services, these purposes eventually boil down to somehow inducing us to buy more products through advertising. The success of the online advertising business certainly seems to indicate that these machines are 'learning about us', and doing rather well.

Limits of Labelling

Still, it seems reasonable to ask, what kinds of things can machines learn? An important negative conclusion was discovered by Mark Gold in 1967.[43] He showed that it was virtually impossible to learn most concepts from positive examples alone. For example, it is not at all possible to learn to distinguish grammatically correct sentences from incorrect ones if one never sees an incorrect sentence. Gold's result was used by many to argue for the Chomskian view that grammar was innate to humans. Be that as it may, the scientific conclusion to be drawn from Gold's analysis is that both positive and negative examples are required to learn a concept. Thus, Gold's result in a sense also vindicates the model of learning from labelled examples, such as we described earlier with dogs and cats, or buyers and browsers.

Machine learning using a classifier is concerned with making distinctions between different classes; animals being dogs or cats, sentences being positive or negative. Similarly, the core idea of information, the 'bit', which essentially makes a binary distinction, one from zero, good and bad, 'yin and yang'. Perhaps, therefore, it makes sense to look a bit more closely at whether we can couch the scenario of machine learning in Shannon's language? We might well expect that machine learning can be viewed in terms of information theory.

Recall that Shannon's original focus was on communication of signals via a noisy channel, such as a telephone. Mutual information measured the accuracy of such a communication. Shannon was concerned with how best to encode signals so as to maximize the mutual information between signals at two ends of a noisy communication channel. It turns out that we can view machine learning in Shannon's language, merely by changing our interpretation of communication, a channel, and signals. The source signal, instead of a voice at one end of a telephone connection, becomes our intent, i.e., whether or not to buy, for the earlier example of Google, or whether an animal is a dog or a cat, in our recent illustration. Instead of telephone wires, the channel is the lens through which Google views us, i.e., the features it uses for learning, such as queries in the earlier scenario. In the dog-cat problem, the features we observe about animals, i.e., size, shape, etc., are the channel. The classifier that we attempt to learn is the equivalent of a coding scheme used to reproduce the signal, along with any pre-processing of features, such as the grouping of negations with nearby words as in the case of learning tweet sentiments. Finally, the accuracy of transmission is exactly the *mutual information* between the reproduced signal, or guessed labels, and the source signal, i.e., our actual intent, whether dog or cat, positive or negative. So, in the language of information theory, when Google classifies browsers from buyers, it is trying to *maximize* the mutual information between what it can observe about us, e.g., our queries, and our intent, of which it is otherwise oblivious.

You might also recall Shannon's famous notion of 'channel capacity', which indicated exactly how good communication across some channel could *ever* be. Armed with the previous analogy, we are ready to ask whether there is an analogue of Shannon's channel capacity in the world of machine learning? Can we say with certainty how well something can be learned, now allowing for both positive and negative examples?

It is easy to conclude using our previous analogy that the best accuracy one can achieve with any learning system is exactly the mutual information between the concept to be learned and the features from which we seek to learn it. In recent years researchers have unearthed even deeper relationships between mutual information and learning accuracy:[44] it turns out that we can theoretically guarantee that under reasonable conditions simple Bayesian classifiers will eventually learn a concept with an accuracy closely related to the mutual information between the concept and the chosen features. This is quite a strong statement, since it says that any concept, however complex, can be learned by a machine with a high degree of accuracy. All we need to ensure is that the features we choose are close enough, i.e., have a high-enough level of mutual information to the concept itself.

From a computer science perspective, however, these results connecting machine learning and mutual information are far from satisfactory. First, whatever we have said earlier depends heavily on the features that we choose. If we choose better features, then we can learn better. Suppose one of the features we choose is exactly the concept itself. In the case of our animals example, this would be as if each dog or cat came with a label identifying what it was; clearly there is nothing left to learn.

More disturbing is that we don't have any idea how long it takes to learn a concept. Consider our dog-cat example itself; as we have calculated earlier, with four features each taking at most five values, there are at most 5^4, or 625, combinations. Once a machine observes enough examples that cover the 625 combinations, it has learned everything that there is to learn about this example. With more features, the number of combinations grows rapidly; e.g., 10 features leads to more than 9.7 million combinations. Large, but certainly not infinite. Once more, having observed sufficient examples of each of these combinations, the machine will certainly have learned to distinguish concepts with 100% accuracy. There must be something more to it, surely? Would it not be better to ask whether a concept can be learned 'fast', without requiring training on too many examples?

* * *

Every year the computer science community confers the prestigious Turing Award for outstanding contributions to the field. The Turing Award is the equivalent of the Nobel Prize for computing. In 2011, Leslie Valiant won the Turing Award for, among other achievements, developing a 'theory of the learnable'. Valiant's theory, called 'probably approximately correct learning', or PAC learning, is to learning what Shannon's channel capacity is to communications.[45]

Valiant's PAC learning model defines what it means for a concept to be learned 'fast'. A concept that requires a training set that is almost as large as the total number of possible examples, such as 5^n for a class with n five-valued features, is definitely not fast. On the other hand, suppose we could learn with just n examples, or even n^2; this would certainly be much better. In the language of computer science, the fact that 5^n grows very rapidly as n becomes large is referred to by saying that it grows *exponentially* with n. On the other hand, something like n^2, or n^3, which grows much slower as n grows, is said to grow *polynomially* with n.

Additionally, since learning from a small number of examples cannot be perfect, the accuracy with which a concept is learned also needs to be considered. Accuracy is usually measured in terms of the probability of the learned classifier making a mistake; the larger the chance of a mistake, the lower the accuracy. The inverse of the mistake probability can be used as a measure of accuracy. Valiant defined a concept to be 'properly' PAC-learnable if the number of examples required to learn a classifier for that concept grows only polynomially with the number of features involved, as well as with the accuracy. The actual mathematical definition is a shade more complicated, but we need not delve into that here. It suffices to note that PAC learnability defines the limits of learning from a practical perspective. Subsequent to Valiant's work, a rich theory has developed to delineate what kinds of concepts are PAC-learnable 'properly', i.e., with only a polynomial number of examples. At the same time, PAC learnability, like Shannon's channel capacity, serves only to define what is possible and what is not, rather than tell us how to actually develop the required fast classifiers.

Whatever be the limits of learning as defined by theoretical models such as PAC learning, in practice it is certainly true that machines are able, using classifiers such as NBC, to do quite well at the various versions of the 'generalized reverse Turing Test' that we defined in Chapter 2. But is learning labels 'really' learning? Surely there is more to learning a concept than mere labelling?

* * *

Machine learning using a classifier certainly learns a concept, at least from a utilitarian point of view. However, concepts in real life, especially in human language, are surely more complex than mere tools to distinguish instances, such as dogs and cats. But more complex in what way? The instance [size:large, head shape:square, sound:roar, legs:4, animal:lion] was suspected to be problematic. Why? Because a lion is also a cat, i.e., a member of the cat *family*, rather than the animal cat. Thus labels have context. When labels are used in language they might be used vaguely, such as 'a big cat', or 'an American flight'. The context is not clear. Complexity arises in other ways also: a dog *has* legs, so does a cat. The concepts 'dog' and 'legs' are related. So are, indirectly, 'dog' and 'cat', since they both 'have' legs.

To see how context and structure in concepts might be tackled, we return once more to our analogy with Shannon's information theory. Instead of a physical medium, the message being transmitted is the actual class label, i.e., 'dog' or 'cat', while the message we receive consists only of features, i.e., size, shape, etc. The interesting thing we notice in our analogy between machine learning and communications is that, unlike in the case of actual communication, we have far more flexibility in choosing the channel itself. In the case of a physical medium, such as a telephone line, the physical properties of the channel are largely out of our control. However, in the case of machine learning we can change the 'channel' itself by simply choosing the right set of features to use for learning. In particular, we are not bound to use all possible features that might be available. It turns out that mutual information tells us exactly which features to use.

Suppose we tried to learn to distinguish dogs and cats using only one feature, say 'size'. Using sufficient training data, we can actually compute the mutual information between the type of animal and its size. If this mutual information is high, it makes sense to use this feature in our NBC. However, consider the feature 'legs'. Almost every instance of a dog or cat has four legs. Knowing the number of legs of an animal therefore serves little to reduce the uncertainty about whether the animal is a dog or a cat. Consequently, the mutual information between the animal type and number of legs will be very low. Note however that the computer has no knowledge of the real world when it computes mutual information. It does not know that dogs and cats have four legs. However, as long as it knows how to count 'legs', it *can* figure out that number of legs is not important to distinguish between dogs and cats, just by mere calculations, which computers are quite good at. What this small but significant example illustrates is that the machine can indeed learn a structural property of the world, i.e., that size is more important than number of legs in distinguishing between dogs and cats, entirely by itself from training data alone. The machine was never explicitly told this property, unlike the labelling of animals. Indeed, this is our first example of *unsupervised* learning, which is all about learning *structure*.

Of course, it is important to note that this argument rests on a fundamental assumption, i.e., that the machine somehow knows that 'legs' is a feature, as is 'head shape', etc. The problem of how features might themselves emerge in an unsupervised manner, i.e., 'feature induction', is a deep and important subject to which we shall return very soon. For now, let's see what other insights follow merely from mutual information, albeit using already known features. Instead of using one feature and the concept 'animal name', the computer can just as well calculate the mutual information between any pair of *features*. For example, suppose we had used colour as a feature. The mutual information between colour and, say, sound is likely to be low, since knowing the colour of an animal rarely tells us much about which animal it is. Thus the machine learns that these two features, i.e., colour and sound, are independent.

What about Google's possible efforts towards separating buyers and browsers? Certain words, such as 'cheap' and similar adjectives, will have a high mutual information with the desired distinction, while others might not. Google's computers learn this using mutual information, and therefore Google 'learns' to ignore such words in its classification scheme. Similarly, Google figures out which words are used together with others, and in which context: 'want cheap clothes' indicates a likely buyer, whereas 'taking cheap shots' does not. Such knowledge can be used to decide which features to use, as well as, for example, how to group words while computing likelihoods. The machine has learned some structure, and is also able to exploit it, at least somewhat.

Rules and Facts

Analysing mutual information between features can lead to some structure, but this is still far from satisfying. For example, even though the machine can discover, automatically, that the number of legs does not help us distinguish between cats and dogs, it should also be able to figure out that a 'cat (or dog) *has* four legs'. In other words, can the machine learn rules, such as '*if* an animal is a cat, *then* it meows'? Or more complex ones such as, '*if* an animal has two legs, feathers, and chirps, *then* it also flies'? Further, we would like the machine to also estimate how confident it is about any rule that it learns, since after all, some birds do not fly.

Such rules are more than mere correlations, and form a basis for reasoning, which is at the core of thought, and to which we shall turn in detail in Chapter 4. The field of machine learning deals mostly with techniques for learning concepts, such as the naive Bayes classifier we have seen earlier, as well as their theoretical underpinnings, such as PAC learning. On the other hand, learning deeper structure from data is usually thought of as the field of data mining, which aims to 'mine' knowledge from available data. At the same time, the two fields are so closely interrelated that the distinction is often moot.

It is probably reasonable to expect that if a machine is going to learn rules, it should be on the basis of reasonably large volumes of data. So, to learn anything with any degree of certainty about two-legged creatures that chirp and have feathers, presumably the machine needs to have seen a large number of examples of such animals. In the language of data mining, there should be a large number of data items that actually prove the rule; such a rule is said to have large *support*. Further, in order to infer our rule, it should also be the case that of the two-legged creatures that have feathers and chirp, a very large fraction of them do indeed fly. In technical terms, this rule has a high *confidence*. Finally, and quite importantly, our rule would be rather useless if almost all animals also flew, instead of only the two-legged, feathered chirping variety that our rule seeks to distinguish. Fortunately, what makes our 'association rule' *interesting* is that the fraction of fliers is far higher amongst the two-legged, feathered, chirping variety of animals, as compared to animals in general.

It might appear that we are spending a lot of time dealing with this rather simple rule about feathered creatures flying. The point is that in the course of actual experiences humans observe a multitude of objects, including animals of course, but a lot of other kinds of data as well. A child does not need to be told that most flying creatures have two legs, feathers, and chirp. She 'learns' this 'rule' from experience; most importantly, she learns this rule along with a myriad of other rules about animals and objects in general. The number of rules is neither predetermined nor constrained in any way, such as 'rules involving three features'.

It certainly appears that we unconsciously learn many rules, some simple and some far more complex: 'Birds of a feather flock together!' More seriously, while we don't see machines as developing idiom, we would like to somehow discover all possible 'interesting association rules that have large support and confidence', from any collection of objects described by features, however large, regardless of how many features there may be. Last but not least, it would be useful if the algorithm for this seemingly complicated task were also efficient, in that it could deal with very large volumes without taking forever.

In 1994, Rakesh Agrawal and Ramakrishnan Srikant published a now famous technique, called the Apriori algorithm,[46] for efficiently computing *all* interesting association rules in very large volumes of data. The key to understanding this rather elegant algorithm is how we define the rules themselves. Recall that we are looking for rules with large *support*, i.e. rules involving combinations of features that occur fairly often in a large data set.

Once we have found such a combination enjoying large-enough support because of its frequency, everything else required to learn a rule from this 'frequent set' of data items can be calculated fairly directly. Suppose a combination involves four features, say, 'has two legs', 'has feathers', 'chirps', and 'flies'. There are now four possible ways of defining a rule of the form '*if* feathers, flies, and two legs *then* chirps', i.e., by choosing one feature in turn as the conclusion of the rule with the remaining forming the conditions.

Once we have a possible rule, we can calculate its confidence and 'interestingness' in a rather straightforward manner: confidence is calculated by comparing the support for this combination with the support enjoyed only by the three conditions, e.g., 'feathers, flies, and two legs'. In other words, what fraction of instances with 'feathers, flies, and two legs' also 'chirp'. (If you notice some similarly with the likelihoods we computed for naive Bayes, your intuition is correct; this 'confidence' is merely an estimate of the likelihood of 'chirp', given the features 'feathers, flies, and two legs'.)

Whether or not a rule is 'interesting', on the other hand, requires us to examine whether its confidence is significant enough. We therefore calculate the support enjoyed by the conclusion 'chirp', as a fraction of possible items; of course, this is merely the probability of the feature 'chirp' in all our data. Our rule is deemed to be interesting only if the confidence with which it asserts that 'chirp' is likely, having observed 'feathers, flies, and two legs', is significantly larger than the probability of 'chirp' in general, i.e., the support of 'chirp' alone as a fraction of the total number of data items.

Finally, just as we examined four rules, each having three features implying the fourth, there could be rules with two features implying the other two, or one feature implying the other three. However, in order to limit the number of such possibilities, one normally looks for rules that involve only one consequent feature, such as 'chirp' in our example.

Still, the difficult part remains to figure out all possible frequent (i.e., high-support) combinations of features in the first place. As we have seen before, the number of possible combinations of features grows rapidly as the number of features increases. For four features, each taking one of five possible values, it is only 625, but grows to almost 10 million for ten features. Thus, checking every possible combination of features for its support is practically impossible. Agrawal and Srikant made the rather obvious observation that if we confine ourselves to looking for rules with a fixed support, i.e., those that occur say more than a thousand times in the data set, then if a combination occurs at least a thousand times, so must each of its features. Similarly, if a combination of, say, four features occurs at least a thousand times, so must every triple out of these four. Obvious though their observation was, it was crucial, as it allowed them to devise a technique that did not need to look at every possible combination of features.

The Apriori algorithm of Agrawal and Srikant computes association rules from any collection of data, as long as each such item is characterized by a set of features. The algorithm determines all possible association rules that enjoy a minimum support, confidence, and interestingness. Apriori first scans the entire data and counts the frequency of each single feature. It then scans the data once more and retains only those instances containing single features that occur with at least the required support. Next the process is repeated, this time with pairs of features. Because of Agrawal and Srikant's observation, all possible frequent pairs are bound to be found during this second pass. The process continues, with triples, groups of four features, and so on, until no more combinations with the required support can be found. At this point, all possible frequent sets have been found, and rules for each frequent set can be enumerated and tested for confidence and interestingness. Most of the hard work, i.e., scanning the large data volume, has been done. Further, at each step, the data retained decreases, hopefully significantly, and therefore the process becomes efficient.

The Apriori algorithm works efficiently since in practice combinations involving a large number of feature values are rare and don't enjoy any reasonable support. But there is no guarantee of this other than an expectation that feature values are reasonably random, and that the algorithm is used with a sufficiently high support value. To see how Apriori itself might be inefficient, we might consider using a support value of one, i.e., any combination that occurs needs to be considered. In this extreme case, Apriori will go on to compute all possible combinations of features, resulting in too much work as the number of features becomes large. It is important to understand this behaviour, which is typical of many practical data-mining as well as learning techniques. Their *worst-case* behaviour is much poorer than for an 'average' case. (This is why theories such as PAC learning that focus on worst-case behaviour often have little to say about the performance of learning algorithms in practice.)

Using techniques such as rule mining we can now understand how a computer might be able to learn structural properties of the world purely from the statistical frequency with which features co-occur together in experiences. Such rules take the familiar 'if . . . then . . .' form, which makes it possible for a machine to *reason* using them (as we shall discuss in Chapter 4). Further, statistical confidence lends credence to the directionality of the rule. For example, the rule 'birds have two legs' is learned with a high confidence, since most instances of birds would have two legs. On the other hand, 'two-legged creatures are birds' should enjoy low confidence. In contrast, both the rules 'birds chirp' and 'chirping animals are birds', might be found to hold equally high confidence from real-world observations.

As we have argued throughout this book, significant progress in computing techniques is often driven more by practical applications than lofty goals of mimicking human intelligence. Thus it makes sense to ask why association rules might be important for the web-based economy or otherwise? There is the, by now classic, story about 'beer and diapers' that explains the origins of interest in mining associa-tion rules. As the story goes, a large chain store used association-rule mining to learn a rather unintuitive rule that 'consumers often bought beer and diapers together'. The purported explanation of this pecu-liar finding is that people who have babies are more likely to drink at home rather than go to a bar. The story is most certainly fabricated, but serves to illustrate the potential of data mining. Presumably, by placing beer and diapers together near each other in a store, sales of both items might be boosted. Traditional bricks-and-mortar stores have made significant investments in data mining since the popular-ization of this anecdote, which has been generalized and referred to as 'market-basket analysis'. Whatever the results on their sales, the field of data mining certainly received a boost with all their interest.

* * *

Apart from marketing, rule mining is also used in many other appli-cations. In Chapter 1 we recounted the 26/11 Mumbai terrorist attacks of 2008, and mentioned the work[23] of V. S. Subrahmanian and others in computationally analysing the activities of terrorist groups such as the Lashkar-e-Taiba (LeT). They enumerate 61 'temporal' rules in their book, all learned from hard data. These are similar to association rules, except that they also include a time element. For example, a number of rules demonstrate that 'deaths of LeT commanders seem to be positively correlated with some subsequent actions (in the next 1–3 months) by LeT such as attacks on Indian civilians'.[23]

In the context of the 26/11 Mumbai attacks, we know of at least five LeT operatives killed during September 2008, in different encounters with Indian security forces in Kashmir. These include* Qari Usman (6 September), Abu Sanwariya (21 September), Tahir Pathan and Abu Maaz (both on 22 September), and Abu Khubaib (26–7 September). These facts, together with a number of rules described in the book, could have pointed to an increased chance of terrorist activities by the LeT in subsequent months.

An example of such a temporal association rule is the PST-3 rule documented in Subrahmanian's book: 'LeT attacks symbolic sites three months after any month in which 0–5 LeT commanders are killed and LeT has [training] locations across the border.' The important thing to note is that this rule is supported by 40 pieces of information, with a confidence level of 90.8%; in other words, out of all the 40 documented months when the antecedents of this rule were true, including September 2008, in 90.9% cases, i.e., 36 instances, LeT attacked symbolic sites. Equally important is that this rule has 0% negative probability, which means that there was no month when attacks were carried out that was not preceded by a situation three months prior when LeT commanders were killed and LeT had locations across the border (of course, the latter condition has been true for years on end).

Of course, rules such as PST-3 say nothing about *where* attacks might take place. Nevertheless, related work[47] by V. S. Subrahmanian and Paulo Shakarian used geo-spatial data-mining techniques to detect the most probable locations of secret explosives caches maintained by Iraqi insurgents, based on the spatial pattern of actual bomb attacks on US and Allied forces.

The potential for data mining to aid in intelligence and counter-terrorism is vast. Early initiatives such as the US's TIA program met with scepticism as well as justifiable privacy concerns. Now that the

* Source: SATP.org.

power of large-scale data mining has been demonstrated in so many applications, many of which each of us experience every day on the web, there is far less scepticism in the technology, even as privacy concerns have gone up.

* * *

In much of market-basket analysis, the directionality of the rules is less important than the fact that selected items are grouped together. Thus, it may well be that the beer-and-diapers combination enjoys high *support*, and that is all that matters. *Confidence* in either of the statements 'people who buy beer also buy diapers', or 'people who buy diapers also buy beer' may well be only moderate. Only one of these rules may be *interesting*, however, in that people who buy diapers are unusually likely to buy beer as compared to all those who normally buy beer.

Like traditional bricks-and-mortar stores, e-commerce sites also need to position related items near each other on their websites so that consumers are likely to purchase more items during each visit. You might be tempted to believe that association rules should work for e-commerce just as well as for traditional retail. While this is true to a certain extent, the opportunity for co-marketing related items on the web is actually much wider than implied by traditional association rules designed for the bricks-and-mortar economy. Exploring these opportunities has resulted in new data-mining techniques, such as collaborative filtering and 'latent feature' discovery. Later on we shall find that such techniques also point the way towards addressing the difficult question of 'where features come from'.

Collaborative Filtering

By their very nature, association rules rely on high *support*, i.e., a large volume of evidence grounded in data. Rules enjoying lower levels of support rapidly become both excessively numerous as well as statistically insignificant, making them all but useless. This is true regardless of whether one is dealing with a customer buying patterns or learning properties of the world around us. At the same time, there are many important structural properties that might never enjoy large support in any reasonable collection of experiences.

While shopping online at a site such as Amazon.com, we are regularly presented with a list of 'people who bought this book also bought . . .'. These look like association rules reminiscent of market-basket analysis. Looking closer, however, there are significant differences. First, the 'support' enjoyed by any particular combination of books is likely to be close to zero, whatever that combination is, just going by the number of possible combinations. So no frequent set will work; in fact there are no frequent sets. Next, the recommendation system is contextual, i.e., the set of books shown depends on the one you are currently browsing.

But that is not all. Who are the 'people' who 'bought this book . . .'? Clearly there are many people, and the books they each bought probably span a wide variety of interests as well as the different purposes for which books are bought, i.e., work, leisure, for kids, etc. Merely combining the set of all books bought by people who bought 'this' book would likely yield a rather meaningless potpourri. So how does Amazon decide which books to show you along with the one you are browsing?

It is indeed possible to group books based on the similarity of the people buying them. Further, and most interestingly, the similarity of people can in turn be computed based on the books that they buy. This seemingly circular argument is at the heart of what is called *collaborative filtering*. No features are used other than the relationship between people and the books they buy. Unlike association rules, collaborative filtering allows groups with low support to be discovered.

Collaborative filtering addresses what is often referred to as the 'long tail' of online marketing. In traditional marketing that is based on placing products on shelves or advertising to a broad audience on TV, association rules based on frequent sets enjoying high support are useful since they point to groups that might attract the largest volume of buyers given the fact that in the end the retailer has to choose one particular way to organize their shelves, or finally decide on a single TV ad to commission and broadcast in prime time. The online world is very different and presents marketers with the opportunity to target specific ads for each individual. We have seen one example of this in Google's AdSense. Recommendation systems, such as for books on Amazon, are another example of the same phenomenon, using collaborative filtering to target ads instead of content similarity as in the case of AdSense.

The recent story of the Netflix competition[48] illustrates how difficult the collaborative filtering problem becomes on large complex data sets. In October 2006, the online DVD rental service Netflix announced a prize of 1 million dollars to any team that could beat its own in-house algorithm, called Cinematch. The problem posed by Netflix was to accurately predict film ratings based on past data. The data consisted of over 100 million ratings given by almost half a million users to just over 17,000 films. Based on this data contestants needed to predict the ratings of a further two million entries, which were also provided sans the rating values. Notice that this is also a collaborative filtering problem. In the case of Amazon, the accuracy of the recommendations given are best measured by how well they match actual purchases by the same users in the future. Instead of predicting purchases, which may be viewed in binary terms—as zero or one values, the Netflix challenge is to predict ratings, between 1 and 5. The million-dollar prize, to be given for improving over the performance Cinematch by just 10%, was finally awarded only in September 2009, to Bob Bell, Chris Volinsky, and Yehuda Koren from the Statistics Research group of AT&T Labs.

* * *

Even though collaborative filtering appears tough, let us take a stab at it nevertheless: how might we group books based on the people that buy them? When you buy a book on Amazon.com, you need to supply your user ID. One way to think about this is to characterize a book not by the words it contains (which would be the natural 'features' of a book), but instead by the user IDs of the people who bought it. The 'closeness' of two books is then measurable by the number of common people who bought both books. Now Amazon can find and display the few books that are most similar, according to this measure, to the one you are currently browsing. Of course, Amazon stocks well over 10 million books (14 million is the current estimate as per Amazon itself). It is needlessly expensive to have to search for similar books each time a viewer browses a title. Instead, Amazon could group books into *clusters* by calculating which ones are most similar to each other.

Clustering, i.e., grouping items that are similar to each other, is another basic technique for *unsupervised* learning. All that is needed is some way to compare two items, in this case books. A simple algorithm for clustering might proceed by first placing each book in its own group of one. Next, two such single-item groups that are closest to each other are merged into a group of two. The process is then repeated until groups of the desired size are obtained. In the case of Amazon, it might be enough to form groups of a dozen or so books. Note however that in all but the first step we need to compute the similarity between *groups* of books, rather than pairs. The similarity between two groups of books might be taken as the average of the similarities between each pair. Alternatively, one particular book in the group might be chosen as a representative, perhaps because it is more or less equidistant to others in the group, i.e., it serves as some kind of 'group centre'.

How long does this above clustering algorithm, also called *hierarchical clustering*, take to complete? If we have 10 million books, the first step itself requires us to compute the distance between 10 million × 10 million, i.e., 10^{14} books.* Now, 10^{14} is the number 1 with 14 zeros, so perhaps clustering was not such a good idea after all. Fortunately there are other, much faster, clustering techniques. In particular, the technique of 'locality sensitive hashing' allows us to somehow get away *without* ever having to compute distances between each pair.

Random Hashing

As you may recall from Chapter 1, locality sensitive hashing (LSH), invented as recently as 1998 by Indyk and Motwani,[17] is a quite remarkable and general approach that allows one to cluster n data items in only $O(n)$ steps, as opposed to the n^2 steps needed to exhaustively compare all pairs. We discussed then how you might compare two volumes to decide whether they were identical copies of the same book by randomly comparing a small number of pages rather than checking all pairs.

LSH generalizes this approach using random 'locality-sensitive hash functions', rather than random page numbers. An interesting example of using LSH to cluster similar books together is called 'min-hashing'. Consider all possible words (there could be millions), and imagine arranging them in some random order, e.g. 1-'big', 2-'outside', 3-'astounding'. Now take one of the books and figure out which of the tens of thousands of words in it have the smallest numbering according to this random ordering. Let's say the word is 'outside' (i.e., the volume does not contain 'big'); then the min-hash of the book will be 2. Do the same for another volume. If the two books are very similar, maybe even identical, then its min-hash should also be 2, since both books will contain identical words.

Now, instead of using random page numbers, we use many random orderings of all words and calculate the min-hash of both volumes each time. The only way such a pair of min-hash values can differ

---

* Ten million is 10^7, so $10^7 \times 10^7 = 10^{14}$.

is if a word is present in one of the volumes but missing from the other; otherwise both min-hash values will always be equal. If we repeat the process, say, 20 times, i.e., using 20 different orderings of words, the percentage of time the min-hashes match will be directly related to how many common words the two books have. So LSH using min-hashing is a means to cluster similar books together. (Note that we are no longer worried about whether the copies are identical; similarity will do, since min-hashing ignores the order of words in each book.)

The really important part about LSH is that the min-hash values for each book (i.e., all 20 of them) can be computed once for each book, independent of any other book, making it a linear algorithm that takes only $O(n)$ steps. Books having the same min-hash values are automatically assigned to the same cluster, without having to individually compare each pair of books.

Because of the way min-hashes are calculated, books in the same cluster are highly likely to be very similar to each other. It turns out that if two books are, say, 80% similar, the probability that they have the same min-hash value for any one of the random orderings is also 0.8, i.e., 80%; the proof is not too complicated, but still a bit involved so I'm omitting it here. Now, there is a further very important trick to LSH: by using many hash functions we can force the probability of similar books getting into the same cluster to be as close to 100% as we want, while at the same time, the chance that dissimilar books are mapped to the same cluster remains small. We shall return to LSH in Chapter 5 to describe how this is done; interestingly we shall also find that LSH is closely related to techniques that try to model human memory.

Latent Features

Let us step back now to return to our problem of grouping books based on the people that read them. It is quite easy to see that clustering achieves the same result just searching for the 'closest' few books, as we had initially thought of doing. Further, if we use an efficient clustering algorithm, it will certainly be faster to pre-cluster books so that instead of searching for nearby books among all possible ones we need only search within the pre-computed cluster to which a book belongs.

Still, clustering ultimately results in a book being assigned to exactly one cluster, or group. In reality, this may or may not be reflective of reality. For example, the book you are reading right now, i.e., this book itself, might possibly be bought both by computer science students as well as readers of popular science. Of course, unless Amazon knows something more about a particular browser of this book, the best it can do is to recommend other books that are 'close' to this one, which might be a mix of elementary computer science texts together with some popular science books. On the other hand, Amazon does know more, such as the query you used to access this book; and alternatively, if you are logged in with your user ID, it can actually identify you. In this case it should be possible to use such knowledge to give better recommendations.

Suppose we allow ourselves to assign books to multiple groups; let's call them *roles*. Similarly, people are assumed to play multiple roles. Roles might represent computer science students, popular science readers, etc. So a role is nothing but a group of books, and each book is a member of some such roles (groups). At the same time, each person can also belong to many roles. Further, each book or person might be thought of as belonging to different roles with different degrees of affinity. The degree of affinity of a person to a role measures, via a fraction (or percentage), the extent to which that role represents her, as compared to others. Similarly, a book's degree of membership in different roles is also some fraction (or percentage).

If we somehow had a list of such roles and the affinities of each book and person to them, we could use this information to give better recommendations. We would simply find out the major roles a person plays, as well as the books in these roles. The list of recommendations would be chosen from the books across all roles that a person has high affinity to, using the role-affinities of both people and books as probabilities driving the random selection process. Thus, the books 'most closely linked to the roles that a person plays the most' would appear in larger numbers than others. The resulting recommendations are both more relevant as well as more personalized. It is easy to experience this phenomenon for oneself. The books that Amazon recommends to you against any particular book title are visibly different depending on whether or not you are logged in.

* * *

Now comes the interesting bit: *we don't really know what roles there actually are.* Instead, we would like to find what roles make sense given the available data, i.e., the facts about people and the books they have bought. And what is a role, after all? A role is nothing but a label; but there is no way the computer can assign a label such as 'computer science student'. Instead, the computer gives roles meaningless labels. We only need to decide up front how many roles there should be. The problem then becomes one of finding a 'good' mapping of books to roles, and people to roles. But what is a 'good' mapping?

Let us recall what constituted 'goodness' in the case of simple clustering, where each book was assigned to exactly one cluster. We tried to ensure that each pair of books within a group were 'close' to each other, in terms of the number of common people that bought both books in a pair. By the same token, clustering algorithms also try to ensure that books in different clusters are not too close. We can extend this concept of goodness to our case of multi-way clustering in a similar manner. For example, we might still consider minimizing the distance between pairs of books within a cluster, or *role*, but now adjust the calculations to account for the fact that each book in a pair, as well as the people that bought them, belongs to that role to a different degree.

Similarly, we would try to maximize the distance between books that do not belong to clusters, once more with adjusted distance measures.

* * *

The algorithms that achieve such multi-way clustering are far too complex to explain here. Further, the best of these techniques are derived from what are called 'generative' models rather than analogues of clustering. Among the most popular of these techniques is the Latent Dirichlet Allocation, or LDA algorithm.[49] LDA and similar techniques, such as Latent Semantic Analysis, which we also came across in Chapter 2, were actually designed for a very similar problem that we have also seen earlier, i.e., that of automatically discovering *topics* in a collection of documents.

A document can be thought of as a mere collection of words, and words as co-occurring in documents. The analogy to the collaborative filtering problem is almost self-evident: if documents are books, then words are people. Buying a book is akin to including a word in a document. Instead of assigning roles to books and people, we view a document as being a collection of topics, each to a different degree. Similarly, each word can be thought of as contributing, to a certain degree, to each of a set of topics. Finally, just as for roles, we really don't know the topics beforehand; rather, the algorithm needs to discover what set of topics best represents the data at hand, which is in turn nothing but the documents we started out with.

There are close relationships between collaborative filtering, topic discovery, probabilistic ('generative') models, information theory, clustering, classification, and other applications and techniques. Deeper connections between these techniques have recently been explored. As is often the case in science and mathematics, very similar techniques are discovered for different problems in different areas of application. Only later do their relationships emerge. The subject of 'latent' topic-like models is one such area, with a variety of techniques originating independently being found to reveal similarities, deeper insight, as well as ideas for new applications and opportunities for improved performance.[50] Moreover, as we now proceed to explore, collaborative filtering and topic models might teach us something about our pressing question regarding how we ourselves learn features.

* * *

Let us step back and compare the collaborative filtering problem with that of recognizing a category or class of objects, such as 'dogs', based on its 'features', i.e., shape and size. In collaborative filtering, there is no distinction between 'objects' and 'features', as was required in the case of machine learning using classifiers. Books are objects with the people who buy them as features. Conversely, people are objects with the books they buy being their features. Similarly for films and ratings. The features that emerge out of collaborative filtering are hidden, or 'latent', such as the roles people play. While we have described only one latent feature in our discussion earlier, there can be many layers of latent features. For example, books may belong to one or more genres, which in turn are favoured by different roles that people play. The most important aspect of latent learning techniques is that they can learn hidden features, be they roles, genres, or topics, merely based on the co-occurrence of objects, e.g., books, people, and words, in 'experiences', be they book purchases or documents.

Now let us return to a question that came up even while we figured out how to learn classes using machine learning, as well as rules that characterized such classes using data mining. Each of these techniques relied on data being described by crisp features; we had postponed the 'problem' of feature induction for later. Can latent learning teach us something about how features themselves emerge from the world around us?

The study of how humans learn categories along with the features by which to distinguish then is an important area of research for cognitive scientists and psychologists. Systematic studies[51] on infants have shown that the categories they learn are different depending on which items they see occurring together, i.e., co-occurrence is important. For example, when presented with pairs of dogs, and then pairs of cats, the infant is surprised (i.e., gives more attention to) a picture of a dog and a cat together. On the other hand, when presented with pairs of white animals followed by pairs of black animals, they learn the black-or-white feature, and are surprised only when presented with one black and another white animal, even if both are dogs.

A common question posed to kindergarten children is to identify items that 'go together'. Presented with a number of animal pictures, some common pets, others wild animals such as lions and elephants, the child somehow groups the domestic animals together, separately from the wild ones. How? Based on the empirically established[51] importance of co-occurrence as an important element of learning, we might well speculate that children recall having seen wild animals during experiences such as visiting a zoo or watching the Discovery channel, while pets are seen in homes, i.e., during different experiences. Animals are seen in experiences: different experiences contain different animals. Might such a categorization process be similar to how people and books get grouped into many different, even 'personal', categories, in the context of Amazon?

The number of scenes a child experiences and the variety of objects they contain are huge. So is the number of books and the people buying them on Amazon. Yet books get grouped, as do animals. Surely animals can be grouped together based on how similar their features are? But what about wolves and dogs? Should they be grouped together because they look similar, or separately: one wild and the other domestic? Similarly, one might expect that books containing similar content should be grouped together. If this were the case, one should be seeing recommendations for college textbooks on physics when browsing Stephen Hawking's popular science books. But we don't see those.

What we see is uncannily what we expect to see, seemingly due to collaborative filtering techniques that are able to learn latent features.

At the cost of dipping our toes in philosophical waters, let us ask what exactly is required for a technique such as collaborative filtering to work? In the case of books and films, people need to interact with these objects in well-defined *transactions*; further, the objects themselves, be they people, books, or films, need to be *distinguished*.

In the case of scenes and animals, the presence of an object in a scene needs to be distinguished. Exactly what the object is might come later; our built-in perceptual apparatus merely needs to distinguish an object in a scene. Experiments with very young infants have shown that movement is something they recognize easily.[51] Any part of their visual field that moves automatically becomes a candidate object worthy of being distinguished from its background.

Next, scenes themselves need to be identified, perhaps as contiguous periods of time. It has been observed that even babies appear to have the innate capability to subitize, i.e., distinguish between scenes with say, one, two, or three objects.[52] Subitizing in time in order to identify distinct experiences is also presumably innate.

The ability to discern objects in a scene, as infants do using motion, and then to subitize in time, is all that is needed for collaborative filtering to work. Collaborative filtering then neatly sidesteps the distinction between 'objects' and 'features'. Latent features can be learned merely by co-occurrence of objects in experiences. Thus the feature needed to distinguish black animals from white ones, i.e., black or white colour, might be learned when infants see groups of similarly coloured objects. More complex features that can distinguish a dog from a cat might be learned when infants experience many dogs, and many cats, and also many 'legs', which are also identified as objects in a scene because they move rapidly.

Speculating further, consider another kindergarten exercise where a child is asked to 'find the odd man out', i.e., identify which object does not 'fit in' with the rest. Given a collection of curved shapes and one pointy shape, such as a star, the child is easily able to determine that 'pointedness' is the feature to look for. In another exercise though, when presented with stars, circles, and squares, she accurately finds an irregular convex polygon as the odd one out; here regularity was the feature used. Perhaps such exercises themselves form the experiences with which the child automatically learns latent features such as 'pointedness', regularity, or even convexity, smoothness, and connectedness. Collaborative filtering is also a plausible explanation for how we learn relationships between low-level visual features, such as angles or smoothness, so as to form higher-level concepts such as 'pointedness'.

Does collaborative filtering serve as a rational model for how humans learn features such as 'wild animals', pointedness, or convexity as just alluded to? We don't know. Speculation on these matters is still in the domain of the philosophy of cognition, as exemplified in Andy Clark's book *Natural-Born Cyborgs: Minds, Technologies, and the Future of Human Intelligence*.[53] Clark asks: 'How does human thought and reason emerge from looping interactions between material brains and bodies, and complex cultural and technological environments?' He uses collaborative filtering as an example of how 'concepts finely tuned to the desires and needs of consumers are learned as an "emergent phenomenon" of the unplanned by-products of the primary activity, i.e., online shopping'. In a review of Clark's book, Leslie Marsh asks how 'the principles of [collaborative filtering] [could] be integrated into theories of memetics of ideas'.[54] The term 'meme' itself was introduced by Richard Dawkins in his 1976 book[55] to denote an idea, or a 'unit of culture', that is transmitted between people and generations in a manner similar to biological genes. In this sense, a 'meme' is similar to a 'topic'; and, as we have seen, collaborative filtering can automatically learn a set of topics from a collection of documents. Thus, Marsh appears to be asking the same question that we are, i.e., whether collaborative filtering sheds any light on how humans learn memes from conversations and experience.

Nevertheless, in spite of interest from philosophers of cognition such as Clark and Marsh, many more systematic psychological experiments need to be carried out before we can decide if latent feature learning via collaborative filtering forms a reasonable model for how humans learn features. Be that as it may, i.e., whether or not it has any bearing on understanding human cognition, collaborative filtering is certainly a mechanism for machines to learn structure about the real world. Structure that we ourselves learn, and sometimes define in elusive ways (e.g., topics and genre), can be learned by machines. Further, the machine learns this structure without any active supervision, i.e., this is a case of *unsupervised* learning. All that is needed is the machine equivalent of subitizing, i.e., distinct *objects* occurring or co-occurring in identified *transactions*.

Learning Facts from Text

We have seen that machines can learn from examples. In the case of supervised learning, such as for browsers versus surfers, or dogs versus cats, a human-labelled set of training examples is needed. In unsupervised learning, such as discovering market-basket rules, or collaborative filtering to recommend books on Amazon, no explicit training set is needed. Instead the machine learns from experiences as long as they can be clearly identified, even if implicitly, such as purchase transactions, or scenes with features.

We began this chapter with the example of the *Jeopardy!*-beating Watson computer. While we might be convinced, based on our discussions so far, that a machine such as Watson could in principle *learn* various kinds of facts and rules, it does seem that it would need to learn such knowledge from a far richer set of experiences than, say, e-commerce transactions, or idealized scenes. Instead, it might be far better for Watson to learn directly from the 50 billion or so indexed web pages that already document and describe so many human experiences and recollections. Of course, web pages are mostly unstructured text, and we know that text can be analysed using natural language processing (NLP) techniques as we have seen in Chapter 2. NLP, together with various machine-learning techniques, should allow the machine to learn a much larger number of 'general knowledge facts' from such a large corpus as the entire web.

Watson does indeed use web pages to learn and accumulate facts. Many of the techniques it uses are those of 'open information extraction from the web', an area that that has seen considerable attention and progress in recent years. Open information extraction seeks to learn a wide variety of facts from the web; specific ones such as 'Einstein was born in Ülm', or even more general statements such as 'Antibiotics kill bacteria'. Professor Oren Etzioni and his research group at the University of Washington are pioneers in this subject, and they coined the term 'open information extraction from the web' as recently as 2007.

The REVERB[56] system most recently developed by Etzioni's group is simple enough to describe at a high level. Recall that NLP technology, itself based on machine learning, can fairly accurately produce a shallow parse of a sentence to identify the part of speech for each word. Thus, a shallow parse of a sentence such as 'Einstein was born in Ülm' would tag each word with its most likely part of speech, based on a combination of classifiers which in turn would have been trained on a vast corpus of sentences. The result would probably be something like, [Einstein/noun-phrase was/verb-descriptor born/verb in/preposition-in Ülm/noun-phrase]. While deeper parsing as we have seen in Chapter 2 could also be done, this may or may not reveal the actual scenario that is conveyed by the sentence. REVERB takes a simpler approach, and instead looks for verbs, or verb phrases such as 'was born', along with surrounding prepositions. Here REVERB would focus on 'was born in', and try to learn a 'fact' with this verb-based group as the central element. The facts being sought are triples of the form [Einstein, was born in, Ülm]. Having identified the longest verb-based sequence to focus on, REVERB then looks for nearby nouns or noun phrases. It also tries to choose proper nouns over simple ones, especially if they occur often enough in other sentences. Thus, for the sentence 'Einstein, the scientist, was born in Ülm', REVERB would prefer to learn that [Einstein, was born in, Ülm] rather than a fact that a [scientist, was born in, Ülm]. Of course, REVERB is a bit more complex than what we have described. For example, among other things, it is able to identify more than one fact from a sentence. Thus, the sentence 'Mozart was born in Salzburg, but moved to Vienna in 1781' extracts the fact [Mozart, moved to, Vienna], in addition to [Mozart, was born in, Salzburg].

Open information extraction techniques such as REVERB have extracted a vast number of such triples, each providing some evidence of a 'fact', merely by crawling the web. REVERB itself has extracted over a billion triples. In fact, one can search this set of triples online.* A search for all triples matching the pattern [Einstein, born in, ??] results in a number of 'facts', each supported by many triples. For example, we find that REVERB has 'learned' that Albert Einstein was born in Germany (39), Ülm (34), 1879 (33), where the numbers in brackets indicate how many independently learned triples support a particular combination.

Of course, REVERB very often fails, perhaps even on most sentences actually found in web pages. Recall we had considered the following sentence to highlight how difficult a task Watson had before it: 'One day, from among his city views of Ülm, Otto chose a watercolour to send to Albert Einstein as a remembrance of Einstein's birthplace.' What do you think REVERB does on this more complex, but certainly not uncommon, sentence structure? Well, REVERB discovers

* <http://openie.cs.washington.edu>.

the pretty useless fact that [Otto, chose, a watercolour]. To give it some credit though, REVERB attaches a confidence of only 21% to this discovery, while it concludes [Einstein, was born in, Ülm] with 99.9% confidence from the easier sentence 'Einstein was born in Ülm'. The REVERB system is but one fact-discovery engine. Different techniques, such as those used in an earlier system called TextRunner,[57] also built by Etzioni's group, can discover a variety of other constructs, such as the possessive 'Einstein's birthplace', or 'Steve Jobs, the brilliant and visionary CEO of Apple, passed away today' to learn [Steve Jobs, CEO of, Apple] in addition to [Steve Jobs, passed away, 5 October 2011].

One may have noticed our use of the terms confidence and support in this discussion, just as in the case of association rules. This is no coincidence. Sentence-level analysis such as REVERB can discover many triples from vast volumes of text. These can be viewed as transactions, each linking a subject to an object via a verb. Frequently occurring sets of identical or closely related triples can be viewed as more concrete facts, depending on the support they enjoy. Association rules within such frequent triple-sets can point to the most likely answers to a question. For example, of the many triples of the form [Einstein, was born in, ?], the majority of them have either Germany or Ülm as the object; only one had Wurttemberg, while some others point to the year 1879.

Facts become more useful if they can be combined with other facts. For example, it should be possible to combine [Einstein, was born in, Ülm] and [Ülm, is a city in, Germany] to conclude that [Einstein, was born in a city in, Germany]. Verbs from triples learned from different sentences can be combined just as if they occurred in the same sentence, with the two triples being 'joined' because the object of one, i.e., Ülm, is the subject of the other.

It is even more interesting to ask whether more general rules can be learned by combining triples other than what appear to be simple statements. For example, many triples of the form [*some person*, is born in, *some place*] might yield a higher-level rule, or fact, that 'persons are born in places'. Another set of higher-level facts, learned from many sentences including the definition of 'birthplace', might be that 'persons have a birthplace', 'birthplace is a place', and 'persons are born in their birthplace'. A system such as Watson would require the exploration of many different combinations of such facts, each of which the machine 'knows' with a different degree of confidence. Watson uses a variety of mechanisms, possibly these and many more, to discover facts, both preprogrammed ones as well as many learned *during* the question-answering process. Watson also uses direct keyword-based search on the vast volumes of raw web-texts it has stored in its memory. Searches are often issued dynamically, in response to facts it has already found, so as to gather more data in an effort to garner support for these facts, while continuously juggling with a set of hypothetical answers to the quiz question it may be trying to answer.

Combining specific facts with more general rules, learning additional facts in the process, while also taking into account the uncertainty with which each fact is 'known', is actually the process of *reasoning*, and is at the heart of our ability to 'connect the dots' and make sense of the world around us. Representing rules and facts and then reasoning with them, as Watson appears to do, is the subject of Chapter 4, 'Connect'.

Learning vs 'Knowing'

However, before proceeding to reasoning, let us reflect on what we might conclude about a machine's ability to learn using the techniques discussed so far. All our discussions required the computer to be presented with objects or experiences that in turn may include or be related to other objects or experiences. These relationships, be they of containment or shared presence in a transaction, determine the *features* on which machine learning of all forms relies. Attributes of dogs, cats, or birds, of buyers and browsers, are features. Similarly, the books people buy are features of people, just as the people themselves are features of books.

All our machine learning is based on first being able to distinguish objects along with some of the features describing them. The ability to distinguish different objects or segregate experiences is probably an innate ability of humans. Computers, on the other hand, derive this ability directly through our programming. Classifiers can then distinguish different classes of objects, dogs from cats, buyers from browsers, provided they have been trained suitably. Unsupervised rule learning can discover important features and frequently observed associations between features, thereby learning some structure of the world. 'Latent' learning techniques such as collaborative filtering can similarly discover even infrequent correlations between objects (e.g., books) based on their features (e.g., people who bought them), as well as between features (e.g., topics in words) based on objects (e.g., the articles they occur in). Finally, the computer can learn 'facts' of the form [subject, verb, object] from vast volumes of text available on the web.

Classes, rules, groups, facts—all surely very useful forms of 'knowledge' that can well be exploited for certain types of applications. At the same time, many philosophers have asked whether the acquisition of such rules and facts has anything to do with 'knowing' anything, or with how humans actually learn knowledge. Our goal in this book is far more limited to highlighting the similarities between human capabilities and what machines can now do in the web age, rather than seeking to comment on such philosophical matters. Nevertheless, I do feel the need to describe two somewhat recent and diametrically opposite viewpoints on this topic, if only for the sake of completeness.

In a highly debated 1980 article entitled 'Minds, Brains, and Programs',[58] the philosopher John Searle severely questioned whether a machine knowing rules and facts such as those we have seen it can learn, knows anything at all in the sense humans do. Searle makes his arguments through a variation of the Turing Test, in a thought experiment wherein an English-speaking human is taught how to recognize and manipulate Chinese characters using programmed rules, facts, etc., armed with which the man is then able to answer simple questions, also presented in Chinese, about a paragraph of Chinese text given to him. The man himself has no knowledge of Chinese. To an external Chinese speaking interrogator though, he, along with all his rules and facts, does appear to display some abilities of comprehension in Chinese. Perhaps the interrogator might even believe that the man inside this 'Chinese room' was indeed a Chinese speaker. Searle's point was that in spite of this external behaviour, in no way could the man, even with all his tools, be considered as 'knowing' Chinese. Searle in effect refutes that the Turing Test has anything to say about such a machine's 'understanding' as being in any way related to 'real' human understanding or knowledge.

Searle's criticisms were directed at the proponents of 'strong AI', who believed that a suitably programmed machine, even if highly complex, could in fact be considered as conscious as a human or at least some higher animal. Searle was however ready to admit and accept that such knowledge and its manipulation could be highly useful, and might even assist us in understanding how minds function:

> If by 'digital computer' we mean anything at all that has a level of description where it can correctly be described as the instantiation of a computer program, then again the answer is, of course, yes, since we are the instantiations of any number of computer programs, and we can think.[58]

Yet he also asserts strongly that the knowledge maintained by a computer and manipulated by its programming cannot actually be said to be doing anything akin to human thinking:

> But could something think, understand, and so on solely in virtue of being a computer with the right sort of program? Could instantiating a program, the right program of course, by itself be a sufficient condition of understanding? This I think is the right question to ask, though it is usually confused with one or more of the earlier questions, and the answer to it is no.[58]

Searle's argument was itself strongly criticized by Hofstadter and Dennett in their 1981 book on consciousness, *The Mind's I*,[59] which also reprinted Searle's article. Hofstadter and Dennett essentially reaffirm the strong-AI view that pure programs could eventually learn and achieve 'understanding' equivalent to humans, possibly via facts and rules, as well as the ability to reason sufficiently well using them.

When we are describing Google, or Watson, as having 'learned about us', or 'learned facts about the world', the Searle–Hofstadter debate does come to mind, and therefore deserves mention and reflection. Whether or not the facts and rules learned by machines operating using web-scale data sets and text corpora 'actually' understand or not will probably always remain a philosophical debate. The points we will continue to focus on are what such systems can do in practice, as well as aspects of their programming that might occasionally provide rational models of some limited aspects of human thought, and that too only when borne out by psychological experiments.

At least one of Searle's primary arguments was that a system that 'only manipulates formal symbols' could have 'no interesting connection with the brain'. The absence of any direct link to sensory perception is one of the things that makes mere symbol manipulation suspect: 'visual experience[s], are both caused by and realised in the neurophysiology of the brain'.[58]

An interesting counter to this argument is now somewhat possible based on recent studies of how human babies learn: 'Consider a baby on a day trip to the city, observing cars and people on the road . . . How does she make sense of this blooming buzzing confusion?' writes Amitabha Mukerjee,[60] a senior AI professor at the Indian Institute of Technology in Kanpur. Studies have shown that 4–7-month-old babies can distinguish foreground and background, identify distinct objects, and direct their attention based on visible motion. They understand occlusion, i.e., 'are surprised by a tall object disappearing behind a short barrier [i.e., one too short to actually occlude it]'.[60] They can also 'understand' that one object is 'contained in' another, but only later, at 7 months or more of age.

Now, what is interesting is that Mukerjee and his student Prithwijit Guha have shown how a computer can also learn similar 'visual concepts' by processing videos of the real world. No human supervision is needed, only basic low-level computations on pixels in images, much as performed by neurons in our visual cortex. The machine learns higher-level visual concepts using grouping, or clustering techniques similar to those we have described earlier, all by itself. This work shows that 'starting with complex perceptual input, [it] is [possible] to . . . identify a set of spatio-temporal patterns (concepts), in a completely unsupervised manner'.[60]

Mukerjee and Guha then go on to show how such visual concepts might get associated with language: students were asked to write textual descriptions of each of the real-world videos. Multi-way clustering is then able to learn relationships between visual concepts and words. Mukerjee and Guha's work provides some evidence that 'language is . . . a mechanism for expressing (and transferring) categories acquired from sensory experience rather than a purely formal symbol manipulation system'.[60] Does visual concept acquisition as demonstrated by Mukerjee and Guha's work address at least one of Searle's arguments, i.e., that direct perception about the real world is required for any learning to be 'real'? Perhaps, if only to a small extent.

* * *

What does all this have to do with the web? Consider this: in 2010 alone 13 million hours of video were uploaded to YouTube. In contrast, the amount of visual sensory input available to any one of us over an entire lifetime is about 525,000 hours (90 years $\times$ 365 days $\times$ 16 hours/day). How much could Google (which now owns YouTube) learn using such a vast volume of real-world videos. Could the machine learn and acquire concepts in the real, yes, real world? Just as a baby might, using ideas such as Mukerjee and Guha's, independent of language and 'mere symbol manipulation'? Further adding to the possibilities are the 50 billion web pages of text. Missing, of course, is any direct link between so many videos and all that text; but there is certainly potential for deeper learning lurking somewhere in this mix.

Could Google's machines acquire visual concepts to the extent that they would 'be surprised by a tall object disappearing behind a short barrier'? Of course, rather than 'be surprised', the machine might merely identify such a video as being a bit 'odd', or an 'outlier' in mathematical terms.

But what causes a machine to expect one thing and 'be surprised' if it is not found? Why should the machine learn any facts at all? So far, all we can say is 'because we programmed it to do so'. Here we come up against Searle's second and deeper objection to 'strong AI'. Where does *intention* or purpose arise in a machine? We postpone our discussion on 'purpose' to the end of this book. For the moment, we resume where we left off before our excursion into philosophy; i.e., having learned facts and rules, albeit symbolic, how might a computer *reason* using these to achieve some fairly complex goals, even if these be only what we ask of it?

4

CONNECT

On 14 October 2011, the Apple Computer Corporation launched the latest generation of the iPhone 4S mobile phone. The iPhone 4S included Siri, a speech interface that allows users to 'talk to their phone'. As we look closer though, we begin to suspect that Siri is possibly more than 'merely' a great speech-to-text conversion tool. Apart from being able to use one's phone via voice commands instead of one's fingers, we are also able to interact with other web-based services. We can search the web, for instance, and if we are looking for a restaurant, those nearest our current location are retrieved, unless, of course, we indicated otherwise. Last but not least, Siri talks back, and that too in a surprisingly human fashion.

'Voice-enabled location-based search—Google has it already, so what?', we might say. But there is more. Every voice interaction is processed by Apple's web-based servers; thus Siri runs on the 'cloud' rather than directly on one's phone. So, as Siri interacts with us, it is also continuously storing data about each interaction on the cloud; whether we repeated words while conversing with it, which words, from which country we were speaking, and whether it 'understands' us or not in that interaction. As a result, we are told, Siri will, over time, learn from all this data, improve its speech-recognition abilities, and *adapt* itself to each individual's needs.

We have seen the power of machine learning in Chapter 3. So, regardless of what Siri does or does not do today, let us for the moment imagine what is possible. After all, Siri's cloud-based back-end will very soon have millions of voice conversations to learn from. Thus, if we ask Siri to 'call my wife Jane' often enough, it should soon learn to 'call my wife', and fill in her name automatically. Further, since storage is cheap, Siri can remember all our actions, for every one of us: 'call the same restaurant I used last week', should figure out where I ate last week, and in case I eat out often, it might choose the one I used on the same day last week. As Siri learns our habits, it should learn to distinguish between the people we call at work and those we call in the evenings. Therefore, more often than not it should automatically choose the right 'Bob' to call, depending on when we are calling— perhaps prefacing its action with a brief and polite 'I'm calling Bob from the office, okay?', just to make sure. As we gradually empower Siri to do even more actions on our behalf, it might easily 'book me at the Marriott nearest Chicago airport tomorrow night', and the job is done. Today's web-based hotel booking processes might appear decidedly clunky in a Siri-enabled future.

A recent Hollywood film[61] titled *Horrible Bosses* includes a scene involving an in-car Siri-like device, called Gregory in the film. Voice interfaces and talking cars are already being seen in the real world, but Gregory, like Siri, does more than just 'turn on the heat'. As the protagonists inadvertently drive into a crime-prone locality, Gregory automatically rolls up the car windows and locks their doors, while also warning them of possible dangers lurking ahead. Of course, this is a Hollywood film, so eventually we find that Gregory also records all conversations taking place in and around the car, a fact that it voluntarily reveals in due course, thereby assisting the police in identifying the true killers. However, lest we begin to suspect the film director of extraordinary prescience, Gregory is endowed with an Indian accent, so the scriptwriter probably had in mind an outsourced call-centre employee as the brains behind Gregory, rather than some highly sophisticated Siri-like technology. Nevertheless, now that we do have the real Siri, which will only learn and improve over time, we might well imagine it behaving quite Gregory-like in the not-too-distant future.

The scenes just outlined are, at least today, hypothetical. However, they are well within the power of today's technologies, and will most certainly come to be, in some manifestation or other. Clearly, machine learning is an important element of making such applications come to life. But that is not enough. Notice that in our imaginary future Siri does more than look up facts that it may have learned. It also *reasons*, using its knowledge to resolve ambiguities and possibly much more, especially in Gregory's case.

To figure out 'the same restaurant as last week', Siri would need to *connect* its knowledge about where you ate last week with what day of the week it is today, and then apply a *rule* that drives it to use the day of the week to *derive* the restaurant you are *most likely* referring to. There may be other rules it discards along the way, such as possibly the fact that you mostly prefer Italian food, because of the *concepts* it manages to extract from the natural language command you gave it, which provide the *context* to select the right rule. Thus, reasoning involves connecting facts and applying rules. Further, the results derived may be uncertain, and the choice of which rules to use depends on the context.

Reasoning is an important characteristic of being human. Hardly any other living species that we know of can reason the way we do, and reasoning is one of the key tools we employ for 'connecting the dots' and making sense of our world. We celebrate reasoning prowess: those who reason better and faster are considered more intelligent than others. 'From a drop of water, a logician could infer the possibility of an Atlantic or a Niagara without having seen or heard of one or the other. So all life is a great chain, the nature of which is known whenever we are shown a single link of it,' writes the legendary detective Sherlock Holmes, as related in A *Study in Scarlet*.[62]

At the same time, the ability to reason and 'connect the dots' depends on the dots one has managed to accumulate. Thus looking, listening, and learning are precursors and prerequisites of reasoning. Further, it is equally important to choose and organize the dots one gathers. To quote Holmes once more:

> 'I consider that a man's brain originally is like a little empty attic, and you have to stock it with such furniture as you choose. A fool takes in all the lumber of every sort that he comes across, so that the knowledge which might be useful to him gets crowded out, or at best is jumbled up with a lot of other things so that he has a difficulty in laying his hands upon it. Now the skilful workman is very careful indeed as to what he takes into his brain-attic. He will have nothing but the tools which may help him in doing his work, but of these he has a large assortment, and all in the most perfect order. It is a mistake to think that that little room has elastic walls and can distend to any extent. Depend upon it there comes a time when for every addition of knowledge you forget something that you knew before. It is of the highest importance, therefore, not to have useless facts elbowing out the useful ones'.[62]

The facts we cumulate in our 'attic' form the knowledge using which we reason, and in turn create more knowledge. So it is important to understand how knowledge is stored, or 'represented'. After all, different ways of knowledge representation might be best suited for different kinds of reasoning.

Reasoning involves simple logical inferences, from the oft-repeated Socratic syllogism 'all men are mortal, Socrates is a man, therefore Socrates is mortal,' to more sophisticated mathematical deductions such as Euclid's proof that there are infinite prime numbers, and most interestingly, the reasoning process by which such deductions are discovered. Further, uncertainty or vagueness about the world brings in unexpected complications: 'most firemen are men; most men have safe jobs; therefore most firemen have safe jobs', while apparently a valid chain of inference, yet results in an inaccurate conclusion; after all, most firemen do *not* have safe jobs. Merely replacing 'all' with 'most' creates difficulties. Watson, as we have already seen in Chapter 3, certainly needs to deal with such uncertain facts that apply often, but not universally. There are indeed different kinds of reasoning, which we shall now proceed to explore. After all, any intelligent behaviour which might eventually emerge from a future cloud-based Siri, Gregory, or Watson, will most certainly employ a variety of different reasoning techniques.

Mechanical Logic

When we make a point in a court of law, fashion a logical argument, reason with another person or even with ourselves, our thinking process is naturally comprised a chain of 'deductions', one following 'naturally' from the previous one. Each step in the chain should be seemingly obvious, or else the intervening leap of faith can be a possible flaw in one's argument. Alternatively, longer leaps of faith might sometimes be needed in order to even postulate a possible argumentative chain, which we later attempt to fill in with sufficient detail. Guesses and 'gut feelings' are all part and parcel of the complex reasoning processes continually active between every pair of human ears. Not surprisingly therefore, efforts to better understand 'how we think', or in other words, to reason about how we reason, go far back to the ancient Indian, Chinese, and Greek civilizations. In ancient China and India, the understanding of inference was closely linked to ascertaining the validity of legal arguments. In fact the ancient Indian system of logic was called 'Nyaya', which translates to 'law', even in the spoken Hindi of today.

However, the systematic study of reasoning, merely for the sake of understanding how to think clearly, and thereby discover knowledge about the world, began with Aristotle in ancient Greece. Prior Greek philosophers, such as Pythagoras, as well as the Babylonians, certainly used logical chains of deduction, but, as far as we know, they did not study the process of reasoning itself. According to Aristotle, a deduction, or *syllogism*, is 'speech in which, certain things having been supposed, something different from those supposed results of necessity because of their being so'.[63] In other words, the conclusion follows 'naturally', *of necessity*, from the premise. Aristotelian logic then goes on to systematically define what kinds of syllogisms are in fact 'natural enough' so they can be used for drawing valid inferences in a chain of reasoning.

The study of logic became an area of mathematics, called 'symbolic logic', in the 19th century with the work of George Boole and Gottlob Frege. The logic of Boole, also called 'classical' logic, abstracted many aspects of Aristotelian logic so that they could be described mathematically. Whereas Aristotelian logic dealt with statements in natural language, classical Boolean logic is all about statements in the abstract. (In fact there is a resurgence of interest in the direct use of Aristotelian 'natural logic' to deal with inferences in natural language.[64]) In classical logic a statement, such as 'it is raining', is either true or false. While this may seem obvious, there are alternative reasoning paradigms where statements may be true only to 'a certain degree'. We shall return to these when we discuss reasoning under uncertainty, such as is used in the Watson system as well as for many other web-intelligence applications.

Boolean logic defines how statements can be logically combined to yield new statements. Thus 'it is raining' can be combined with 'the grass is wet' to yield 'it is raining *and* the grass is wet'. An alternative combination with 'the sprinkler is on' might be 'it is raining *or* the sprinkler is on'. Now, the rules of classical logic define when each of these combinations are true or false depending on the truth or falsehood of their constituent statements. The first *and*-combination is true only if *both* the statements 'it is raining' and 'the grass is wet' are true. If either of these is false, the *and*-combination is also false. On the other hand, the latter *or*-combination is true if *either* (or both) the statements 'it is raining' or 'the sprinkler is on' are true. The operations *and* and *or*, used to combine statements, are called Boolean operations. These operations also form the very basis for how information is represented and manipulated in digital form as ones and zeros within computer systems.

So much for that. Now comes the key to reasoning using classical logic, i.e., how the process of inference itself is defined in terms of Boolean operations. Suppose we wish to state a rule such as

> *if* it is raining *then* the grass is wet.

What does it mean for such a rule to be true? It turns out that we could just as well have said

> it is *not* raining *or* the grass is wet

This statement says exactly the same thing as the if–then rule! Let's see why. Suppose it is raining; then the first part of the implication, i.e., 'it is *not* raining', is false. But then, for 'it is *not* raining *or* the grass is wet' to be true, which we have stated is indeed the case, the second part of this statement must be true, because of the *or*-operation. Therefore the grass must be wet. In effect 'it is *not* raining *or* the grass is wet' says the same thing as '*if* it is raining, *then* the grass is wet'. Thus, by merely stating each 'implication' as yet another logical statement, the idea of one statement 'following from' another, 'naturally', 'of necessity', becomes part of the logical system itself. The consequence 'the grass is wet' follows from 'it is raining' simply in order to avoid an inconsistency.

There is a subtle but very important difference between the implication about rain and grass just described, and the well-known example 'all men are mortal, Socrates is a man, so Socrates is mortal'. Whereas the statement 'it is raining' is a plain and simple 'fact', the statement 'all men are mortal' says something in general about *all* men. We can think of this statement as expressing a property 'mortality' about any 'thing' that also has the property of 'being a man'. Thus, this implication is firstly about *properties* of things in the world rather than directly about things. Such properties are called 'predicates' in classical logic, whereas direct statements of fact, either in general or about a particular thing, are called 'propositions' that can either be true or false. Thus, 'being a man' is a predicate, which when stated about a particular thing named Socrates, results in the proposition, or fact, 'Socrates is a man'.

Secondly, the implication 'all men are mortal' is a general statement, about *all* things. Referring to *all* things is called 'universal quantification'. On the other hand, the statement 'some men are mortal' implies that there is at least one thing that is a man, which is also mortal. This is called 'existential quantification', since it is in effect saying that 'there exists at least one man, who is mortal'. Classical logic without predicates or quantifications is called *propositional calculus*. After adding the additional subtleties of predicates and quantification it becomes *predicate logic*.

Note that every statement in predicate logic is about properties of things, or *variables*, whether they are particular things or unknown ones quantified either universally or existentially. Consequently, in order to state the fact 'it is raining' (i.e., a simple proposition) in predicate logic, one needs to write it as a predicate, i.e., a property; only in this case there is no 'thing' involved, so it becomes a predicate with *no* variables as its 'arguments'. In the language of predicate logic we would write the statement 'Socrates is a man' as Man(Socrates) whereas the fact 'it is raining' becomes a statement of the form Raining().

We note in passing that this distinction between statements using predicates versus those about facts alone is something introduced by modern logicians; original unfettered Aristotelian logic treated statements about the particular, i.e., propositions, together with those referring to *all* or *some* things. Properties of things, or predicates, were also naturally included, just as they occurred in human language. It is for this reason, perhaps, that Aristotelian 'natural logic' is once more finding its way into modern computational linguistics, as we have alluded to earlier.

Bringing in variables and quantification makes the process of reasoning in predicate logic slightly more involved than the natural chain by which one statement follows from another in propositional calculus. The statement 'all men are mortal' reworded in predicate logic becomes 'for all things it is true that, if a thing "is a man", then that thing "is mortal"', which can also be written as the predicate-logic formula

$$\forall\, T \; \textit{if}\; \text{Man}(T) \; \textit{then}\; \text{Mortal}(T)$$

where the symbol $\forall$ stands for 'for all', and T for a 'thing'. On the other hand, as we have seen earlier, the particular statement 'Socrates is a man', expresses the fact that 'the thing Socrates "is a man"', and is simply written as Man(Socrates).

In the case of propositions, such as 'it is raining', we would be able to conclude 'the grass is wet' because of the implication directly linking these two statements. In predicate logic, however, the chain of reasoning needs to be established by a process of matching particular things, such as 'Socrates', with hitherto unknown things within quantified statements such as 'for all things, if a thing "is a man". . .'. Since the latter statement is true for all things, it is also true for the particular thing called 'Socrates'. This matching process, called 'unification', results in the implication 'if Socrates is a man, then Socrates is mortal', written more formally as

if Man(Socrates) then Mortal(Socrates)

which is obtained by 'unifying' the variable T with the particular value Socrates. Now, this implication when taken together with the assertion that Socrates is indeed a man, i.e., that Man(Socrates) is a true fact, allows us to conclude Mortal(Socrates), i.e., that 'Socrates is mortal'.

Whew! A lot of work to merely describe the 'chain of reasoning' that comes so naturally to all of us. However, as a result of all this work, we can now see that reasoning using classical logic can be simply automated by a computer. All one needs are a bunch of logical statements. Some statements are facts about the world as observed, which can be independent propositions such as 'it is raining', or propositions stating a property of some particular thing, such as 'John is a man'. Along with these are statements representing 'rules' such as '*if* it rains *then* the grass is wet', or 'all men are mortal'. As we saw earlier, such rules can be merely encoded in terms of *or*-combinations such as 'it is *not* raining *or* the grass is wet', or 'a thing x is not a man *or* the thing x is mortal'.

Thereafter, a computer program can mechanically reason forwards to establish the truth or falsehood of all remaining facts that follow from these statements. Along the way, it also attempts to 'unify' particular things such as 'John' with unknowns, or variables, such as 'a thing x', which occur within logical statements. Reasoning forwards in this manner from a set of facts and rules is called 'forward-chaining'. Conversely, suppose we wanted to check the truth of a statement such as 'the grass is wet', or 'Tom is mortal'. For this we could also reason backwards to check whether or not any chain of inferences and unifications leads to a truth value for our original statement, or 'goal', a process referred to as 'backward-chaining'.

* * *

Unlike in the simple examples just discussed, real-world applications require dealing with hundreds or even thousands of facts and rules. Rule engines are computer systems that perform forward- or backward-chaining on extremely large sets of rules and facts. Now, unification on sets of rules with even a moderate number of variables also poses computational challenges. With a mere ten variables and, say, ten things, there are 10^{10}, or 10 *trillion*, combinations, i.e., different ways in which ten things can be unified with ten variables. Of course, we don't search for all possible combinations, and clever algorithms for efficient reasoning unify only where required, both for forward- as well as backward-chaining. We shall return to describe such techniques later in the context of some examples.

Computer systems that used rule engines to evaluate very large numbers of facts and rules became rather widespread in the mid-1970s to late 1980s, and acquired the popular name 'expert systems'. Expert systems were developed and successfully used for diagnosing faults in complex machinery or aircraft by encoding the many 'rules of thumb' used by experienced engineers or extracted from voluminous documentation. Other expert systems were proposed to assist in medical diagnosis: the knowledge of expert doctors as well as facts and rules extracted from large corpora of medical research were encoded as facts and rules. Thereafter less experienced doctors, or those in developing countries or far-flung remote areas, could benefit from the knowledge of others, as delivered through the automated reasoning carried out by such expert systems.

Over time, however, the popularity of expert systems waned. One of the main challenges was in coming up with a large-enough set of rules that encoded enough real-world knowledge to be useful. The process of interviewing experts and manually extracting rules from documents and research papers was not easy to do, and was difficult to scale and replicate across different applications. Thus, the knowledge extracted and encoded once, say, for fault diagnosis of a particular military aircraft, did not in any way speed up the process of developing the next expert system, for, say, a tank. The other very real problem when dealing with large numbers of rules was that more often than not, different rules could lead to contradictory results. Thus, one set of rules might yield 'the patient has diabetes', while another evaluation path might lead to a different conclusion. Establishing the consistency of a large system of rules is itself a very difficult problem. Moreover, dealing with the contradictions that naturally emerge required a different kind of logic that could deal with uncertainty. Good old classical logic, where a statement is either true or false, was no longer good enough. So expert systems went into cold storage for almost two decades.

In the meanwhile, as we have seen in Chapter 3, there have been significant advances in the ability to automatically extract facts and rules from large volumes of data and text. Additionally, the business of reasoning under uncertainty, which was pretty much an 'art' in the days of early expert systems, has since acquired stronger theoretical underpinnings. The time is possibly ripe for large-scale automated reasoning systems to once again resurface, as we have speculated they well might do, even if in the guise of Siri-like avatars very different from the expert systems of old. Let us see how.

* * *

The origins of Siri on the iPhone 4S go back to SRI, a contract research firm on the outskirts of Stanford University, in a project christened CALO, or 'Cognitive Agent that Learns and Optimizes'. CALO's goal was to create a personal digital assistant that could assist a typical knowledge worker in day-to-day tasks such as breaking down high-level project goals into smaller action-items, which in turn might require specific tasks to be completed, meetings to be scheduled, documents to be reviewed, etc. CALO would assist its human master by taking over the more mundane activities of scheduling mutually convenient times for meetings, prioritizing and organizing emails, as well as reminding its master of imminent meetings, impending deadlines, or potentially important emails that remained unattended.

Further, CALO would, over time, *learn* what its master meant by 'important', which people were her 'bosses', peers, or subordinates, and 'how' each category was to be dealt with. In effect, CALO would act much as a human assistant does. CALO was funded by the US

Defense Advanced Research Projects Agency, DARPA, to 'revolution-ize how machines support decision makers'.[65] CALO was to have advanced natural-language understanding capabilities, and interact with its users via speech and vision interfaces, while performing its job as a personal digital assistant. Just before the DARPA project neared its end, in 2007 SRI spun off a company called Siri to commercialize the CALO technology for non-classified applications. Siri was bought by Apple in April 2010, and the rest is history.

From the perspective of CALO's original goals, Siri actually does far less. At least as of today, Siri does not understand projects, tasks, and how meetings or calls fit into the overall scheme of work. Siri is for per-sonal use, and supposed to be fun, not work. Much of Siri's engaging and entertaining behaviour is quite similar to a very early experiment dating back to the 1960s, called Eliza.[66] Joseph Weizenbaum wrote the Eliza program at MIT in the mid-1960s, to demonstrate how fairly rudimentary computer programs could fool humans into ascribing far greater intelligence to them than was warranted. Eliza was based on matching its human conversation partner's comments with simple patterns. For example, suppose you were to utter 'I plan to go to Oxford tomorrow with my wife'. An Eliza-like program would recognize this as being a statement rather than a question, and therefore respond with a question, such as 'What happens if you don't go to Oxford tomorrow with your wife?' The program has 'understood' nothing; it merely matches the incoming sentence with a set of stock patterns that it can recognize, and responds with a stock answer. The pattern, which could be of the form '[I] [verb phrase] [noun phase]', triggers one of a set of stock responses, i.e., 'What happens if you don't [verb phrase]?' Additionally, Eliza applies a simple few rules so as to replace 'my' with 'your'.

Siri certainly has Eliza-like elements: one of Siri's responses to 'what is the meaning of life' is 'all evidence to date suggests it's chocolate'! Moreover, similar entertaining yet obviously stock responses pop up regularly and at startlingly appropriate moments during one's conversations with Siri. Of course, Siri could potentially do more than merely entertain. 'I plan to go to Oxford with my wife' should be accurately recognized as an intent to travel, with Siri then offering to book train tickets for you and your wife. A bit of Eliza, but clearly more as well.

In order to actually accomplish tasks without needing excruciatingly detailed directions, both CALO as well as, to at least some extent, Siri need to *reason* in a fairly human-like manner. For example, consider what it would take for CALO to 'send this email to those who need to see it'. Any of us who use email for work know how much cognitive effort goes into deciding whom to send an email to. Sometimes it's a simple decision, we reply to the sender, and when in doubt, reply to all. (As a direct consequence, much of our daily efforts 'at work' are spent in figuring out which of the many emails we each receive are really meant for us to see and possibly respond to.)

First, CALO would need to figure out the project within whose context the email most likely lies. The project's structure would need to be 'represented' somehow within CALO's memory, including the people involved, their roles, the items and documents being created or discussed, and emails already exchanged. Next, CALO would need to make a hypothesis regarding the role that this particular email might play within an overall project, such as which task it is serving to initiate, report on, or discuss. Based on the structure of the project and the role purportedly played by the email at hand, CALO would finally need to rely on some rule-based understanding of 'those who need to see it'. Perhaps the past behaviour of its master has allowed CALO to learn rules about what she means by 'those who need to see it', and how this might differ from 'those possibly interested in it'.

Last but not least, CALO might also end up learning some real-world rules about office politics, such as which 'rivals' its master does *not* want copied in, regardless of their real need or potential interest. CALO might even go so far as to analyse each email-chain it sees and figure out who the rivals of its master's rivals are—a truly intelligent assistant indeed, perhaps even better than most human ones. Of course, you might justifiably argue that people are unlikely to ever trust office politics to their automated assistants anytime in the foreseeable future, however intelligent these might appear to be. Still, it is interesting to explore what it might take to embody software such as CALO or Siri with such capabilities.

* * *

If reasoning means being able to navigate through logical rules such as 'if it rains then the grass is wet', then we can readily imagine many rules that could assist CALO in deciding which people to send the email to. One rule could state that a person who has authored an earlier version of a document that is attached to the current email certainly needs to see the latest one. Another rule might deem that anyone who is responsible for a task that depends on the one the current email thread is serving to accomplish also needs to see this mail, but only if the current email is reporting completion of the task. We could go on and on. Presumably such rules can be learned from past experience, using techniques such as those we saw in Chapter 3. CALO's master may also correct its actions occasionally, thereby providing more data to learn rules from. Another, similar set of rules might define who 'should be interested' in the email, as opposed to actually needing it. Lastly, there may be a list of 'rivals' that are regularly deleted from every email copy list. It appears that all CALO needs is a reasoning engine that can process such rules, however they might be learned, so as to compile the list of people who need to see the email.

Unfortunately, life is not that easy. Even in the simple world of a personal digital assistant, the number of rules that CALO would need to learn and work with could grow very large indeed. Further, how could one ensure that the rule for 'needs to see' always results in a subset of people who 'should be interested' in any document? And suppose that, while learning and defining large numbers of rules, CALO's rules do not fulfil this natural constraint? How could such an inconsistency be discovered?

Next, any rules that are learned or defined about CALO's world are necessarily 'about' common work concepts such as projects, action items, tasks, meetings, emails, and documents. They would also deal with people and their mutual relationships in an office: managers, team members, consultants, customers, and of course 'rivals'. Surely, one might say, are not computer systems especially good at keeping track of such information in databases, such as those maintained by every bank or even an email program? We could merely keep track of such 'structural' information in a database and let a rule engine reason on such data using a large enough set of rules.

The early AI programs of the 1970s, many of which later morphed into the expert systems of the 1980s, did exactly this, i.e., maintained facts in a so-called 'knowledge base', over which rules would be written and executed by rule engines using forward- or backward-chaining. Often such knowledge bases were also represented diagrammatically, depicting, for example, the 'concept' of an 'expert' by lines joining a circle labelled 'expert' with others labelled 'email', with the line joining the two labelled as 'comments on'. The circle labelled 'email' may in turn be connected, by a line labelled 'talks about', to a circle labelled 'technology'. Such diagrams went by many names, such as 'semantic nets' and 'frames'. But they were far from being semantic in the formal sense of statements in a logical system, such as predicate logic. Any meaning they conveyed was dependent on their readers attributing meanings to the labels they contained. Such diagrams merely assisted programmers in writing the rules that actually encoded knowledge in a manner logically executable by a computer.

Not only were such knowledge representations unsatisfying by not really distinguishing themselves from mere databases of facts, there were further complications indicating that the task of representing knowledge is actually ill-served by such conventional data representations. Suppose we wanted to define 'those interested' in an email to include people who are experts in the same or related technologies as mentioned in the email or attached documents. 'Being an expert' itself could be defined as people who might have commented on emails or edited documents dealing with a particular technology. On the other hand, we may consider a person's work as being 'dependent' on a particular task, email, or meeting if the action-item assigned to them in another meeting is identified as being dependent on any of these activities.

Now, suppose CALO's owner wanted to send an email only to people who 'should be interested in it' *or* were 'experts in a project that was dependent on the current one'. A moment's reasoning reveals, at least to us, that such people are all experts in some technology or other, and we might immediately figure out that posting this mail to an 'expert's' newsgroup might be more efficient than sending it to all the people who fit the description mentioned. This might especially be the case if there is another rule saying that mails to more than ten persons should be directed to news-groups whenever possible. However, how might a computer program *reason* in such a manner? Certainly not by including even more complicated rules atop of 'meaningless' facts stored in a database.

Moreover, what if we later decided to change or expand the definition of 'expert' to include people who had authored independent documents on related technologies? Drawing additional lines in a semantic diagram would scarcely change our system's behaviour. Would we then return to the drawing board, add new database tables or types of files, along with new programming? Even more challenging would be dealing with new concepts which, instead of being defined by humans, are learned from experience.

Thus, it appears that mere rules evaluated using a plain database of facts are not enough if we need to support powerful yet efficient automated reasoning on large volumes of information, as might be needed in tomorrow's world of CALO-like web-intelligence systems. Not surprisingly, it turns out that there are better mechanisms for representing knowledge; true 'knowledge bases', rather than mere databases.

* * *

In the 1970s, the nascent field of artificial intelligence had two schools of thought with respect to knowledge representation. On the one hand lay the world of loosely defined but easy-to-understand semantic nets and frames, which had to be translated into data structures on which logical rules could be defined. On the other side were the proponents of purely logical reasoning without recourse to any separate knowledge representation form. Logic could, in principle, be the basis for reasoning systems, reasoned the logicians. Nothing more was needed. True, in principle. But in practice, relying on pure logic was unwieldy except for the simplest of real-world problems. The purely logical approach did, however, result in considerable progress in some specialized tasks, such as that of automated theorem-proving in mathematics (which we do not deal with here in this book). However, techniques relying on logical rules alone did not easily scale for more general tasks on larger volumes of information.

A breakthrough in the realm of practical knowledge representation came with the invention of 'description logics' beginning with the early work of Ron Brachman in 1977,[67] and formulation of their theoretical underpinnings and limits in 1987, by Brachman himself along with Herman Levesque.[68] The theory of description logic shows how data can be endowed with semantic structure, so that it no longer remains a 'mere database', and can justifiably be called a 'knowledge' base.

So, what does it mean for data to have semantics, so that we can call it knowledge? As in the language of logic, one statement 'follows from', or is 'entailed by', another, naturally, due to the basic laws of logic. Similarly, data in a description logic is stored in the form of facts that automatically 'entail' other facts, even those that are not initially stored or asserted. Additional rules on top of the data are not required; new facts follow, or are entailed, merely because of the structure of the facts themselves. In this manner the theory of description logic, as introduced by Brachman, clearly distinguishes knowledge bases from mere databases. A knowledge base builds in semantics, while a database does not. Databases need to be augmented by semantics, either via rules or programs, in order to do any reasoning at all. Knowledge bases too can be, and often are, augmented by rules, as we shall soon see; but even before such rules come into play, a knowledge base that uses some form of description logic has reasoning power of its own. Last but not least, knowledge bases using description logic form the basis for the emerging 'semantic web' that promises to add intelligent, human-like reasoning to our everyday experience of the web.

The Semantic Web

In 1999 Tim Berners-Lee, the inventor of hyperlinked web pages[13] and thereby the web itself, outlined his vision for its future:

> I have a dream for the Web [in which computers] become capable of analysing all the data on the Web—the content, links, and transactions between people and computers. A Semantic Web, which should make this possible, has yet to emerge, but when it does, the day-to-day mechanisms of trade, bureaucracy and our daily lives will be handled by machines talking to machines. The intelligent agents people have touted for ages will finally materialise.[69]

Over the past decade the technology to realize a semantic web has been developed and put to a variety of practical uses. Today, semantic web technology is represented by the still evolving OWL, or 'web ontology language'. (The word 'ontology' is often used to refer to any mechanism of knowledge representation.) As it happens, the evolution of the semantic web, including OWL and its companions such as RDF ('resource description framework'), has been based on the ideas of description logic as expounded by Brachman and others since the mid-1980s.

To see what a semantic knowledge base using description logic looks like, let us recall our encounter with Watson in Chapter 3. In order to answer a question about, say, places where Einstein lived, Watson would ideally prefer to have at its disposal the answer stated as a fact, such as [Einstein, 'lived in', Ülm], or [Einstein, 'lived in', Princeton]. Unfortunately, as we argued earlier, Watson might not have such facts in its database. Instead, it may have some general knowledge about the world, in the guise of concepts, such as 'persons' and 'places', and possible relationships between concepts, such as [person, 'lives in', place] and [person, 'worked in', place]. Further, the structure of the world may also be encoded using statements about concepts; for example, 'places some person "worked in"' is a sub-concept of, i.e., is *contained* in, the concept of 'places a person "lived in"'.

Of course, concepts, relationships, and statements are written more formally in the syntax of a description logic, such as the OWL language, rather than as informally described here. The important thing to note is that if knowledge about the world is available along with its semantics, it is possible to reason without recourse to external rules. Thus, Watson need only somehow assert the relationships [Einstein, 'worked in', Princeton], along with knowledge that Einstein refers to a person, and Princeton to a place. Thereafter, the knowledge base can itself *derive* the conclusion that [Einstein, 'lived in', Princeton], merely because it 'knows' that places where people work are most often where they live, or at least close by.

* * *

Let us now imagine how a CALO-like personal digital assistant might encode the structure of the office world in a semantic knowledge base, or ontology, so as to give rise to intelligent behaviour, rather than merely better search. The concept of a person 'being an expert', a project 'being dependent' on another, or a document 'relating to' a technology, are all possible to express in description logic. So are concepts such as people who 'should be interested in' a document, which might be defined in terms of other concepts such as experts and people in dependent projects. Once knowledge is so encoded, it should be possible for a CALO-like system to be able to determine that the compound concept of people who 'should be interested in or are experts in a dependent project' is subsumed in the simpler concept of people who are 'experts in some technology'. At the same time, if the user's desire is to send a document to all people who 'should be interested in or *work* in a dependent project', clearly the short cut of using the experts' newsgroup would not work. In the latter case the subsumption of the two concepts, i.e., that asked for and the short cut, does not follow from, i.e., is *not entailed* by, the knowledge available, and thus the short cut is likely to be invalid.

These examples serve to demonstrate that ontologies that allow for reasoning within the semantics of a knowledge base appear valuable. For one, knowledge encoded in a semantic knowledge base is guaranteed to at least be consistent. It is not possible to add facts to such an ontology if they lead to contradictions. Next, using a knowledge base makes it easy to check if a statement, such as that emanating from an external query, i.e., [Einstein, 'lived in', Princeton], or the hypothesized short cut of people to whom to send a document, follows directly from the knowledge available. (Of course, this begs the question of how a computer comes up with a hypothesis such as the particular short cut in the first place; we shall return to the question of generating, or *predicting*, possible hypotheses in Chapter 5.)

* * *

In systems such as Watson or Siri, knowledge about the world will most likely be learned from the vast volumes of information available in the web, using learning techniques that we explored in Chapter 3. While encoding facts learned in this manner within a semantic knowledge base using a formal description logic, we can choose to include rules that appear to be true with high probability. Thus, probable structural properties uncovered in the form of association rules, or concepts learned through collaborative filtering and clustering, can be formally encoded to become part of the knowledge base itself.

Learning rules from many instances is also a form of reasoning, called *inductive* as opposed to deductive reasoning. Deduction, as we have already seen, proceeds 'naturally' from generalities, or rules, to specifics, or conclusions. Induction, on the other hand, proceeds from many specifics, or instances, to generalizations, or rules. Further, induction is almost always probabilistic, and introduces uncertainties (rather than the 'natural', certain entailment of deduction). The fact that such induced or learned knowledge is almost always uncertain, and can therefore be contradicted by future discoveries, introduces new problems; we shall return to some of these issues later in this chapter as well as in Chapter 5.

In recent years there have been large research projects dedicated to *inductively* learning rules and facts from the web, so as to develop ontologies for 'common-sense knowledge'. In Chapter 3, we described the REVERB project as one such example that tries to learn simple subject-verb-object triples, but no further structure. Other projects such as Cyc and Yago use more powerful semantic knowledge bases and are thereby able to capture more structure. Cyc,[70] an older project pre-dating the semantic web, directly uses rules in predicate logic in its ontology. Yago[71] is more recent and its ontology is based on a description logic that is closely related to OWL.

Interestingly, Yago's knowledge base has been constructed using Wikipedia. Yago uses categories as defined in Wikipedia to derive 'is-a' relationships between entities, for example names and concepts such as 'person'. To date, Yago is probably the largest available semantic ontology, with over 6 billion facts, which Yago also claims it 'knows' with an accuracy of 95%. (Cyc and REVERB, the next closest in size, have 2 billion and 1 billion facts respectively. In contrast, WordNet, the publicly available but handcrafted thesaurus, has but 200,000 entries.) Thus, posing a semantic query to Yago, such as 'scientists who were born near Ülm and won a Nobel Prize', yields not only Albert Einstein, but also Hans Spemann and Gerhard Ertl, Nobel laureates in medicine and chemistry respectively. Most certainly any future Watson and Siri-like systems will be served by such large and semantically powerful knowledge bases.

In fact, semantic search is already a part of Siri: when you ask Siri a question it sometimes consults WolframAlpha, a semantic search engine launched in 2009 by the cognitive scientist Stephen Wolfram.[72] Like the semantic-web vision of Berners-Lee, WolframAlpha scours the web for information, which it then curates and stores in a structured form. WolframAlpha claims to use its own proprietary mechanisms to represent such knowledge, rather than languages such as OWL that are more popularly associated with the semantic web. Nevertheless, it is still a semantic search engine in that it extracts knowledge from the web, rather than indexing the web directly using keywords as Google and others do.

Does Wolfram Alpha yield better results than Google? If we ask Wolfram 'who is the prime minister of Canada?', it comes up with the right answer; but so does Google. Unfortunately, if one asks 'who is the president of Canada?', it finds the president of India instead, at least for me: presumably Wolfram figures out that I'm logged in from India and returns the geographically closest 'president' entry in its database. Google, on the other hand, at least points us to Wikipedia. Further, Google associates 'president' and 'prime minister' as related words and therefore throws up the right pages. Yago, on the other hand, does indeed figure out that by 'president of Canada', what the user probably means is the leader of Canada, which is actually its prime minister. However, Yago too is unable to return the exact name. Instead, and not surprisingly given its origins, it points us to Wikipedia.

It appears that the prospects for semantic search competing with traditional search any time soon appear fairly dim, at least today, unless, as we have speculated in Chapter 3, people actually start using complete sentences in their queries leading to deeper understanding of a user's intent. Further, the actual reasoning that such systems do in response to queries will also need to improve significantly. For example, while WolframAlpha correctly recognizes that 'president' is a 'leadership position', it fails to relate it to other leadership positions, such as 'prime minister'. However, it should have been able to figure this out using reasoning techniques, such as those used by the more powerful Yago. However, even Yago fails to zero in on the 'right' answer, at least by itself. Clearly, semantic web technology has a long way to go in practice. Not only will semantic web engines need to use reasoning to extract facts from the web, they will also need to reason in response to queries, much as Watson does.

Nevertheless, it should now be clear that computational reasoning has many potential uses. We have seen that an important component of reasoning has to do with computing *entailments*, i.e., statements that 'follow naturally' from a collection of knowledge and rules. Therefore, it is only natural to also ask whether this is an easy problem to solve or whether reasoning is actually 'hard' in a computational as well as colloquial sense, as aptly implied by Sherlock Holmes: 'the Science of Deduction and Analysis is one which can only be acquired by long and patient study, nor is life long enough to allow any mortal to attain the highest possible perfection in it.'[62]

Limits of Logic

The formalization of logic by George Boole and Gottlob Frege in the late 19th century led to considerable excitement in the small world of philosophy and, in particular, mathematical philosophy. It suddenly appeared that all reasoning, especially that used in mathematics, could be reduced to a set of facts and rules expressed in formal logic. If one were able to do so, all possible mathematical truths should, in principle, naturally 'follow' from these basic facts through the inexorable prowess of logical entailment. Indeed, this was exactly the approach used many centuries earlier by Euclid, the great Greek mathematician, in coming up with the idea of geometric proofs from basic axioms, which all of us have learned in high school. But now, with logic on a firm foundational footing it appeared that much more was possible. In the early 20th century, Bertrand Russell and Alfred North Whitehead published a monumental treatise called *Principia Mathematica*, which attempted to define all the basic facts and rules from which all of mathematics would naturally follow. All reasoning, at least in mathematics, appeared to be reducible to the logic of Boole and Frege. Any mathematical truth could be simply calculated from Russell Whitehead's axioms using logical reasoning.

However, the euphoria, at least in the limited world of mathematical philosophy, was short-lived. In 1931, Kurt Gödel stunned this small world with his demonstration of a mathematical statement that could neither be proved nor disproved.[73] Further, this statement was expressed using the very same logical building blocks that Russell and Whitehead had so painstakingly put together. Essentially, Gödel showed how to write, using the precise formal language of logic, a statement that essentially said '*this* statement cannot be proven'. Here the '*this*' refers to the very same statement itself. The paradox is immediately apparent: if the statement can be proven, then it must be false, and so logical reasoning has proved a falsehood. On the other hand, if it cannot be proven it demonstrates the limits of logical reasoning in that it is a true statement that cannot be proven using logical rules. Consequently, the belief that any true mathematical statement could be proven using logic was shattered. In fact, Gödel went even further: not only could his artfully crafted statement not be proven, it was not even possible to logically prove that it could not be proven. Finally, Gödel showed that such difficulties were inherent in *any* 'sufficiently powerful' logical system, i.e., not only the one proposed by Russell and

Whitehead. Thus, very surprisingly indeed, reasoning using logical rules had very fundamental limits. Some clearly evident (at least to humans) truths simply could *not* follow naturally from logic.

Around the same time that Gödel was busy shaking the foundations of logic in Germany, Alan Turing, the father of computer science, was developing the fundamental theory of computing at Cambridge University in England. As we have seen earlier, the rules of logic can, in principle, be mechanically followed by a computer. So, it seemed natural to expect that a computer should be able to prove *any* logical statement, by mechanically following an appropriate procedure based on the rules of logical entailment. Turing wondered what would happen if such a computer were presented with a true but unprovable statement such as the ones devised by Gödel. The computer would have to go on forever and *never* stop, concluded Turing. Of course, Turing's computers, called 'Turing machines', were abstract ones, nothing but mathematically defined ideas, rather than actual physical computers as we see today. But Turing was concerned with the theoretical limits of computing, much as Gödel was with the limits of logical reasoning. Turing argued that any practical computer, even those not invented in his time, could be simulated by his abstract machine, and therefore faced the same limits on what it could compute.

Turing was not satisfied with the explanation that a computer trying to prove Gödel's statement would never halt. Was this good enough to argue that computers following the rules of logic were subject to the same limitations as logic itself? Suppose he could devise a special Turing machine that could determine if *any* other computer procedure would ever halt. Then he could use this special Turing machine on the computer trying to prove Gödel's statement. The special machine would say 'no, the Gödel-statement-proving computer does not halt', and thereby prove that the Gödel statement was unprovable. But Gödel had shown that this was not possible using the rules of logic. So were Turing machines more powerful than logic?

Fortunately, or unfortunately, this was not the case. Turing used a simple argument to show that his special Turing machine, i.e., the one that could determine if another machine halted, was *impossible*. The key to Turing's argument was being able to represent any computer, or rather its equivalent Turing machine, as a number; think of it as a unique serial number for every possible Turing machine. Thus, the special Turing machine would take a computer's serial number and some input, such as the Gödel statement, and determine if that computer halted on the given input or not.

Turing went about showing that such a special Turing machine was an impossibility; his proof is depicted in Figure 1. Turing imagined a second special machine, T2 in Figure 1, which used the first special Turing machine, called T1 in the figure, as one of its parts. This second special machine T2 takes a number and gives it to the first special machine T1 *twice*, i.e., it asks T1 whether the computer with a particular serial number halts if given its *own* serial number as input. If the answer is no, the second machine itself actually halts. But if the answer is yes, it goes on forever.

A convoluted procedure for sure, but one that also leads to a paradox. The trick is that this second special Turing machine itself also

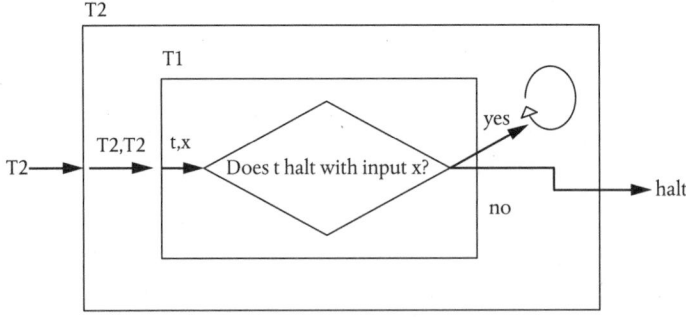

FIGURE 1 Turing's proof. If T1 says T2 halts on input T2, then it deliberately does not halt. If T1 says T2 does not halt on input T2, then T2 halts. Each case leads to a contradiction, so T1 cannot exist.

has a serial number (T2), just like any other computer. Suppose we gave the T2 machine its *own* serial number as input? Would it halt or not? Remember, all that T2 does is pass on the serial number to the first machine T1. Thus it asks the same question as we just did, i.e., would it halt on its own input? If T1, which is supposed to answer such questions, says yes, then T2 stubbornly goes on forever, contradicting this answer. Similarly, if T1 said no, then T2 indeed halts, again contradicting the first machine's answer. Either way there is a contradiction, so the only conclusion to draw is that the special Turing machine T1, i.e, the one that is supposed to check whether any other machine halts or not, is itself an impossibility.

So, just as Gödel found the limits of logical reasoning, Turing discovered the limits of computing: some things just could not be computed by any computer, however powerful. Reasoning using a computer, mechanically following the rules of logic, is not only hard, it can sometimes be *impossible*.

At the same time, the surprising thing is that we humans do indeed reason, and quite well too. Further, we *are* able to reason the way Gödel and Turing did, demonstrating contradictions and impossibilities that themselves do not follow automatically using the rules of logic or reasoning. Does this mean that we do not use logic to reason? How can that be? After all, logic is our own invention, created to reason more carefully and better understand our reasoning processes.

Some authors, such as Douglas Hofstadter in particular, have argued that far from exposing its limits, Gödel-like self-reference, where a logical statement can refer to itself, or a Turing machine referring to its own serial number, might point the way to figuring out how machines might not only be able to exploit self-reference themselves to come up with proofs such as Gödel's and Turing's, but might also serve as a model for how consciousness itself arises.[74] Others, such as the neuroscientist Antonio Damasio, have also quite independently pointed to self-reference as being an important element of consciousness.[75] However, we shall not speculate in these philosophical waters.

Let us now return to our problem of reasoning in systems such as CALO, Siri, or Gregory. Reasoning and computing have their limits. But surely many reasoning tasks are actually possible to encode and execute efficiently in practice using systems such as description logic and rules expressed in predicate calculus. But which ones? First let us imagine an example from a possible Siri-enabled world of the future.

Description and Resolution

Those of us who use social networking sites such as Facebook know how cumbersome it can be to manage privacy in such forums. What one posts on Facebook will likely be seen by all one's friends, who may in turn 'like' the post, thereby propagating it to their friends, and so on. Devices such as the iPhone 4S make it really easy to propagate the contents of, say, an email, to a social website such as Facebook. To send a really private email we need to avoid any of our friends who are friendly with someone we are definitely unfriendly with. (While this does not guarantee privacy, it certainly reduces the probability that our mail is seen by people whom we do not get along with.)

Even for us, such an exercise represents a non-trivial bit of reasoning. It also requires us to search Facebook for our friends' friend-lists. Definitely something we would like an intelligent agent such as Siri to handle if possible. Siri would need to examine our list of friends, as well as a list of people whom we do not get along with. Of course, Siri may not have all the information it needs; for example, all the people we know well enough may not in fact be our friends on Facebook. So Siri would need to ask us a few questions before sending out the email. At the same time, it would be irritating if Siri asked us too many questions; so Siri needs to reason carefully. Let's see how it might do this.

Suppose you are friends with Amy, while Chloe is someone you wish to avoid, i.e., 'block'. You want to ensure that what you say is unlikely to reach Chloe. Siri also knows (possibly by crawling Facebook's site) that Amy and Bob are friends, as are Bob and Chloe. What questions should Siri ask before deciding whether to send the mail to Amy? More importantly, how should Siri go about this reasoning problem? Siri wants to find out if anyone is friends with someone whom we have blocked, and avoid sending the email to that person. In the language of reasoning, Siri needs to check if the following logical statement is true for some X and Y, or show that it is always false:

X is a friend AND X is a friend of Y AND Y is blocked.

At its disposal Siri has the following facts in its knowledge base, 'Amy is a friend', and 'Chloe is blocked'. It also has the binary predicates* 'Amy is a friend of Bob', and 'Bob is a friend of Chloe'.

Siri needs to determine whether the logical statement it is examining is directly entailed by the facts in the knowledge base. In other words, Siri is actually trying to prove or disprove the logical statement '*if* knowledge base *then* logical statement in question'. The entire knowledge base is included in this latter statement, thus making it an independent logical statement that is simply either true or not. Of course, as we have seen in the case of Gödel, there is always the faint chance that logical reasoning cannot prove or disprove a statement. However, we hope that at least in the case of our simple example such an unfortunate situation does not arise. Hopefully Siri should be able to arrive at a definite conclusion either way simply by following the laws of logical entailment.

First, recall that the implication '*if* knowledge base *then* statement to be proven' is the same thing as saying 'knowledge base is *false* OR statement to be proven is *true*'. It turns out that it is easier to *disprove*

---

* *Binary* predicates express a relationship between two things, as opposed to *unary* ones that describe a property of a single object.

a statement than to prove it. We start out with the negation of the statement to be proven and try to reach a contradiction; if we succeed, then the negation is false and the original statement true. Now, the negation* of the statement to be proven works out to

X is *not* a friend OR X is *not* a friend of Y OR Y is *not* blocked.

We'll call this the *target* statement. The next trick we use is called 'resolution'. Imagine we have two statements that we assume are both true, for example

Gary is a friend

and a more complex statement such as

Gary is not a friend OR John is not blocked.

But the two contradicting sub-statements, 'Gary is a friend' and 'Gary is not a friend' cannot both be true, so what remains in the second complex statement must be true, i.e.,

John is not blocked.

This 'resolvent' statement can now be resolved with others.

Returning to our task of proving or disproving the target statement, we need to replace (i.e., 'unify') the unknowns X and Y with some values before any resolution can take place. First we try X = Amy and Y = Bob. The target now becomes

Amy is not a friend OR Amy is not a friend of Bob OR Bob is not blocked.

The first two pieces cancel out with the known facts, i.e., 'Amy is a friend' and 'Amy is a friend of Bob', leaving us with the resolvent 'Bob

* Negating the AND of a bunch of statements is easily done by negating each of the statements while replacing AND with OR; similarly, negating the OR of a bunch of statements results in the AND of their negations; you can easily verify this mentally.

is not blocked'. Next we try the combination X = Bob and Y = Chloe. The target becomes 'Bob is not a friend OR Bob is not a friend of Chloe OR Chloe is not blocked'. This time, the last two pieces cancel with the known facts 'Bob is a friend of Chloe' and 'Chloe is blocked', yielding the resolvent 'Bob is not a friend'.

Siri now knows what to ask us. It first asks whether Bob is blocked. If we say 'yes', then it contradicts one of the resolvents, hence disproving our target, and proving the original statement (since the target was the negation of what we were after). On the other hand, if we say 'no', Siri can ask us if Bob is a friend. If he is, then the second resolvent is contradicted and we prove what we are after. But if again we say 'no', then we are unable to reach a conclusion. It might then try a third combination, i.e., X = Amy and Y = Chloe. You might like to verify that the resolvent will be 'Amy is not a friend of Chloe'. Siri asks us if we know. If Amy is a friend of Chloe, then we have a contradiction, once again proving what we are after. If not, once more Siri is stuck, and cannot conclude a direct one-hop chain from a friend to a blocked person.

Hopefully this scenario has convinced you that reasoning is pretty complex, especially for a computer. Yet there are techniques, such as the combination of unification and resolution just described, which a computer can use to reason automatically. A few questions arise naturally. Do procedures such as unification and resolution always work? Clearly not, since there were situations when Siri could come to no conclusion. Next, what should be done if no conclusion is reached? Should Siri assume that the statement it set out to prove is false? After all, we may not know conclusively that Amy and Chloe are definitely not friends. Suppose they are? In other words, if we can't verify a resolvent, should we not assume the worst case? What are the implications of assuming 'failure equals negation'? We shall return to this question in a short while.

* * *

But first, there are even more fundamental difficulties. It turns out that proving or disproving a complex statement, such as the one used earlier, is inherently difficult. If we have a really complex combination of, say, n statements linked by ANDs and ORs, the resolution procedure requires, in the worst case, on the order of 2^n steps. In other words, there are examples where, using resolution, we really need to try almost all possible combinations of assigning true or false values to each of the n statements before we can decide whether or not there is some *satisfying* combination of values that makes the statement true.

But perhaps there are better procedures than resolution? Unfortunately it appears unlikely. In 1971 Stephen Cook[76] formally introduced the notion of what it means for a problem (rather than a specific procedure) to be computationally intractable. The 'satisfiability problem', or SAT for short, was in fact Cook's first example of such a problem. The theory of computational intractability is founded on the notion of 'NP-completeness', a rather involved concept that we do not go into here except to say there are a large number of such NP-complete problems that are *believed* (but not proven) to be computationally intractable.

However, in the case of reasoning, the theoretical situation is even worse than computational intractability might warrant. The SAT problem only covers statements in propositional (as opposed to predicate) logic, where there are no variables, such as the x and y in our earlier example. In the case of predicate logic, such variables first need to be unified with values during the resolution process, as we did by first choosing $x =$ Amy and $y =$ Bob, etc. Unfortunately, if we allow variables, the resolution plus unification procedure may go on forever, i.e., it may take *infinite* time. This is actually not surprising, since we know from Gödel and Turing that such situations should in fact arise, since there are true statements that cannot be proven, and procedures for which we cannot logically prove termination.

However, before we get all gloomy and give up, all that such 'worst case' results mean is that logical reasoning may not always work, and even it it does, it is highly unlikely it is efficient in all cases. It is important to note that neither Gödel nor computational intractability say that there are no easier *special cases*, where resolution always terminates and does so efficiently. If fact there are, and that is why semantic web systems and rule engines actually work in practice.

* * *

We have already seen an example of a special case, namely, the description logic that was used to represent our knowledge of 'project structure' in CALO. Recall that we also mentioned that the web ontology language, OWL, devised for Burners-Lee's semantic web, is also description logic-based. There are actually a variety of simpler specializations of the OWL language, such as OWL-DL and OWL-Lite, also based on description logic. Such specializations have been designed specifically to make them easier to reason with. In particular, OWL-DL and OWL-Lite, unlike full predicate logic, are in fact *decidable*. Thus, statements expressed in these languages, such as 'all experts are technologists', can be verified to be true or false in finite time. There is no Gödel-like unprovability or Turing-like uncertainty here. (Note however, the *complete* OWL system is actually as powerful as predicate logic, and therefore also *not* decidable.)

It is certainly comforting to know that we can express our knowledge about the world in a manner that computers can process with some degree of certainty. Unfortunately, all is not so well after all. It turns out that while reasoning in such languages is decidable, it is not necessarily efficient. Both OWL-DL and OWL-Lite suffer from worst-case behaviour that grows like 2^n with the size of the knowledge base. Fortunately there is some good news too. While reasoning using resolution and unification is in general intractable for the propositional case (and in fact undecidable if variables are used, i.e., in the predicate-logic case), there are special types of statements that *do* allow efficient reasoning. Luckily, these special cases are exactly right for defining rules about the world, i.e., implications of the form 'if a person is a child and a female *then* the person is a girl'.

Rules where we are allowed to have any number of conditions, but only one consequent (i.e., right-hand side of the implication), are called 'Horn clauses', after the American logician Alfred Horn. Thus, the rule 'if a person is a child and a female *then* the person is a girl' is a Horn clause, whereas 'if a person is a child and a female *then* the person is a girl and she likes dolls' is not, because of the two consequents involved (being a girl *and* liking dolls).

To see why Horn clauses are easy to reason with, let's see how resolution works for them. As earlier, implications are rewritten as logical statements, so the Horn clause defining 'girl' becomes

not a child OR not a female OR girl.

So if we somehow know that the person in question 'is a child', then these two statements resolve, as before, to

not a female OR girl

which is another Horn clause since it has just one consequent, i.e., a 'positive', unnegated term—'girl'. Resolving two Horn clauses results in another Horn clause; so we can imagine a procedure that continuously resolves clauses in this manner until our desired goal is either verified or proved false.

For example, suppose our knowledge base had a few more statements: 'not toddler OR child', which essentially says 'if a toddler then a child'. Also 'not male OR not child OR boy', 'not infant OR child', etc. Finally we have two facts about a person, i.e., that (s)he 'is a toddler' and 'is a female'. How would we test what other facts this knowledge base entails? Or suppose we want to check if the person in question 'is a girl'; how would a reasoning procedure go about such a task?

In fact the two questions we have posed direct us to two different approaches to reasoning, which we have also mentioned briefly earlier. The latter task, i.e., checking whether 'is a girl' is true, leads us to backward-chaining, in which we check if there is any rule that implies 'is a girl', and then check in turn whether each of the conditions of that rule are satisfied, and so on until we are done. In this case, we find one such rule that leads us to check for 'is female' as well as 'is a child'. These in turn cause us to 'fire' the rules that imply these conclusions, including facts, such as 'is female', which is already given to us. Once we reach 'is a toddler' and find that it too is a fact, we are done and have proved that 'is a girl' holds true. Unfortunately, and contrary to expectations, backward-chaining can lead to circular reasoning. For example, suppose we had a rule such as 'not a child OR is a child'. The backward-chaining procedure might end up firing this rule indefinitely and getting stuck in a cycle.

On the other hand, it turns out that there are forward-chaining procedures that can compute all the conclusions from a set of rules without getting stuck. All we need to do is keep track of which facts have been calculated and which rules are 'ready to fire' because all their conclusions have been calculated. Thus, in the case of forward-chaining we begin with the facts, 'is a toddler' and 'is a female', and mark these as calculated. This makes the rule 'toddler implies child' fire, so 'is a child' becomes known. Next, the rule 'female and child implies girl' fires (since all its conditions are calculated), allowing us to correctly derive 'girl'. At this point, there are no rules left ready to fire, and so there is nothing else to derive from the knowledge base.

Such a forward-chaining procedure might need to check facts and rules many times, but at worst as many times as there are 'things' about which the knowledge base expresses facts. Each time it needs to check at most the number of rules in the knowledge base. Thus, this forward-chaining procedure takes at most 'number of things' × 'number of rules' steps, which is certainly very efficient as compared to procedures whose behaviour is 'exponential', such as 2^n. (In fact, with a few tricks it can be shown that forward-chaining can be done in *linear* time, i.e., number of things + number of rules steps: this is the famous Rete algorithm devised in 1982 by Charles Forgy.[77])

Wow! Does that mean that we can reason efficiently with rules based on Horn clauses and need look no further? But wait, we have only discussed simple propositional Horn clauses. As expected, when we introduce variables and require unification, even Horn-clause reasoning need not terminate, and can go on forever in peculiar cases. Recall that this was not the case for description logics, such as OWL-DL and OWL-Lite. So, what is often done in practice for semantic web systems is that description logics are used to capture and reason about *structural* properties of the world being represented, whereas Horn clauses are used for other rules, such as to describe *behavioural* properties of the system, e.g., 'deciding when to *do* what'.

* * *

Recently there has also been a resurgence of interest in using mechanisms based on Aristotelian 'natural' logic to reason directly in natural language, without necessarily having to translate every sentence into a logical statement. In 2007,[64] Christopher Manning and his team at Stanford revived interest in using natural logic for 'textual inference', i.e., the problem of determining whether one natural language sentence 'follows from', or is entailed by, another. Entailment in natural logic, as per Manning, is quite different from one statement implying another, as in, say predicate logic. It is closer, in fact, to a description logic, in that we can say what words entail others, just as for concepts in description logic. A specific word or concept is entailed by a more general one.

So, *shark* entails *fish*, *swim* entails *move*. In other words, a shark is a fish, and something that swims is also something that moves. Words such as *every*, on the other hand, express relationships between other concepts. So, as an example of the rules of Manning's natural logic, one can *formally* conclude from 'every fish swims' that 'every shark moves', because of a rule regarding how the word *every* behaves with regard to the two concepts it relates: the first concept, i.e., *fish* in this case, can be made more specific, i.e., specialized 'downwards' to *shark*, whereas the second, i.e., *swims*, can be generalized 'upwards' to *moves*. A moment's reflection reveals that the reverse does not hold, at least for the word 'every'.

* * *

There is one more important issue that will lead us down our next path of explorations in the realm of reasoning. Even though reasoning using Horn clauses is not guaranteed to work, we might imagine a computer procedure that simply stops if it spends too much time trying to evaluate a statement using the resolution-unification process. Suppose it now assumes that just because it has failed in its efforts, the fact is *false*. Let's see what happens if we begin to allow this kind of behaviour.

Suppose we have a rule saying '*if* something is a bird and not a penguin, *then* it flies'. Now suppose we also know that 'Tweety' is a bird. Unification of the unknown 'something' with 'Tweety' leads us to check whether the conditions of the rule are satisfied. Unfortunately, while one of the conditions, i.e., 'Tweety is a bird', turns out to be true, we are unable to say anything about whether Tweety is a penguin. Thus, using normal logical reasoning it is not possible to reason further. However, if we take the failure to show that Tweety is a penguin as meaning its negation, i.e., that 'Tweety is not a penguin', then we can indeed conclude that 'Tweety flies'. However, we might later come to know that Tweety is in fact a penguin. In normal logic this would lead to a contradiction. However, we might like to imagine 'retracting' the conclusion we derived by treating 'failure as negation', i.e., to assume that Tweety is not a penguin. This in turn leads to our having to retract our earlier conclusion about Tweety being able to fly.

In standard logic, a statement is either true or not. Further, once it is established to be true, it remains true forever, whatever new knowledge might come our way. However, as we have seen in the example in the previous paragraph, we can treat failure as negation as long as we also *retract* any resulting conclusions when new facts emerge. If one thinks about it, this is actually how we humans reason. We form beliefs based on whatever facts are available to us, and revise these beliefs later if needed. Belief revision requires reasoning using different, 'non-monotonic', logics. The term 'non-monotonic' merely means that the number of facts known to be true can sometimes *decrease* over time, instead of monotonically increasing (or remaining the same) as in normal logic. Dealing with beliefs also leads us to mechanisms for dealing with uncertainties, such as those which Watson might need to handle as it tries to figure out the right answer to a *Jeopardy!* question.

Beliefs and uncertainties are essential aspects of human reasoning. Perhaps the Siris and Gregories of the future will need to incorporate such reasoning. Traditional logical inference may not be enough. To better understand what such reasoning might involve, we turn to a very different world where humans need to reason together. Hopefully, our own belief revision process gets exposed by studying such a scenario, leading us to computational techniques that mimic it.

Belief albeit Uncertain

During the night of 9 August 2006, British police arrested 24 people in and around London and Birmingham. These were al-Qaeda terrorists suspected of planning a massive terrorist plot to bomb at least ten airliners heading from Britain to various US destinations. Fortunately a major disaster was avoided. In fact, intelligence operations leading to these arrests had been going on for months. At its peak, the investigation involved as many as a thousand intelligence officers and policemen. Many possible suspects were under surveillance, not only in Britain but also Pakistan, for which CIA intelligence was also used. While we may not wish to delve into the entire history of this affair, it is perhaps instructive to focus on the process, which at least in such a case is largely documented,[78] unlike similar reasoning processes that go on all the time inside each of our heads.

First some suspicions arise. This is followed by increasing degrees of belief that something sinister is afoot. During the process new probes are activated to validate suspicions, gather more information, and expand the scope of surveillance. At the same time, it is important to keep all options open as to exactly *what* the terrorists are up to, certain hypotheses get ruled out, while others become more probable with new evidence. Finally, and probably most importantly, there is the need to remain always vigilant as to when the suspected attack becomes truly imminent, so as to decide on taking action: wait too long, and it might be too late; after all, one could never be 100% sure that no other terrorists remained free who might still carry out an attack. (Luckily, this was not the case, but it *could* have been.)

Post-9/11, worldwide continuous surveillance of any and every possibly suspicious activity had become a necessity. One of the plotters, Ahmed Ali, was under routine surveillance because of his numerous trips to Pakistan in the past year. In June 2006, police secretly opened Ahmed's luggage at Heathrow as he was returning from one such trip. In it they found a power drink along with a large number of batteries; not enough to surmise mala fide intent, but enough to raise the level of surveillance on Ahmed. As a result, the people he met often, such as Assad Sarwar and Tanvir Hussain, were also put under light surveillance, and it was then found that Tanvir had also recently visited Pakistan. Sanwar was observed disposing of a large number of hydrogen peroxide bottles at a recycling centre; then further surveillance revealed that he was buying many items that appeared unrelated to his daily needs. Meanwhile, Ahmed and Tanvir were also often seen shopping together, and frequenting a flat in east London. The flat was found to have been recently purchased in cash for £138,000. The accumulated circumstantial evidence was determined to be cause enough for the police to covertly enter this flat, where they found a chemical lab that appeared to be a bomb-making factory.

Let us take a step back and examine the reasoning involved in this police investigation. First, listening leads to new facts, which serve as feedback to enlarge the scope of listening to cover more individuals with surveillance. Next, facts being unearthed are continuously being connected with each other to evaluate their significance. Reasoning with multiple facts leads to further surveillance. Eventually, 'putting two and two together' results in the unearthing of the bomb factory.

So far, the reasoning process used in the course of investigations is largely *deductive*, in the sense that one fact leads to the next steps of surveillance, which in turn uncover more facts. Established rules, regarding what kinds of activities should be considered suspicious, are evaluated at each stage, almost mechanically. No one is trying to figure out exactly what these people are up to; after all, there is no concrete evidence that they are really conspirators. Further, these three are a few among the thousands under continuous investigation throughout the world; wasting too much effort speculating on every such trio would drown the intelligence apparatus.

But everything changes once the bomb factory is found. Both the investigation and the reasoning process move to a new level. Now, deduction alone is not enough. What kind of bomb plot was under way? The 2005 bombing of the London Underground was fresh in everyone's memory. Naturally there were suspicions that a repeat was being planned. However, other potential targets could not be ignored either. Shopping malls, government buildings, and of course, airports and airlines: any of these might be targets. More importantly, how large was the conspiracy? Were there more terrorists involved who had so far managed to escape surveillance? If so, cracking down on the particular trio and shutting down the bomb factory might alert the others, and thereby fail to avert an eventual attack.

In fact the bomb factory was *not* shut down, and the surveillance continued. The reasoning process moved to one of examining all possible *explanations*, which in this case consisted of potential targets, terrorists involved, and the timing of the attack. Further investigations would need to continuously evaluate each of these explanations to determine which was the most probable, as well as the most imminent.

Determining the most probable explanation given some evidence is called *abductive* reasoning. While deduction proceeds from premises to conclusions, abduction, on the other hand, proceeds from evidence to explanations. By its very nature, abduction deals with uncertainty; the 'most probable' explanation is one of many, it is just more probable than any of the others.

* * *

Actually, we have seen a simple form of abduction earlier in Chapter 3, when we described the naive Bayes classifier and its use in learning concepts. Recall that a classifier could, once trained, distinguish between, say, dogs and cats, shoppers and surfers, or positive versus negative comments on Twitter. Given the evidence at hand, which could be features of an animal or words in a tweet, such a classifier would find the most probable explanation for such evidence amongst the available alternatives. The naive Bayes classifier computes the required likelihood probabilities during its training phase and uses them during classification to determine the most probable class, or explanation, given the evidence, which in this case is an object characterized by a set of features.

However, the classification problem deals with choosing exactly one of two (or in general many) class labels, or explanations ('dog' or 'cat', positive or negative), and ruling out the other one (or ones). More generally, however, abduction needs to entertain *simultaneous* belief in many possible explanations. For example, investigators would have explored many different potential targets of the planned bombing: Underground trains, shopping malls, airports, etc. Each new fact, such as Ahmed and Tanvir browsing for backpacks and camping equipment in a store, would impact their degree of belief in each of these possible explanations, possibly to a different extent in each case. Backpacks could be used for attacking any of these targets; flash-lights however, might increase belief in a repeat attack on the Underground. In the end, when Ahmed was observed researching flight timetables for over two hours from an internet cafe, belief in an airline attack became the most dominant one.

Just as earlier for simple classification, abductive reasoning can be understood in terms of probabilities and Bayes' Rule. Since we are dealing with humans rather than machines, past experience takes the place of explicit training. Investigators know from specific experience that backpacks were used by the London Underground bombers, whereas common-sense rules might tell them their potential utility for other targets. Recall that in the language of Bayesian probabilities, experience, specific or common, is used to estimate *likelihoods*, such as 'the probability that a backpack will be used for an underground attack'. Bayes' Rule then allows one to efficiently reason 'backwards' to the most probable cause, i.e., reason abductively. At some point, as when Ahmed browses flight schedules so intently, the probability of an airline attack becomes high enough to warrant specific actions, such as increasing airport security (rather than policing shopping malls), and, as it turned out in this particular case, triggering the actual arrests. Such abductive reasoning across many possible explanations can be thought of as many different classifiers operating together, one for each possible explanation. In such a model it is possible to have a high degree of belief in more than one explanation, i.e., the belief in each explanation is independent of the other.

At the same time, beliefs are not completely independent either. Note that the detection of flight-schedule browsing not only increases belief in an airline attack, it also *decreases* our belief in a shopping mall or Underground attack. As a result, we are more confident about diverting resources from policing malls and train stations to securing airports. This 'explaining away' effect has actually been observed in experiments on human subjects.[79] In spite of allowing ourselves to entertain varying and largely independent degrees of belief in many possible explanations at the same time, we also allow our belief in one explanation to affect the others somewhat. (At the same time, our beliefs in different causes are not as closely correlated as in the either-or model of a single classifier, where if our belief in one cause is 80%, belief in the others necessarily drops to 20%.) As it turns out, the 'explaining away' effect, which is an important feature of human reasoning, is also observed in Bayesian abduction using probabilities and in Bayes' Rule.[80]

How does the seemingly very human 'explaining away' phenomenon take place in the cold world of probabilities and Bayes' Rule? Imagine only two explanations, i.e., the hypothetical targets 'shopping mall' and 'airline'. For each of these we construct a naive Bayes classifier with many features, such as 'scouting a mall', 'browsing flight schedules', and also 'making a bomb'. However, the last feature, 'making a bomb', is shared amongst the two hypotheses. Therefore, even though the likelihood that 'making a bomb' is observed is high whichever of the two cases is true, it is *even higher* in the unlikely event that both of the explanations are true, such as if there were actually two attacks being planned. It turns out that the common feature 'making a bomb' which was already observed, is the key to the 'explaining away' effect. Because of this commonality, as soon as the probability (or belief) in an airline attack rises due to some other feature, such as 'browsing flight schedules', being observed, the belief in 'shopping mall' as a possible target automatically reduces. While we will not do the maths here, surprisingly the 'explaining away' effect arises merely as a consequence of Bayes' Rule and simple arithmetic.

A few important conclusions emerge from our discussion here. First of all, Bayesian inference appears to be a surprisingly good rational model for the kind of human abductive reasoning that took place in the 2006 airliner investigation, as also in similar collaborative problem-solving situations. Consequently, researchers have also speculated on the fruitfulness of using Bayesian approaches for directly modelling human thinking.[81]

Second, Bayesian models comprised of different explanations for a large set of factual evidence, with some explanations sharing evidence, are best viewed as a *network*. Nodes in such a Bayesian network are either explanations or facts, and the links between them likelihoods. The structure of the network, determined by which nodes are linked to others, results in complex 'explaining away' effects. A complex Bayesian network can result in phenomena such as where disparate pieces of evidence affect one's degree of belief in seemingly unrelated explanations.

Finally, as demonstrated by phenomena such as the 'explaining away' effect, abductive reasoning using Bayesian networks is quite naturally non-monotonic, in that belief in a hypothesis can both increase or decrease as new evidence is unearthed. Therefore, there is growing interest in using probabilistic networks, Bayesian or otherwise, to model complex abductive reasoning under uncertain conditions, such as the emergent behaviour of large groups of investigators, as well as the unconscious reasoning that takes place within each of our individual brains.

Collective Reasoning

Barely a few months after the 2006 airliner plot was successfully foiled, on 11 October 2006 a small aircraft collided with a skyscraper in New York. Was another terrorist attack under way? The memories of 9/11 were indelible; the security agencies were naturally concerned.

However, unlike the 2001 situation when different intelligence and law enforcement agencies struggled to communicate rapidly enough with each other, this time they used a tool called Intellipedia,[82] inspired by the web's Wikipedia. Within 20 minutes of the incident it had a page of its own on the Intellipedia site, accessible to all concerned agencies and departments. Within the next couple of hours, this page was updated over 80 times. Each update was accompanied by commentary and discussion, as is the case on Wikipedia as well. Such discussions both revealed and provided a platform for a highly collaborative, multi-agency abductive reasoning exercise, which finally, and rapidly, established that the unfortunate crash was in fact an accident and not another terrorist attack.

The Intellipedia approach represented a radical alternative to the traditional process of intelligence gathering and analysis. First and foremost, Intellipedia allowed instantaneous information-sharing between agencies, rectifying a defect made apparent after the 9/11 post-mortem enquiry.[83] However, equally important was the fact that discussions and debate were laid bare for anonymous others to build on. By contrast, in the traditional intelligence model information moves up and down in an organizational hierarchy. Each level in the hierarchy is responsible for collating and *fusing* information from multiple sources. Analysts at each level apply abductive reasoning and communicate their most probable explanations up the hierarchy, while simultaneously also directing lower levels to look for additional facts that could increase or decrease current degrees of belief in the most probable set of explanations at a given point in time.

One obvious advantage of the Intellipedia-based approach to information-sharing is speed. Instead of having to wait until a fact is processed and collated at each level of a complex hierarchy, every fact becomes available immediately to anyone searching for related concepts. Moreover, searches reveal not only all related facts, but also any discussions between or conclusions drawn by human analysts.

As a result, connections to be explored using related sets of facts or hypotheses are discovered dynamically during the process of investigation, rather than as a part of a strict, hard-wired hierarchy. By contrast, information moves upwards in a traditional hierarchy only if belief in its importance is high at any particular level. Thus many potential high-level explanations can get missed out merely because the facts they rely on somehow did not make it up the prescribed hierarchy. As brought to light after the fact, such a situation was in fact seen to have occurred prior to the 9/11 attacks, with information residing in disconnected silos never being connected together in time.

Of course, a flat 'everybody shares everything' architecture can also get unwieldy to navigate. One increasingly has to rely on the serendipitous discovery of related pieces of information, as users look for information using keyword-based search. By 2009, Intellipedia had over 900,000 pages and 100,000 users, with roughly 5,000 page edits taking place every day.[82]

One can imagine users setting up 'permanent' searches that are fired regularly so that information of interest to them naturally flows to them. Similarly, a user might wish to be informed whenever any of a selected set of co-users edits a page, merely because of past experience that found those particular users' comments to be interesting. In this manner the initially flat Intellipedia architecture begins to acquire features found on social networking sites such as Facebook. Imagine if you were presented with every post of each of the now billion-or-so Facebook users. Besides being technically impractical, it would also be useless, as this volume of information would be impossible for any user to digest. Instead, as we all know, users on Facebook define who their friends are, so as to limit the information they receive and disseminate information. A similar situation naturally evolves on Twitter, with its follower–followee relationships. In short, information-sharing at scale naturally requires a complex and dynamic *network*. Only recently, however, has belief revision in such a human network been modelled using abductive reasoning using an analogous Bayesian network so as to develop a better theory for improving human fusion centre operations.[84]

Perhaps you are wondering what all this has to do with automated reasoning by computers. The point is that complex reasoning with vast quantities of information requires not only reasoning techniques and mechanisms for representing knowledge, but also an *architecture*. As we shall soon see, the Intellipedia architecture is closely related to a well-researched model for building intelligent systems. Further, the natural evolution of such an architecture into a network is essential to handle scale, and in fact points us to closely related research in neuroscience and related speculations on how large-scale knowledge representation and reasoning possibly works in the human brain.

* * *

The hierarchical structure of most large human organizations, including those for gathering intelligence, did indeed motivate a powerful idea dating back to the early days of artificial intelligence research. In 1958, Oliver Selfridge, one of the pioneers of AI research, proposed his 'pandemonium' model of how cognition might be organized in the brain, and how intelligent systems should therefore be structured.[85] Selfridge's model involved many 'demons', each responsible for some specific reasoning activity. Lower-level demons would act on direct sensory input. Each such demon would 'shout' if it found evidence of some specific pattern that it was responsible for discovering; if the evidence was strong, it would shout louder. Higher-level demons would listen to the shouts emanating from lower levels, and look for more complex patterns, connecting the dots, so to speak, and in turn shout out their findings. The cacophony of demons shouting, which motivated the name 'pandemonium', would eventually lead to some higher-level cognitive output, such as recognizing a sound, letter, sentence, or even a face.

In spite of this early and prescient idea, AI research through the 1970s continued to focus on problem solving by 'lone agents' using specific techniques, be they of the symbolic-logical or statistical, machine-learning variety. Looking back on this era in his 1991 address as president of the American Association for Artificial Intelligence (AAAI), Daniel Bobrow reflected disparagingly on the limitations of the lone agent approach: 'The agent was disconnected from the world with neither sensors nor effectors, and more importantly with no connection to other intelligent goal driven agents. Research results in AI consisted primarily in the determination of the principles of construction of such intelligent, but deaf, blind and paraplegic agents.'[86] Even if this was a rather harsh assessment, it did serve to highlight the need to embrace the changing paradigm of AI research, the seeds of which had already been laid in the 1970s and 1980s.

The first steps towards just such a collaborative architecture as described by Selfridge had already been taken in the mid-1970s, by Raj Reddy and his group at CMU, while developing the first reasonably successful speech recognition system, Hearsay II.[87] Of course, the fruits of that labour are apparent for all to see in the Siris of today. To understand the advantages of the pandemonium-like hierarchical, collaborative, architecture used in Hearsay II, a simple example serves to illustrate why speech recognition turns out to be so difficult, or even impossible, with a more traditional 'lone agent' approach.

Imagine a spoken sentence such as 'bring the bill please'. If spoken very fast and possibly with a foreign accent, you may well hear it as 'ring the bell please'. It is easy to imagine a 'lone agent' computer program, using a classifier such as naive Bayes to recognize words from speech waveforms, making just such an error quite often. However, if you were hearing this sentence in a restaurant, it is unlikely that you would make such an error. The context in which the utterance was heard would make the first interpretation far more probable than the latter. A similar argument holds at finer levels of disambiguation.

You are unlikely to confuse the utterance with 'ring the bill', because the chance of this word combination is far rarer than 'bring the bill', regardless of context; after all, one does not 'ring' a 'bill'. Similar mechanisms are at work down to the level of discerning distinct words, syllables or phonemes. The speech waveform may well sound like 'ringthe bill', or even 'bring thebill'. However, you know that neither 'ringthe' nor 'thebill' are words, and so these interpretations are discarded even though the 'bottom-up' processing of the speech waveform throws up both these possibilities, along with many others, including the correct word sequence. In fact, if you were not a native speaker of English you may well get confused by such alternatives, as you lack some of the higher-level knowledge about what sounds are definitely not words, and what sequences of words are clearly impossible. This lack of higher-level knowledge is why it is more difficult to understand a foreign tongue when spoken, as opposed to its written form.

The Hearsay II system employed many different 'knowledge sources', operating at different 'levels'. Some processed the speech waveform directly using signal processing techniques. Others detected phonemes and syllables using statistical classifiers of various types. Higher-level knowledge sources detected probable words using a dictionary. At even higher levels, *predictions* were made about as-yet undetected words using logical reasoning based on the context, such as being in a restaurant. These predictions are then propagated down to lower levels to verify their presence. At the highest level, multiple hypotheses regarding the possible sentence being spoken are generated and continuously evaluated as to their likelihood of being correct. In fact, multiple hypotheses are generated and maintained at each level recursively, with each level receiving the outputs of lower levels as well as predicting possibilities that are propagated back downwards for further verification.

The Hearsay II system introduced the notion of a 'blackboard' where all these multiple hypotheses would be written, and from which different knowledge sources would read and in turn write back. This 'blackboard architecture' formalized Selfridge's earlier pandemonium idea, and has since been used in a variety of applications of knowledge-based techniques.[88] The key elements of the blackboard architecture include the combination of bottom-up and top-down processing, exploring multiple hypotheses in parallel, combining many different kinds of knowledge sources, and last but not least, making *predictions* of as-yet undetected elements during the collaborative reasoning process. These elements have been found to be be immensely useful in a wide variety of disparate applications ranging well beyond speech and natural language understanding to expert systems, computer vision, and even robotics.

* * *

Further, besides its proven utilitarian value, the blackboard architecture has also been proposed as a plausible rational model for how the human brain reasons to 'connect the dots', make sense of the world, and even be creative. In particular, the well-known cognitive scientist Douglas Hofstadter has repeatedly used blackboard-like architectures to build models that purport to explain human thinking and reasoning.

In 1984 Hofstadter used the following problem to illustrate how non-obvious, possibly even creative, thinking might be simulated.[89] We are given a pair of letter sequences, such as 'abc' and a supposedly related sequence 'cba'. Now we are presented with a third sequence, such as 'ijk', and asked to find another one that is related to this sequence in 'the same manner' as 'abc' is related to 'cba'. A moment's thought leads us to 'kji' as the most likely prediction in this particular case.

Relationships can be fairly arbitrary, so given a pair like 'abc' and 'aabbcc', we would guess that 'ijk' and 'iijjkk' are 'similarly' related. The game becomes more interesting with 'abc' and 'abd': now we need to know about the alphabet in order to guess that, 'ijl' is a better guess than, say, 'ijd'. But things become difficult even for us when we seek to 'copy' the relationship between 'aabc' and 'aabd' to 'ijkk'. This time we might be confused with the doubling of 'k'; should we replace both 'k's by their successor, yielding 'ijll'? Alternatively, should 'k' be 'linked' to 'a' because of this doubling, consequently leading us to link 'c' with 'i' and replace 'successor' by 'predecessor', so as to finally give 'hjkk'?

Hofstadter argues that 'being a copycat', by constructing *analogies*, as illustrated in this toy scenario, should be regarded as a key, even the primary, ingredient of intelligence. In 1990, Hofstadter's student Melanie Mitchell described a computational solution to the sequences puzzle using what is essentially a blackboard architecture with a combination of top-down and bottom-up reasoning.[90] Instead of detectors and classifiers, their knowledge sources were agents looking for patterns, such as 'alphabetic order', 'successor', and 'numeric order'.

Further, some patterns are related to others, such as 'successor' being the 'opposite' of 'predecessor', and 'first letter' being the opposite of 'last letter'. Such relationships were captured in a semantic network, which they call a 'slipnet'. During the reasoning process, elements of this slipnet are activated, i.e., assigned higher degrees of belief, based on patterns that are discovered in the given letter sequence, and relationships between them. All these knowledge sources explore many alternatives in parallel, evaluating them for the 'strength' of the analogy being proposed by each. Finally, the most appropriate analogy discovered is used to predict the answer sequence. Hofstadter refers to the process of top-down, bottom-up, parallel exploration of multiple hypotheses as a 'parallel terraced scan', which, he speculates, is a key element for understanding how humans reason by discovering analogies. Quite surprisingly, the copycat program manages to come up with fairly complex analogies, very similar to those produced by humans, and sometimes even better.

Let us now compare these pandemonium-like blackboard-based systems to our earlier example of collaborative problem-solving and analysis using Intellipedia. Instead of a 'blackboard', Intellipedia uses a user-editable website, better known as a wiki, which is also the basis for the well-known Wikipedia. Of course, unlike Hearsay II and Copycat, Intellipedia relies on human 'knowledge sources' rather than computational ones. But in other respects they are remarkably similar. Intellipedia provided a shared environment where an inherently hierarchical collective, such as the intelligence community, could freely share ideas and insight.

Similarly, the blackboard architecture provided a means for different 'lone agent' knowledge sources, performing different 'levels' of analysis, to cooperatively solve a larger problem in a non-deterministic manner. In fact, a key aspect of the blackboard architectures of both Hearsay II and Copycat, was how they decided which knowledge source to apply next. In each case, knowledge sources that were most likely to produce new hypotheses would be evaluated first, given the state of the 'board' at any point of time. Similarly, human analysts using Intellipedia would use their own intuition and the data already seen by them to decide which topics or pages they might be most interested in reading, as well as decide upon that to which they had something new to contribute.

Finally, it is exactly in the crucial point of deciding (or choosing) which knowledge source (or analyst) works on what data and when, that both the blackboard architecture and Intellipedia face a challenge when dealing with *scale*. In the case of Intellipedia, human analysts would need to be presented with the 'right' information, i.e., which they would be able to either contribute to or use for other analysis. At the same time, they must not be swamped with so much data that merely sifting through it to find what is relevant consumes all their time. The scale challenge for the blackboard architecture is very similar, even if articulated in a different manner. The blackboard system needs to choose which knowledge sources are most likely to be relevant given the data posted on the blackboard at any point of time, but *without* actually trying out all knowledge sources on all available data. This is currently an area of active research; in fact this author and his team have recently suggested some approaches to automatically cluster blackboard data and knowledge sources, without having to try all combinations,[91] by applying locality sensitive hashing (LSH[17]), which, you may recall, was also mentioned in earlier chapters as a surprising way to group n data items into sets of similar items in only $O(n)$ steps, i.e., *without* having to compare all n^2 pairs. We shall return to the LSH algorithm in Chapter 5, and also discuss its connections to related techniques that model memory and how the brain works.

More generally however, the problem of scale is probably better addressed by replacing the shared wiki, or blackboard, with a network of connections. As we have mentioned earlier, the need for selective connections as opposed to complete sharing is already evident in social networks such as Facebook and Twitter, and similar ideas are likely to percolate into Intellipedia as well. Similarly, the problem of scale naturally leads us from a fully shared blackboard model to network-based 'connectionist' architectures for automated reasoning. Connectionist models are also motivated by neuroscientific studies of how brains are themselves comprised of very large networks of neurons, as well as by the success of Bayesian networks in modelling human abduction, including phenomena such as the 'explaining away' effect that we have seen earlier.

* * *

We began our exploration of reasoning with Siri's need to eventually reason about our world. This led us into the world of logic, its limits, and its incorporation into the very fabric of the emerging semantic web, in the form of OWL and its variants. Logical rules are the basis for deductive reasoning, from generalities to specifics. We saw how such rules might be used to power intelligent web-linked agents such as future Siris. At the same time, inductive reasoning, i.e., going from many specifics to a generalization, is needed to first learn such rules themselves. We found that even inductive learning can be automated, especially by exploiting the web-based data, using the machine-learning techniques of Chapter 3, to produce large-scale knowledge bases such as Yago, Cyc, and REVERB. Next, the limits of deductive reasoning were once more tested in having to deal with uncertainties of the real world. Abduction rather than mere deduction appeared to be equally prevalent in human thought, both individual and collective. Bayesian networks yielded yet another rational model, this time one that appeared to mirror human abduction and its properties.

Still, practical problems requiring machines to mirror human analysis (as in Intellipedia), or insight (as in Copycat), continue to remain very difficult. Multiple modes of reasoning need to be brought to bear on such problems to have any hope of success, just as collective and collaborative analysis by groups of humans is required in many endeavours, not the least of which is the intelligence (as in CIA) arena itself.

Finally, we have seen how collaborative reasoning using social platforms mirrors the blackboard architectures of Hearsay II and Copycat, with all of the embodying aspects that appear key to intelligent reasoning: multiple knowledge sources, combining abduction and deduction, top-down and bottom-up reasoning, parallel 'terraced scan' explorations, and, last but very importantly, the role of *prediction* in the reasoning process. In Chapter 5 we shall go even further in these directions and explore how predictive power can be brought about in web applications, and why it is so important yet elusive. In fact, we shall argue that *prediction* is not only required for intelligent thought, but is one of its central characteristics.

5

PREDICT

'Predicting the future'—the stuff of dreams one might imagine; the province of astrologers and soothsayers, surely. Perhaps not, the scientific mind might retort: after all, is it not the job of science to discover laws of nature, and thereby make precise, verifiable predictions about the future? But what if we were to claim that prediction is neither fanciful nor difficult, and not even rare. Rather, it is commonplace; something that we all accomplish each and every moment of our lives.

Some readers may recall the popular video game, pong, where the goal is to 'keep the puck in play' using an electronic paddle. Figure 2

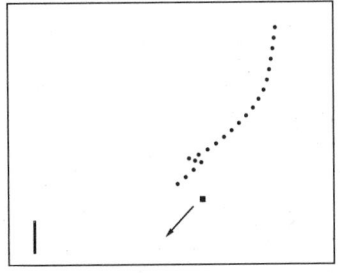
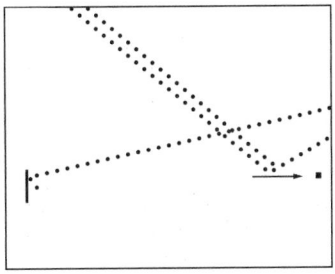

Reactive Player   Predictive Player

FIGURE 2 Pong games with eye-gaze tracking.

With permission from Dr Pawan Sinha, MIT Dept. of Neurosciences.

shows images of two different pong games in progress. In addition to the paddle and puck, the players' eye gaze is also being tracked. The image on the left shows the player's eyes tracking the puck itself. On the other hand, in the right-hand image, the player is already looking at a point where she *expects* the puck to travel *to*. The player on the left is *reactive*; she simply tracks the puck, and as the game gets faster, she eventually misses. The right player, in contrast, is able to *predict* where the puck will *be*, and most of the time she gets it right. Further, we often see her eyes dart faster than the puck to multiple regions of the field as she appears to recalculate her prediction continuously.

What kind of player do you think you are? As it happens, almost all of us are predictive players. Even if we have never played pong before, we rapidly begin predicting the puck's trajectory after even a few minutes of playing. The 'reactive player' in this experiment was in fact autistic, which apparently affected the person's ability to make predictions about the puck's trajectory. (The neurological causes of autism are still not well known or agreed upon; the recent research from which the images in Figure 2 are taken represent new results that might shed some more light on this debilitating condition.[92]) So it appears that prediction, as exhibited by most pong players, is far from being a rare and unusual ability. It is in fact a part and parcel of our everyday lives, and is present, to varying degrees, in all conscious life. Let us now turn once more to the web and related applications, and see where they stand in the arena of predictive abilities.

* * *

When we search the web using a search engine such as Google, we are inadvertently disclosing some of our intentions, such as possibly being interested in buying some product or other. However, we also search for many other reasons. As it happens, health-related queries form a significant fraction of online search. Whenever we or someone we know falls sick, we immediately 'google' their symptoms. If there is a public health warning, such as the H1N1 pandemic that struck the world in 2009, we search even more frantically at the slightest sign of infection.

In 2008 Google launched *flu-trends*, where it measured search activity on flu-like symptoms across the world and made the data available to public health officials as well as the general public. In a 2009 article published in *Nature*,[93] Google's researchers along with CDC* scientists showed that the results from Google's flu-trends predictions were highly correlated with manual surveys conducted by CDC officials. Further, predictions based on search trends came one to two weeks *earlier*, and were of course far cheaper to obtain as compared to physically interviewing samples of physicians and door-to-door surveys of people at large. Google flu-trends proved especially useful the following year, during the H1N1 pandemic, and was used by public health agencies to focus vaccination drives towards areas that were most likely to become centres for the spread of the disease in the near future.

In their recent book *The Two-Second Advantage*,[94] Vivek Randive and Kevin Maney relate the story of the East Orange, New Jersey, police department. This crime-ridden county installed smart surveillance cameras throughout its jurisdiction. Smart cameras not only fed their video streams to a centralized monitoring centre manned by policemen, they also detected and correlated unusual events. Suppose a camera is witness to a lone person walking down a street, as well as a car slowing down as it approaches the person. A smart camera can detect and classify objects, i.e., a person walking and a car slowing down, as well as note the locations of these events. The central system correlates the two events, which get escalated to an alert if they happen to be taking place late at night. At this point 'I want to know about it', says police director Cordero. The system then finds a nearby police car and asks it to turn on its siren, which in many cases prevents a crime from taking place by scaring off the potential criminals. Compare

---

* Centres for Disease Control and Prevention, USA.

this scenario with the as-yet hypothetical NATGRID system described in Chapter 2. The East Orange system is actually in place; perhaps NATGRID-like *predictive* early-warning systems are less futuristic than we imagined.

The progress of technology is inexorable, and along with it we now have access to incredibly detailed and voluminous data, which can be used for the good, as just shown, but also misused. As of this writing, Twitter is used in 200 countries with over 500 million tweets being posted daily. Further, the number of smartphones equipped with GPS* is growing by the day. People use such phones to post messages on Twitter. Moreover, such Twitter posts are, by and large, free for anyone to access. In fact, it is possible to ask Twitter to give us a stream of feeds from any rectangular region in the world. Many of these users are also high-volume tweeters, and seemingly tweet at the slightest opportunity.

Imagine what can be done with such a stream of data. For one, it reveals the daily movements of all the Twitter-users who tweet from GPS-enabled devices. From this data a computer program can easily figure out where each such person's home and office are. For the more incessant tweeters, it can also determine when they are travelling out of town, how often they visit a mall, or which restaurants they eat at. Spooky indeed. But there is more: once a person's daily habits are revealed, the computer can also predict where they *will* go in the immediate future, at least with high probability. The possibilities for misuse of such information by criminals are obvious, as is the need for law enforcement agencies to likewise ensure similar predictions to pre-empt criminal behaviour.

In spite of these dangers, there are many less alarming and potentially beneficial possibilities as well. As more and more people use

---

* Global Positioning System, which uses satellite signals to pinpoint a device's exact latitude and longitude; used in car-navigation systems as well as many mobile applications.

smart, location-aware devices, the behavioural patterns of people at large begin to get revealed at an aggregate level. Retailers, restaurant chains, and oil companies can use such insight to locate new facilities in the most optimal locations. Tweeters also reveal their interests and friends, from the content of their tweets as well as their profiles, followers, and friends. Marketers in the bricks-and-mortar world of malls and restaurants are increasingly viewing such data as a potential goldmine of insight with which to target consumers better, just as web-based retailers are able to target their services based on the behaviour of consumers while online.

Last but not least, Twitter in particular has also become a rich source of local news. Many events of local importance are first reported on Twitter, including many that never reach news channels. Even though such events may be primarily of local importance, they can also be of critical interest to some specific but possibly far-flung entities. For example, a fire or labour strike near a supplier's factory halfway around the world may be of interest even from afar, as it can be used to *predict* a possible supply disruption a few weeks into the future.[95]

Organizations today, be they public-health and law-enforcement agencies, or large commercial retailers, banks, and manufacturers, are only just beginning to explore many such ways to exploit social media as a means to make *predictions* about the future and act on them, in much the same manner as the 'predictive' pong player is able to look ahead to where the the puck is *going to be*, rather than merely track the puck as it moves. As aptly put by Randive and Maney, 'A little bit of information ahead of time is more valuable than a boatload of information later on'.[94] Prediction, however limited, is often far more useful than perfect analysis with 20-20 hindsight after the fact. Instead, the goal of analysis needs to be the creation of predictive models, which can then be used 'just in time' to make better decisions.

The power of predictive analysis is often underestimated, and so is the need for its responsible use, as Andrew Pole of the Target retail chain found out quite recently. Target's ability to predict the future needs of its shoppers, merely by analysing their past purchases, was so good that their system predicted that a teenage customer was pregnant even before her father came to know. This highly publicized event resulted in a scandal of sorts when the girl's father lodged a strong complaint.[96]

One final example before we explore what it takes to make predictions: in his 2007 book[97] on using data to make predictions, called *Super Crunchers*, Ian Ayres recounts a story of how a wine critic named Orley Ashenfelter has successfully used large volumes of historical data on weather conditions during the wine growing season to accurately predict the eventual selling price of a particular wine. Ashenfelter uses basic statistical regression, which we shall explain soon, to arrive at a seemingly simplistic formula such as: wine quality $= 12.145 + 0.00117 \times$ winter rainfall $+ 0.0614 \times$ average temperature $- 0.00386 \times$ harvest rainfall. Quite surprisingly, Ashenfelter's predictions are remarkably accurate and have often astonished the supposed 'experts' of the wine-tasting community.

Statistical Forecasting

To begin our exploration of the science of prediction, let us see what is involved in analysing historical weather data to predict wine quality. Suppose you are Orley Ashenfeter and have got hold of temperature and rainfall data from the past ten years for the wine region. How would you go about creating a *model*, such as the equation just described that purports to predict wine quality?

Suppose for the moment that Ashenfelter has, somehow, guessed that average winter rainfall, average temperature during the growing season, and average harvest rainfall are the right *features* that could be predictors of the final wine quality for a region. He is looking for an equation *like* the one described, i.e., wine quality $= a + b \times$ winter rainfall $+ c \times$ average temperature $+ d \times$ harvest rainfall, just that he does not know what numbers to use as a, b, c, and d. Of course, once he figures out the 'best' values for these numbers, he has his model and can go about making predictions using recent weather conditions. Those familiar with statistics would recognize this as a *regression* problem, for which there are well-known formulae. However, for reasons that will become clearer later on, we shall describe another, albeit more roundabout, route to arrive at the same model.

Imagine we are Ashenfelter looking for the right model 'parameters', a, b, c, and d. To begin with, we just guess some values out of the blue; any values, even all zeros, will do. (In this particular case it is true that *any* initial guess will do, because the equation is 'linear', i.e., does not involve powers of the parameters, such as a^2. In more general cases, as we shall see later, our initial guess itself cannot be too far off.)

Next, we remember that we do have a lot of historical data, with wine quality as well as weather conditions for many past years and different wine-growing regions. All we do is test our guessed model on past data and see what wine quality it predicts. Clearly, our first guess for a, b, c, and d will probably produce results that are way off, with the predicted wine qualities differing greatly from the actual ones. But the nice thing is that we can easily *measure* how far off we are. For each past year and region, we measure the difference between the predicted wine quality and the actual historical value; these are just two numbers, and we subtract them from each other.* By adding up all these differences we get an idea of how far off we are.

The next step is crucial, and will also form an important piece of our understanding of prediction later on in this chapter: we make a small change to each of the guessed parameters a, b, c, and d, say by adding a fixed but tiny increment. We can also subtract this increment

---

* Since we don't know which is larger, what is usually done is to blindly subtract the numbers and take the *square*: e.g., $(15 - 20)^2 = (-5)^2 = 25$. This way we don't get fooled by negative numbers.

from each parameter; or add the increment to *a* and subtract it from all the others. There are two choices to make, i.e., add or subtract the increment, for each of the four parameters; this gives us 2^4 or 16 different sets of parameters. For each of these 16 'nearby' parameter choices (they are all near the guess that we began with), we can recalculate how far off the predicted wine qualities are from the actual ones. Most likely, one of these choices will be better than our initial guess, i.e., will predict values that are just slightly closer to the actual wine qualities. All we do next is replace our initial guess by this new choice, and repeat the entire procedure, and continue doing so.

At each step of the algorithm, we are, hopefully, getting closer and closer to accurately predicting the actual historical wine qualities. At some point we should reach a stage where none of the 16 neighbouring parameter choices improve our model; at this point we stop. By this time we will find that our model is predicting qualities pretty close to historical facts, so we should feel comfortable using the model to predict the future as well.

Most importantly, not only does the model help us predict the future wine quality for the current year, the model also tells us how *confident* we should be about our prediction. Let us see how: even using our 'best' model, our predictions on the historical samples will differ from the actual values of quality, in fact we would have calculated the sum of all these errors during our model-finding procedure in any case. Dividing by the number of historical samples we used, we get the average error per sample. This 'residual error' gives us an estimate of how far off our future prediction might be. But there is more; we can also figure out how much the model's errors on historical data deviated from this residual error—once more we just average the differences between the model errors and the residual error. This 'error in the errors' tells us whether our errors vary widely or not, i.e., how good our *error* estimate is, which in turn gives us a precise measure of how confident we should be in our prediction of future wine quality. Without going into more detail, such calculations allow us to make precise statements about the confidence of our prediction, such as 'there is a 95% chance that predicted wine quality lies between the two values . . .'.

Similar prediction models work for other scenarios as well. Consider the case of predicting flu outbreaks using search trends. Our historical data would include the frequencies with which certain keywords are searched by users, the locations from which these searches are issued,* and of course the actual flu-incidence volumes as measured after the fact. Again, a regression model, very similar to the one used for wine quality, would give us the multipliers to use with different keywords in a simple formula to predict flu-volume for each region.

Of course, as we have mentioned already, there are much better and faster ways of finding the best possible model, and also better ways of estimating the error in our prediction. The reasoning behind why precise statements of confidence are possible is also quite straightforward; however we won't go into these topics here. The important aspect of the algorithm just described is that it makes guesses and then improves them using historical data; when no further improvement is possible, we are left with the 'best' model that can be found using the historical data available.

Neural Networks

Of course, the question arises as to whether and how our brains also form models such as the ones described in the previous section. Such questions were very much a part of early discussions about artificial intelligence, dating back to the 1940s, when McCulloch and Pitts suggested that the neurons present in their billions in every brain could

---

* Google knows the internet address of the internet service-provider you are using, which actually lets it figure out *where* you are in the world!

be understood, in a logical sense, by certain abstract mathematical models. Thereafter, if such abstract 'neuronal elements' could indeed be shown capable of tasks normally associated with brain-like capabilities, such as recognition, recollection, or prediction, then perhaps we would come closer to understanding how brains actually worked. The field of 'neural networks' was thus born. While initially motivated by the hope of producing rational models of brain-like behaviour, neural networks have also been successfully used in many practical applications. Let us see what a neural network looks like, and how it might possibly learn to predict wine quality by producing a model similar to Orley Ashenfelter's.

Each real-life neuron is connected to many other neurons via its unique structure, as depicted in Figure 3. The neuron receives input signals from a large number, often thousands, of other neurons via its *dendrites*. It also sends out its own signals via its *axon*, which in turn connect to the dendrites of other neurons via *synapses*. Some synapses are stronger than others, and so transmit or amplify signals better than weaker synapses. Further, synapses change their strength over time, and this is how the brain *learns*. Lastly, the output signal that a

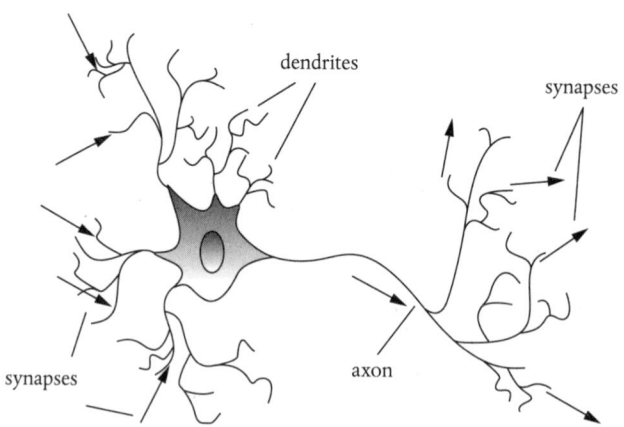

FIGURE 3 Neuron: dendrites, axon, and synapses

neuron transmits along its axon depends on the cumulative input it receives from other neurons via its dendrites.

McCulloch and Pitts suggested that this behaviour of a neuron could be modelled as a mathematical equation linking its output signal to its inputs, with the strengths of its incoming synapses playing the role of multiplication factors in this equation, in much the same manner as the number a, b, c, and d did in Orley Ashenfelter's model of wine quality. Thus, the output signal of a neuron could be viewed as an equation that combines its input signals based on incoming synapse strengths, in much the same manner as Ashenfelter's equation combines different pieces of weather data. Of course, the natural question arises as to how such a neuron might *learn* 'correct' synapse strengths for a particular purpose, such as predicting wine quality.

Well, we might be able to adjust the synapse strengths in such a simple single-neuron model in much the same manner as we did earlier for Ashenfelter's model. We merely compare the wine quality predicted by our current guess of synapse strengths with what we observe in real life, and make small adjustments to each synapse strength so as to reduce the error, i.e., the difference between our prediction and our observation. We make such an adjustment each time we consider a new year's data; further, we cycle back to revisit all the data again and again, continuing to make adjustments until our predictions come close enough to our actual observations.

It turns out that our simple single-neuron model can 'learn' to predict wine quality and come up with an equation, or model, in much the same manner as our earlier procedure did. The success of abstract neural elements in learning predictive models led to the development of the field of *neural networks*. Neural networks could be much more complex than a single neuron, with complex structures involving larger numbers of 'neuronal elements' connected with each other in a variety of different ways.

An important technique for efficiently readjusting synapse strengths, called 'back-propagation', was first suggested by Werbos in 1974,[98] and popularized over ten years later in 1986 by Rumelhart, Hinton, and Williams.[99] Instead of trying out all possible adjustments to the many synapse strengths involved in a neural-network model, the back-propagation technique suggested a far simpler way, essentially using simple high-school calculus to figure out the relative proportion in which to adjust all the synapse strengths in one fell swoop. To see why this was a major achievement, even if in hindsight fairly obvious, imagine a neural network with m synapses; our simplistic approach of trying out all possible ways to adjust m synapse strengths, each upwards or downwards, would need to explore 2^m combinations. Using back-propagation instead, not only can we determine the best combination immediately in one step, but also the *relative proportion* in which each synapse is to be adjusted, which eventually results in the network being able to learn the final model much faster.

Over the years the field of neural networks has grown substantially. Today the ability of neural networks to learn predictive models is unquestioned, and neural models are used in a variety of practical applications in diverse domains ranging from early detection of fraudulent financial transactions to controlling complex machinery in manufacturing plants or detecting dangerous substances in airport security scanners.

However, in spite of their success in so many different arenas, it remains an open question as to whether neural networks are at all *better* than the many other mathematical learning techniques available, especially those carefully tailored to the problem at hand. Further, the theoretical underpinnings of neural networks remain fairly weak, leading many researchers to view the field as a form of 'black art'. At the same time, the strongest advantage enjoyed by neural networks is their ubiquity, i.e., providing a common approach to solving a vast variety of prediction problems, in much the same manner as the seemingly uniformly structured brain does. We shall return to neural models shortly. Before that however, let us see the role predictive models play alongside the most apparent functions that large collections of real neurons (i.e., our brains) perform amazingly well, in particular logical reasoning and recalling memories.

Predictive Analytics

Let us return once more to the pong videos; how might we explain the predictive pong player being able to predict the puck's trajectory? Let's recall some of our earlier explorations in the arena of learning, such as the basic naive Bayes classifier we discussed in Chapter 3. In principle, such classifiers could, if trained on many, many pong videos, learn to recognize and distinguish between concepts such as 'puck moving left', 'puck moving right', 'puck moving 30° upwards-right', 'puck close to top wall', 'puck far away from wall', and so on. More complex variations of such classifiers can learn to recognize and track the exact angle, speed, and direction of movement of the puck, at least when it is moving straight rather than bouncing off a wall.

However, as you might well imagine, using learning techniques such as these, even very rapidly, merely reproduces the behaviour of the reactive pong player, who tracks the puck with her eyes rather than predicting where it is going to be a few seconds into the future. So, can we do more using additional techniques to mimic the predictive player?

Having learned basic concepts such as 'puck close to wall', one might further imagine learning a vast number of 'rules', again by crunching past data from many observations of past pong games. For example, we might learn a rule such as 'if the puck was moving upwards-right at a 30° angle at time $t-1$ *and* it hits the top wall at time t, *then* it moves downwards-right at $-30°$ at time $t+1$'. Recall the reasoning techniques we discussed in Chapter 4, such as rules and description logic. Reasoning tells us what facts 'follow from', or are entailed by, what is already known. Thus, we could imagine a process of reasoning, using rules such as those described earlier, to predict where the puck might be a few seconds later.

Now imagine another system, one that exploits the physics of the puck-world, i.e., one that knows that the puck will continue to move in a straight line unless it hits a wall, and how it will rebound when it does hit a wall. Newton's laws of motion, which we all learn in high school, give us exactly such a set of equations. Using the shape of the arena and these laws of motion, we can write down equations that can predict the exact trajectory of the puck. In other words, we have an exact *model* for this particular world, using which the future can be predicted. Clearly such a model is probably simpler to write down and follow than a vast number of logical rules. What do our brains do? Classify and reason, or learn models? Or a combination of all three?

Models need not always be exact of course. Orley Ashenfelter *learned* a model from past data, rather than a classifier or rules. This model was in the form of a *linear* equation between wine quality and weather parameters.* Prediction, at least in this case, involves learning a *model* that can produce values, such as the puck location or wine quality. Such models differ somewhat from classifiers that recognize concepts, or rules that express relationships between concepts.

In a certain sense, models based on equations might also be thought of as more precise rules—ones that allow exact calculations. Could precise models of the world in general, such as Newton's laws of motion, be *learned* from past data, instead of being 'discovered' while sitting under a tree and having an apple fall on one's head? Surprisingly, two Cornell University researchers, Michael Schmidt and Hod Lipson were able to get a computer to *learn* Newton's laws

---

* *Linear* merely means that the weather parameters are not multiplied with, or squared with, *each other*; i.e., there is no rainfall^2 etc. in the equation.

of motion for a pendulum, merely from data regarding its movements.[100] Moreover, and most importantly, they did *not* tell the computer anything about what 'kind' of equation these laws would require, e.g., 'linear' or otherwise. This is an example of a far more powerful statistical learning technique than Ashenfelter's use of linear regression. Schmidt and Lipson's approach used not only experimental data, but also some general principles about what 'kinds' of equations were 'elegant' and simple; their approach thus was a mix of learning and reasoning.

There are other, practical situations where a combination of a classifier, rules, and reasoning can also predict. Imagine a bank on the lookout for fraudulent credit-card transactions. Over time, a classifier may learn to recognize different patterns of behaviour. Further learning may reveal rules that point to certain combinations of patterns being more likely to indicate fraudulent behaviour in the future.

It is important to recognize that different techniques and combinations thereof can be used for prediction, including all of the tools we have come across so far—classifiers, rules, reasoning, and models. Here 'model' is used in the strict sense that it predicts the future *value* of a desired quantity, or even many values. Further, as we have already seen, such models themselves can be learned from data, as can concepts or rules.

The term *predictive analytics* has become popular in the business world to broadly describe computing systems that use any of these techniques. In practice, predictive analytics models usually combine classifiers, rules, and the statistical models just described. Further, not all applications of so-called predictive analytics systems need to be 'predictive', in the strict sense. For example, in the case of bank fraud we can also use the same set of techniques for detecting, i.e., recognizing, a fraud in progress, which is somewhat different from predicting one in the future.

However, neither of these mechanisms are close to being a rational model of how human brains actually make predictions. The average person, even a small child, begins playing pong in a predictive manner within minutes of learning what pong is all about. They certainly don't need to observe hundreds of prior pong games such as the learning-plus-reasoning proposition demands. Nor do they need to have gone through high-school physics. (Conversely, they *don't* learn Newton's laws just by observing the world, unlike Schmidt and Lipson's computer; and do *need* to learn these explicitly in high school!)

Something *else* is needed to build a good prediction system, one that is closer to what is going on in the brain.

* * *

In his best-selling book *Outliers*,[101] Malcolm Gladwell quotes the neurologist Daniel Levitin: 'ten thousand hours of practice is required to achieve the level of mastery associated with being a world-class expert—in anything'. He goes on to describe example after example of successful people, from composers to basketball players to ice skaters and pianists. In each case their mastery of their field, which makes them 'outliers', can be explained by the extra opportunities for practice that they each happened to find and take advantage of. Randive and Maney also quote this 'ten-thousand-hour rule' in *The Two-Second Advantage*,[94] to explain the seemingly extraordinary predictive powers of the ice-hockey player Wayne Gretsky, who somehow always seems to know *where* the puck is going to be, just a few seconds before anybody else. Gretksy is a *really* good predictive player of real ice hockey, just as our earlier predictive pong player was much better than the reactive one.

What is going on in those ten thousand hours of practice that makes someone an expert? Perhaps the brain too is building a predictive *model* of some kind using all the data it collects during these many, many hours of practice, similar to Orley Ashenfelter's statistical model using many years of weather data, or the Google flu-trends' statistical model using volumes of past search queries correlated with actual flu outbreaks. Further, more experience means more data, and therefore a better predictive model:

> Such deliberate practice is how a lot of talented people become so accomplished . . . all that practice generates mountains of data that these people's brains are able to chunk into an efficient mental model. So the tennis pro winds up being able to anticipate her opponents's shots in uncanny ways. The musician can hear notes before they are played. The CEO can foresee the outcome of a decision with amazing accuracy,[94]

submit Randive and Maney, while discussing the ten-thousand-hour rule.

We came across another, much more commonly possessed predictive model way back in Chapter 3, 'Listen'. Recall Shannon's wife being able to guess the next letter in some text chosen at random: she could accurately predict the next letter in 'the lamp was on the d . . .'. Why? Because her experience of using language, like most adults, far exceeded ten thousand hours. As a result, she had probably formed a strong *statistical* model of how letters appeared in words, and how words appear in sentences. Even more importantly, she would have learned classifiers that could identify objects such as lamps and desks, as well as rules that would state that lamps are most likely found on desks, rather than, say, doors (even though both begin with a 'd').

Our predictive models are not perfect, though—even those learned over thousands of hours of 'practice'. As explained in the recent popular book by Daniel Kahneman, *Thinking, Fast and Slow*[102] our immediate reactions, presumably based on learned models, which he refers to as our 'System 1', can often be very very wrong. One of the many examples he uses to illustrate the fallibility of System 1 is a simple puzzle: 'A bat and ball cost $1.10. The bat costs a dollar more than the ball. How much does the ball cost?'

Many people's instinctive answer is '10 cents'. But a moment's reflection later, one sees one's error. The correct answer is 5 cents (so that the bat costs $1.05, both together adding up to $1.10). In this moment of reflection we rely on slightly deeper abilities, involving some simple logical reasoning. Kahneman attributes such reasoning abilities to our 'System 2'.

Over time, and with extensive practice, our continued use of System 2 lets us develop System 1 abilities that work faster, and, most often, give the right answer. The speed of System 1 makes it closer to a predictive model that uses a small, compact representation, such as the simple formula that Ashenfelter derived for wine quality. System 2, on the other hand, involves more complex analysis, using logic and rules, such as might be used by wine 'experts' and agriculturists reasoning from first principles to predict how good a wine is likely to be.

* * *

Now let's see if the web displays similar predictive powers. Type 'the lamp is——' in the Google search box and it instantly provides a few alternatives to complete your query: 'lamp is *lit*', the 'lamp is a lie',* etc. Try this again with 'the lamp was——', and the possible completions now include 'the lamp was a lie', 'the flame was lit', and 'the lamp was invented'. At first glance at least, these look like the *statistically* most probable completions. But let us look closer.

Let's take another example, and see what comes first to our own minds: 'one small step'—what does this evoke? Most of us familiar with history might instantly recall Neil Armstrong's words as he took the first steps on the moon: 'One small step for a man, one giant leap for mankind'. So does Google's query completion; just try it. However, *statistically* speaking, this sentence is probably far rarer than the vast number of times the words 'one small step' occur in various texts having nothing to do with Neil Armstrong. As a final example, consider the phrase 'yes we——'. Until 2008, this

---

* Referring to a much-discussed, and rather risqué, optical illusion.

sequence of words probably had no special meaning to most of us. After the US presidential campaign of 2008, though, most of us might instantly complete this phrase as 'yes we can', echoing Obama's oft-quoted refrain. Google too now recalls this phrase instantly, which it might not have done prior to 2008. Of course I did not verify this back then—after all, how could I have known that this phrase would become so well known?

Something more than a statistical model is at work here. In the case of our own prediction, we instantly *recall* Armstrong's famous quote from *memory*. Google's query completion instantly looks up its vast search index and not only finds those documents that contain this phrase, but also chooses the most *important* of these (via its famed PageRank algorithm) to form the most likely completions. It thus appears reasonable to conclude that *memory* also plays an important role in prediction. Additionally, going back to Kahneman's two systems, apart from reasoning his System 2 also relies on recalling facts from memory.

Just what kind of memory though? And how do memories, predictive models, and reasoning work together? Further, the web certainly has a vast 'memory'; after all, it appears to store every bit of recorded human knowledge today. So how does this web memory compare with human memory, especially when it comes to making predictions? It looks like we are back where we started, with 'Looking' in Chapter 1.

Sparse Memories

Recall our excursion into the world of 'classifiers' in Chapter 3, 'Learn'. We considered how a computer might learn to distinguish a dog from a cat based on features, such as 'it barks' and 'is large', versus 'it meows' and 'is small'. Our naive Bayes classifier there accumulated statistics regarding the features of all the animals it observed into a small set of probabilities. These 'likelihoods' together with Bayes' Rule allowed it to successfully *decide* whether the next animal it saw was a dog or a cat, or for that matter, some other animal amongst the many it may have observed. At that point we emphasized that our classifier did *not* need to store the details of every animal it ever saw. The small set of likelihoods were enough for it to disambiguate the future animals it encountered.

However, if one thinks about it, we experience more than mere recognition when seeing a dog. If it happens to be a large and fierce one, we may, at times, instantly recall similar encounters we might have had with other equally formidable creatures. Most importantly, we easily and instantly recall images of these earlier seen dogs. At the same time, our recollections are most likely faint, or hazy, and certainly not as clear and detailed as the fresh image of the dog in front of us.

Way back in 1988, Pentti Kanerva, then a scientist at the NASA Ames research centre in Mountain View, California, proposed an intriguing *mathematical* model of how a system resembling human memory might work. Kanerva's model was called 'Sparse Distributed Memory', or SDM[16] for short. There has been renewed interest in SDM and related models derived from it in recent years. In particular, a number of different approaches to modelling the human brain appear to be closely related both to each other and to SDM. Further, the mathematics behind these models *also* turns out to be that of Bayesian networks, closely related to our naive Bayes classifier, as well as to the Bayesian 'blackboard' reasoning architecture we saw in Chapter 4. Thus, memories and predictive models appear to be intimately related, both mathematically and with regard to their actual instantiation in the human brain. Finally, techniques based on these brain-like memory-prediction models are just beginning to get applied in a variety of applications, and eventually maybe even the web. Let us see how, beginning with Kanerva's SDM.

Each of us view many hundreds of millions of images each year as part of our normal waking existence. For instance, within 12 waking hours we might see and process over a million images (assuming our retina captures 25 images per second, which is the rate at which a high-quality film needs to be played). If our memory worked like Google, we would store each of these images as a separate document, or at least as a video sequence, so that any picture could be retrieved whenever we need it.

Clearly our memories do not store every single image in full fidelity; rather, we may be hard pressed to remember the clothes worn by a colleague who just walked out the door. Kanerva's SDM also does not explicitly store all the images it experiences. Yet, when presented with a fresh image, the SDM reconstructs a closely related image that somehow 'represents' the sum total of similar images it may have experienced in the past. Thus, presented with a large, fierce dog, the SDM produces a *similar* dog-like image constructed from its past memory, but which may not be exactly the same as any image it actually experienced. In a sense, our own memory behaves in a similar manner; the images we recall are rarely exact replicas of our actual experience.

Imagine our animal-viewing computer once more, but this time instead of a few summarizing features such as size or shape, our computer is presented with a complete image of the animal in all its detail. However, for simplicity, in our discussion we assume it is a true 'black-and-white' image, not even greyscale. In other words, however dense in pixels the image may be, each pixel in the image is either black or white. Suppose each image is a 100×100 grid of such pixels; then each image is defined by a bit-pattern comprised of 10,000 bits, with a one indicating a black pixel and a zero a white one. (Note that to incorporate colour, we merely need more bits per pixel, instead of just one.)

Kanerva's SDM relies on some interesting and counter-intuitive properties of very large bit-patterns, also called 'high-dimensional spaces', such as the 10,000-bit patterns representing each moderately sharp 100 × 100 image. First of all, there are an awful lot of possible such patterns: just as there are four two-bit patterns (00, 01, 10, and 11), eight three-bit patterns, and so on, so there are 2^{10000} possible 10,000-bit patterns. This is more than the number of electrons in the universe, more than the number of seconds since the beginning of the universe, and certainly far more than the number of images we might ever need to process.

Next, and perhaps quite obviously, any two *randomly chosen* patterns differ, on the average, in about 5,000 places. Just as obvious might be the fact that half of all possible patterns, i.e., half the entire 'space', is further than 5,000 bits from a chosen pattern, or 'point' in this space, with the remaining half being closer than 5,000 bits to this point.

Now come the most unexpected set of facts about high-dimensional spaces: how many patterns are within, say, 4,700 of a chosen pattern? Surprisingly, only 10^{-10}, or less than a one ten-billionth of the total space is 300 bits closer than the average (i.e., 5,000) to any point. In other words, by merely requiring 300 more bits of agreement with our chosen pattern (as compared to the average distance of 5,000), we eliminate all but one ten-billionth of possible patterns. If we increase our tolerance to say 4,800, we get many more points, but still less than one ten-thousandth of the space is within 4,800 of our initial point.

What do these observations mean from the perspective of storing and retrieving 10,000-bit patterns? The properties of high-dimensional spaces mean that once we have observed an image, we can be sure that any subsequent image of the same animal that is even slightly close to resembling the original, even differing in as many as 47% of the bits, will still be far closer to the original one as compared to any other unrelated image.

In a sense, this behaviour resembles our own human ability to recognize and recall from the faintest of clues. For example, imagine a (pure) black-and-white picture of your dog; if we randomly change all the bits, i.e., the chance that a bit remains the same is only 50%, the image becomes unrecognizable. However if fewer, but still a reasonable fraction, of the bits are scrambled, say as many as a third, then a very faint outline of our dog becomes recognizable even in the highly distorted image. Notice however, the maths doesn't quite add up: we should be able to flip 47% of the bits and still recognize our dog, since *almost* no other image is even within the generous tolerance of 4,700 bits in the space 10,000 bits. In reality we cannot tolerate so much noise. Why?

The trouble is that we need to compare our new image with the past set of images we have seen and stored, somehow. The space of 10,000-bit patterns is, as we have seen, huge indeed. But so is the collection of images we may possibly observe. Searching such a vast collection of images using a conventional index, such as the one that Google keeps for documents, is close to impossible. Kanerva showed how such extremely large collections of high-dimensional bit-patterns can be stored and retrieved efficiently. His procedure further exploits the properties of high-dimensional spaces; however, in the process we find that multiple images 'experienced' by his 'memory' system get blurred, much as do our own memories. So the actual amount of noise that can be tolerated is lower than the 47% suggested by the pure mathematics of high dimensions.

Kanerva's scheme uses only a fraction of the possible high-dimensional space, say 'only' 10 million randomly chosen points, called 'hard locations'; it is therefore called a *sparse* memory. Instead of storing all the bit-patterns it observes explicitly, each pattern is mapped to a small number of these hard locations, so the memory of any pattern is *distributed* across all these locations. Hence the name 'Sparse Distributed Memory'.

This is how SDM works. Whenever it sees a new pattern, the SDM finds all hard locations within, say, 4,800 bits of the input pattern. Since at most a ten-thousandth of the space is within this distance, it will contain a few hundred hard locations, on average. Each hard location keeps count of the number of times it sees a pattern that matches, or fails to match, each of its 10,000 bits. In other words, 10,000 numbers are kept alongside each hard location. These numbers serve as 'counters' that are either incremented or decremented based on whether the new pattern matches or does not match in the respective bit location. Note that an input pattern only affects a few hundred hard locations out of the total of 10 million, so the computational cost of storing a pattern remains tractable. Now, when we want to retrieve a pattern corresponding to a new input, all bit-counters in the hard locations to which this pattern maps are summed up, resulting in a set of 10,000 numbers. The output pattern is obtained by placing a one in any location where the sum exceeds a fixed threshold.

So, images are not explicitly stored in the SDM. Instead they are 'remembered' via a distributed representation across the few hard locations to which each maps. The large number of hard locations, together with the special properties of high-dimensional spaces, result in the SDM being able to recall complete images even when presented with highly distorted or partial inputs, in much the same manner as humans do.

So far we have described using an SDM as a memory. In fact it is an example of an 'auto-associative' memory, where a pattern is retrieved using an approximate version of itself as input. Another way to use the SDM is in a 'hetero-associative' manner, to store a *sequence* of patterns, such as a sequence of images. In such a case, each pattern is used to store the next pattern in the sequence: when incrementing the counters at hard locations, the next pattern in a sequence is used rather than the one used to choose the hard locations themselves. In this avatar, the SDM becomes a sequence memory, which can remember complex sequences of patterns, and also *predict* the next few patterns in a sequence. For example, Rao and Fuentes[103] have used an SDM to train a robot using a sequence of images of what it 'sees' and 'does' on its mission. On subsequent missions the robot is able, via its SDM, to not only remember what it had seen before but predict the image it expected to see as well as its next actions, and all this using real camera images with errors due to noise, orientation, lighting, etc.

Returning now to the web. Another interesting application of SDM has been in the arena of 'web analytics'. Every time a user visits a website, he leaves a trail of information that traces his behaviour on the site: each button clicked, each page navigated to, how much time spent on each page, etc. All these activities of a user surfing the site are logged, along with the internet address from where the user connects, or any cookies* that could serve to identify the same user reappearing again in later web-surfing sessions. Researchers from China and Sweden recently[104] used a technique called random indexing, which is based on Kanerva's SDM, to remember, understand, and ultimately predict the behaviour of web users.

Sparse Distributed Memories can be used to remember and predict behaviour in a variety of situations, and are capable of exhibiting behaviour that resembles human 'remembering', which is both approximate as well as represents cumulative experience. In this sense we can view SDM as a rational model for some aspects of human memory. But what about the way SDM is constructed? Does this have anything to do with how brains consisting of billions of neurons work? As it turns out, the SDM architecture itself is also closely related to the neural network models we have seen earlier that attempt to mimic brain structure.

Suppose an SDM has N hard-locations (we used 10 million in our earlier example), with which incoming bit-patterns are compared. Think of each hard location as a neuron connected to all the bits of the input. Each such neuron compares its input to its particular bit-pattern, and becomes 'active' if the input pattern is close enough to

---

* A 'cookie' is a secret number that a website asks a user's browser to remember, so that the site can track the same user across his multiple visits.

its own. Further, the *outputs* of all the hard-location neurons are also connected to an 'output-layer' of *n* neurons (where *n* is the size of the bit-patterns that the SDM stores; in our example it was 10,000), with their synapse strengths being the 'counters' of the SDM. When a bit-pattern is 'observed', the active neurons adjust their output synapse strengths. Those corresponding to matching locations are adjusted upwards, and non-matching ones downwards. This constitutes the learning process. During prediction, on the other hand, an output-layer neuron 'fires' only if the cumulative input it experiences, which is nothing but the sum of all the synapse strengths of hard-location neurons active for that input, is large enough. The bit-pattern retrieved by this neuronal version of SDM is a one in those positions corresponding to 'firing' output locations and a zero otherwise.

So, not only does the SDM model of memory mimic some aspects of human memory, but it can also be represented as a neural network that 'learns' to remember. It thus appears that neural networks can also remember, recall, and abstract from a vast number of experiences, in addition to learning predictive models, as we described earlier.

* * *

If you think about what SDM is doing, it is mapping a high-dimensional object onto a relatively smaller number of hard locations. This is in some ways similar to locality sensitive hashing (LSH), which we have seen earlier in both Chapter 1, 'Look' and Chapter 3, 'Learn'. Just as SDM uses a number of hard locations, LSH, if you recall, computes a small number of hash values for each object. Such a hash function could be the contents of a random page when one is trying to find duplicate books, or a 'min-hash' value, as described in Chapter 3, when one wants to club similar books, or, more generally, any similar objects together. All we ask is that it be highly likely (but not certain) that two similar objects, be they books, or even 10,000-bit patterns, have the same hash value.

To understand the relationship between these two techniques, LSH and SDM, let us see how they might be used with some 10,000-bit patterns arising in an important security application—fingerprint matching. Figure 4 shows a human fingerprint. Fingerprints are characterized by particular features such as ridge endings, bifurcations, and short ridges, which are also high-

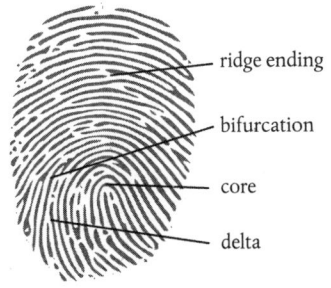

FIGURE 4 Minutiae (fingerprint)

lighted in the figure. Two fingerprints match if their minutiae match, i.e., both have the same kind of minutiae points at the same position. Suppose we lay a 100 × 100 grid on a fingerprint image. These 10,000 grid cells can be converted into a 10,000-bit pattern that has a one if a grid cell contains a minutiae point, and a zero otherwise. Let us see how we might group a large number of such 10,000-bit patterns into clusters containing similar fingerprints using LSH. (For simplicity, we do not worry about which kind of minutiae is where; in other words, we assume only one type of minutiae.)

Suppose the chance of any random grid position having a minutiae is 0.2, i.e., 20%. However, if we have two prints from the same person, and one of them has a minutiae-point at a particular position, then the chance that the other print also has a minutiae at that position is much higher, say 0.9.

Now let us choose three grid cells at random; each fingerprint is hashed a value of 1 if all three of these positions have minutiae, and to 0 otherwise. The chance that two prints from different persons get a hash value of 1 is $0.2^3 \times 0.2^3$, because the chance of a random position having minutiae is 0.2, and we want six unrelated cells to all have minutiae. This works out to 0.000064, a rather small chance indeed. But if the two prints are from the same person, then the chance of the first print getting a hash value of 1 is still 0.2^3, but the second print now has a 0.9^3 chance of having minutiae in all three positions. So for prints that are supposed to 'match', the chance of them both getting a hash value of 1 is $0.2^3 \times 0.9^3$, which works out to 0.006, slightly larger than before.

Still, the prospect of clustering fingerprints using these two hash values does not inspire confidence, if the chance of matching prints getting a hash value of 1 is a mere 0.6%. In other words, there is a $1 - 0.006$ or 99.4% chance that they do not get hashed to a 1.

But there is still hope. After all, there are many ways to choose three random grid cells to define our hashing strategy; in fact there are 161,700 ways. (For the mathematically minded, there are $^{100}C_3 = 161,700$ ways to choose three things out of a hundred.) Suppose we use just a thousand of them, i.e., a thousand different hash functions, each defined using a different triplet of grid positions. Now, the chance that two prints from the same person do *not* match in all thousand hash values is 0.994^{1000}; conversely, the chance that at least *one* of the thousand hash values match is $1 - 0.994^{1000}$, which works out to 0.997, or 99.7%. On the other hand, if the two prints came from *different* persons, then the chance that they do *not* hash to the same value for one particular hash-function is $1 - 0.000064$, or 0.999936. So the chance that these two prints get matched in one of the thousand hash-values is $1 - 0.999936^{1000}$, which works out to 0.062, or a mere 6%.

Now our calculations do indeed inspire confidence: prints are put in the same cluster if they match in at least one of the thousand hash values. The chance that two prints from the same person end up in the same cluster is 97%, whereas prints from two different persons will get into the same group only 6% of the time.

It is important to note that the LSH technique never explicitly compares pairs of fingerprints. It only requires computing a thousand hash values per print independently of others. Thereafter similar prints end up being grouped together, albeit implicitly by their hash values. Another way to think about this process is that it is similar to building an inverted index as we did for documents in Chapter 1. Instead of millions of words we have a thousand triplets of grid cells. A print is said to contain one such 'word' if it happens to have minutiae at all three positions, i.e., has a hash value of 1 according to this procedure. Once we have such an index, checking for matching prints is easy. Given a fresh print, we note those hash functions for which this print gets a hash-value of 1, and merely collect other prints from the index that also hash to a 1 for any of the same hash functions.

Last but not least, the LSH procedure is related to SDM in the sense that they both compute *sparse* representations of high-dimensional objects such as fingerprints or documents. In the case of SDM, a relatively small number of hard locations are used, whereas in LSH we use a small number of hash functions to index objects. Of course, a major difference between the two approaches is that LSH explicitly stores every object, merely indexing it with hash-values. In contrast, SDM stores 'impressions' about each object that it 'sees' in the counters associated to every hard location. As a result, whereas LSH can retrieve each object that it has previously stored, SDM can only reconstruct objects based on past experience, somewhat similar to how human brains presumably recall memories. We return now to techniques that attempt to mimic the brain, which, as we shall see, also happen to share the property of using sparse representations.

Sequence Memory

There has been a resurgence of interest in neural models of the brain in recent years, along with their utility as computational memories and prediction engines. This is due also in part to recent progress in more faithfully modelling the neocortex of the human brain. Additionally, such neocortical models have, most surprisingly, been shown to be closely related to another emerging set of techniques called *deep belief networks* based on good old Bayesian mathematics. Last but not least, some properties of the brain's internal wiring appear to have a similar structure to how the web itself is wired. Thus, many threads are coming together, many of which are beginning to be referred to as 'Deep Machine Learning' techniques;[105] and all of these have something to do with predicting the future.

One of the unlikely pioneers in furthering and reviving the cause of research on neural computational models is Jeff Hawkins. Unlikely, because Hawkins is probably better known as an entrepreneur and pioneer in the realm of hand-held computing: he is the inventor of the Palm Pilot and Handspring Treo, and was the founder of both these companies in the 1990s. In 2002 Hawkins founded the Redwood Centre for Neuroscience at the University of California, Berkeley. As he lucidly explains in his 2004 book[106] *On Intelligence*, Hawkins believes that the brain is essentially a 'memory-prediction' engine. Hawkins's neural model, called 'hierarchical temporal memory' (HTM) combines both aspects of neural networks that we have seen earlier, i.e., prediction and memory. Further, HTM also postulates and justifies a large-scale structure for neural networks that mimics properties of the real human brain as recently established by neuroscience studies. Most recently, in 2005 Hawkins founded Numenta, a start-up dedicated to building predictive computational technology based on models of the human neocortex and the HTM-based memory-prediction algorithm.

Neuroscience researchers have studied the physical anatomy of the brain for years. Using a variety of imaging technologies they have been able to pinpoint regions of the brain associated with vision, speech, hearing, movement control, short-term and long-term memories, etc. One important fact that emerges from such studies is that all high-level, or 'intelligent', tasks such as seeing, listening, language, and planning appear to be performed by the *neocortex*, a thin outer layer of brain tissue that is unique to mammalian brains. Further, and not surprisingly, humans have the largest neocortex amongst all mammals. Given the diverse nature of functions performed by the brain, and especially the neocortex, one might expect that the brain itself, including the neocortex, would be comprised of a number of sub-organs with vastly different structures, much as the stomach differs from the liver, or the lungs from the heart. However, this is not the case, as discovered and documented by the neuroscientist Vernon Mountcastle in 1978. In his paper[107] co-authored with Gerald M. Edelman, Mountcastle pointed out that the neocortex is remarkably uniform in appearance and structure. He goes on to propose that because all parts of the neocortex look the same, perhaps they are also operating a common procedure that nevertheless miraculously accomplishes all these diverse high-level functions.

In fact, clinical studies corroborate Mountcastle's supposition. It turns out that in totally blind people, regions of the brain normally active during visual tasks are instead activated by auditory input. It is known that blind people develop an enhanced sense of hearing; perhaps it is because larger parts of the neocortex, including unused portions normally dedicated to vision, are instead used to process sound. But how can that be? How can such seemingly different tasks be performed by the same kind of structure? We have seen the ability of neural networks to learn models. The fact is that the basic structure of neural networks is the same; they just end up performing different memory-prediction tasks depending on which input patterns are presented to them. Hawkins's hierarchical temporal memory, or HTM, proposes how such neural networks are wired together in a manner resembling the brain, so as to not only perform simple prediction tasks but also possibly produce higher-level 'thought'. As of today however, no evidence of 'higher-level thought' has emerged from any HTM implementation. Nevertheless, the HTM model is an interesting potential rational model to understand how high-level pattern recognition arises in brains.

* * *

While the details of HTM are fairly involved, the core HTM algorithm combines aspects of SDM in both space and time so as to learn to recognize not only complex patterns, but simultaneously also *sequences* of patterns.

An HTM is comprised of a hierarchy of *regions*, each consisting of a large number of neurons, or cells. We can view each cell as being connected to a set of inputs that receive bits from sensory organs or from other regions in the HTM hierarchy. For comparison with our SDM example, a region might have 10,000 inputs, representing, for example, a small 100 × 100 pixel region of the visual field. Each cell in such a region is connected by synapses to a few hundred inputs from amongst the 10,000 possible ones, seemingly at random. When the region observes an input pattern (i.e., an image) each cell sums up its random sample of the pattern's bits to decide whether it is ready to 'fire'. If the sum of its inputs crosses a threshold, a cell becomes ready to fire, else it remains off. For some input patterns only a small number of cells might be ready to fire. In other cases almost all the cells may be 'excited'. However, the HTM also ensures that in either case, only a small number of cells fire. It does this through a process of *inhibition*, whereby cells that are ready to fire inhibit those in their vicinity, so that only the strongest few of the excited cells actually fire.

As a result, the HTM converts its inputs into a sparse representation, where only a few cells fire, in much the same manner as the SDM mapped each input to a sparse set of hard locations. For example, each 10,000-bit input pattern may result in only 100 cells firing. However, because of the properties of long bit-sequences, two patterns that are close to each other will usually result in a strong overlap in the cells that they trigger, so often over 75 of these 100 will match. At the same time, if two patterns are not close, usually fewer than 25 cells would be triggered by both patterns. However the sparse representation is still able to discriminate between patterns, because of the peculiar properties of high-dimensional spaces, as we saw in SDM.

Before delving into how HTM deals with sequences, let us first see how sparse representations work in a hierarchy of regions. Imagine an image of a room with many objects. The lowest-level regions in the HTM hierarchy will form sparse representations of low-level features such as edges and planes as seen in the small portion of the visual input handled by the region's cells. These sparse representations are passed on as inputs to higher-level regions, which also receive inputs from other similar low-level regions responsible for the rest of the visual field of view. A higher-level region also uses the same HTM algorithm. However, since its inputs are each sparse and come from many different parts of the visual field, the sparse representation it in turn creates will represent higher-level objects, such as eyes and hair. Even higher-level regions might be able to represent a human face, so as to eventually even recognize particular faces.

* * *

Now let us turn to sequences. It may seem that sequences of patterns are important only in temporal input streams, such as the sounds we hear. However, as it turns out, sequences are ubiquitous. If one observes oneself a bit, one will realize that even while looking at an image, such as a human face, one's eyes are always moving; these movements are called *saccades*. Thus, the visual inputs arriving at the neocortex are also sequences, rather than a constant image, even whilst we might be looking fixedly at a single scene.

The way the HTM algorithm learns sequences is its real strength. While earlier we considered a region as comprising a number of cells, now extend this picture to one where instead of a cell we have a *column* of cells, say four. Such a columnar structure is actually observed by neuroscientific studies of real brains, where the number of neurons in a column number varies between five and 15 depending on the region of the cortex one looks at.

Now suppose that the sparse representation learned by this region always involves around a hundred active cells directly triggered by inputs, each of which is now actually a column of four cells; so we should really be talking about active columns, not cells. By using different combinations of columnar cells the region manages to remember sequences of patterns in addition to the patterns themselves. For any particular combination of a hundred columns, there are 4^{100} possible combinations involving exactly these hundred columns with one cell per column being active. In the HTM algorithm, these possible combinations are used to represent *sequences* of patterns in which the particular hundred-column sparse pattern happens to occur. Thus, the region is able to keep track of as many as 4^{100} different sequences in which our hundred-column spares pattern might occur, which is a very large number in indeed.

In actual brains it is found that only 10% of the connections within a region are to other regions, either below or above it in the hierarchy. The rest are lateral, inter-region connections, which Hawkins speculates are responsible for learning sequences of patterns. For example, one of the four 'predictive' cells in a column might have connections to a random set of, say, a thousand columns in the same region. When some of these columns fire in sequence, one after another, such lateral connections are strengthened. Subsequently, if even a small number, as small as say five, of the strongly linked lateral columns are found to be active, the predictive cell becomes 'ready' and 'expects' that it will become active soon. If this prophecy is fulfilled, the lateral synapses are further strengthened, else they are weakened. In effect the predictive cells behave like a sparse memory in 'time' rather than space, and end up learning sequences.

So the combination of ready cells and those that actually become active constitute the output of an HTM region. Not only is this input a sparse representation in space, it is also a sparse representation in time. The columns include predictive cells that are 'ready' to fire, expecting inputs based on past sequences. Further, when sequences repeat, the combined set of both ready and active cells stays 'on' for longer than only the active cells in the actual input image. It is in this sense that we might imagine that our thoughts and memories are comprised, not of static patterns, but of patterns of neuronal firing sequences over time.

Finally, and very importantly, an important feature of both the HTM structure and that of real brains is that the flow of activation from region to region is not only 'up' the hierarchy from lower- to higher-level regions, but also *down* the hierarchy from higher-level regions to lower ones. But what could higher-level regions offer lower ones, since they are not connected to any inputs? The answer is *predictions*. Higher-level regions form aggregated and therefore possibly more *abstract* representations in both space and time. Thus a higher-level region could recognize a sequence of musical notes and predict the next one; or could watch a movie and predict that a person walking towards a banana skin might soon fall down.

When predictions flow down the hierarchy and are reconfirmed by actual experience they reinforce learning. Such reinforcement might even be viewed as mimicking the 'feeling of satisfaction' that we sometimes experience when finally recognizing what we see. On the other hand, when predictions are refuted by experience, such as when hearing a new melody, or staring at a piece of very abstract modern art, they stimulate higher levels of the hierarchy to cause new high-level abstractions to be formed and re-formed, until some level of 'satisfaction' with current experience is achieved. Thus, if one stares at the abstract picture in Figure 5, one might at first be confused as to whether there is any recognizable object in it. But after a while a man's face might appear. If the HTM model is correct, what has just happened is that the predictions made in lower-level regions could not be confirmed, and so higher-level ones get involved. However, higher levels are also slower, because of the aggregation in time that takes place between regions, in addition to spatial aggregation. So it takes longer to 'see' the face in this abstract image.

According to Hawkins, confirmation of predictions, be they at lower levels or higher ones, is the essence of *understanding*; and the process of continuously learning, remembering, and making predictions is the essence of *thought*. Whether or not this is the case remains, as of today at least, in the realm of speculation. Nevertheless the HTM model certainly sheds much-needed fresh light on what could possibly be going on within brains, as well as the almost-ubiquitous role that *prediction* plays in intelligent thought and making sense of the world.

Deep Beliefs

Whether or not Hawkins's memory-prediction architecture is related to how brains function, or even whether or not the cortically inspired learning algorithms

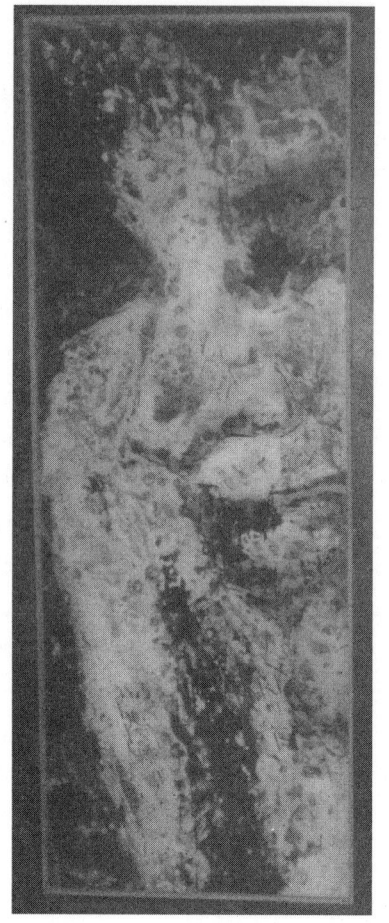

FIGURE 5 Face painting

it proposes actually function better than other mathematical approaches, there are certainly a few important things to learn from the approach it adopts. First, it postulates that predicting the future serves as a unifying *goal* for all cerebral functions. The ability to predict based on past experience is critical for guessing the next few frames received by our visual cortex as we scan a familiar face, as well as to imagine what might soon happen if we dropped a banana skin on the pavement. According to Hawkins, brains are continuously predicting, remembering, and learning. Moreover, he claims that, fundamentally, this is *all* that they do. More complex brains, such as mammals and then humans, do this much better than others, and presumably this gives them an evolutionary advantage, which also explains why this ability is present. Finally, higher-level thought of all forms can be traced ultimately to prediction, coupled with the layered, hierarchical structure of many HTM regions; with higher-level concepts being formed at higher levels of the HTM hierarchy.

Another important point that Hawkins makes is to reinforce Mountcastle's observation of the uniformity of the actual neocortex. Hawkins postulates that a single HTM-like cortical learning algorithm is at work in the brain, processing all types of sensory inputs as well as producing higher-level thought and memory. Precisely because of the variety of sensory input being processed in a seemingly uniform manner, Hawkins speculates that predictions, at least as produced by higher layers of the HTM hierarchy, are based on *invariant representations* of objects. Higher layers aggregate inputs from lower levels in both space and time to form models for higher-level concepts, such as a song, a ball, or a box. These invariant concepts get triggered regardless of the sensory route by which they are experienced, e.g., by touch, vision, or sound. Thus, the 'same' neural structure for 'ball' is triggered whether one looks at a ball with one's eyes, or feels a ball while blindfolded. In fact, a closely related philosophical problem was posed by the 18th-century philosopher William Molyneux:

> Suppose a man born blind, and now adult, and taught by his touch to distinguish between a cube and a sphere of the same metal, and nighly of the same bigness, so as to tell, when he felt one and the other, which is the cube, which is the sphere. Suppose then the cube and the sphere placed on a table, and the blind man made to see: query, Whether by his

sight, before he touched them, he could now distinguish and tell which is the globe, which the cube?[108]

Molyneux is asking whether basic concepts, such as 'cube' and 'sphere', are innate, i.e., something we are born with. If they are, then both his touch and sight would activate the same innate concept. From the perspective of Hawkins's model, the question arises as to the relationship between the invariant representation of the sphere based on touch alone, and that learned from sight. Are these the same or not? If so, why; if not, how are we able to imagine a sphere when touching it while blindfolded?

Quite surprisingly, it recently became possible to test some aspects of both the invariant representation hypothesis as well as Molyneux's problem, *experimentally*, with human subjects. In 2003, Pawan Sinha, whose team also supplied us with the pong images in Figure 2, was able to witness exactly the scenario imagined by Molyneux. Pawan's pioneering clinical work in India was able to return the gift of sight to many children born 'blind'. How he achieved this is a medical and social miracle in itself, which we do not have the space to describe here. What Pawan found is that children who could easily recognize a sphere or a cube based on their experience touching it, could *not* distinguish between the two based solely on their now miraculously restored power of sight. Thus Molyneux's philosophical poser was answered, experimentally, in the negative.[109]

What about the idea of invariant representations, though? It turns out that while the children could not at first visually discern cubes from spheres, they could begin to do so quite soon after they were allowed to touch the objects while also seeing them. Further, within weeks of getting their sight back, they also developed the ability to distinguish between two new objects, first by sight and then by touch when blindfolded, like anyone else. It appears that their visual invariant representations developed very rapidly, and became connected to tactile ones. Their brains rewired themselves to process and account for the new stream of visual input. Pawan's surprising experimental observations appear to confirm Hawkins's ideas on invariant representations, as well as Mountcastle's postulate regarding the uniformity and plasticity of the brain.

Of course, even if the correspondence between Hawkins's HTM structure and that of actual brains is taken as plausible, the connection between the predictive abilities of a hierarchically organized neocortex and higher-level thought has not been explained, either by Hawkins, or by anyone else as of today. It certainly remains an enduring mystery: how do logic, reasoning, or feelings arise from the predictive efforts of billions of neurons connected by quadrillions of synapses? The neuroscientist Antonio Damasio does propose some ideas in his recent book[75] *Self Comes to Mind*; we shall return to some of his ideas in the Epilogue, 'Purpose'.

* * *

At a more scientific level however, the memory-prediction-based learning framework and the role it gives to prediction as a primary goal do serve to unify the two learning paradigms we have discussed often enough so far, i.e., *supervised* versus *unsupervised* learning. Recall that in supervised learning, such as the naive Bayes classifier we saw in Chapter 3, the learning algorithm uses a large number of *labelled* instances to learn its model, which in the case of naive Bayes was merely the likelihood or probabilities. The learned model is then used to assign labels to future instances, i.e., *predict* what they must be, based on past experience. In unsupervised learning, on the other hand, instances are grouped into clusters based on their mutual similarity: there are no labels, only clusters characterized by a set of similar features. Thus, close-up pictures of faces naturally emerge as a cluster amongst a large personal photo collection. However, there is no label, such as 'faces' or anything else meaningful assigned to this subset by the unsupervised learning system.

Now let us re-examine what the memory-prediction model of Hawkins's HTM does. Two kinds of unsupervised clustering are taking place, in 'space', i.e., across pieces of each input pattern as they get mapped to sparse patterns of *columns*, as well as in *time*, so that similar *sequences* of patterns are mapped to similar sets of columnar *cells*. Now imagine for the moment that clusters of patterns and sequences have been learned. In Hawkins's HTM, these are now used to make predictions about future inputs, i.e., as to which previously recognized cluster is possibly being reobserved. If the predictions indeed appear to be confirmed by the input, this confirmation works like a supervised training sample that strengthens, i.e., *reinforces*, the spatial and temporal models that the clusters collectively represent. Thus, the central role of prediction is to enhance unsupervised learning with supervision, using previously learned models as proxy 'labels'. Of course, unsupervised clustering continues in parallel, thus unifying the two modes of learning.

Hawkins's HTM is not the first approach to unify supervised and unsupervised learning. The field of *reinforcement learning* is a rich and promising area of current research that studies many different approaches that have nothing to do with neural models or mimicking brain-like structures. Similarly, hierarchical neural models based on Bayesian mathematics, currently referred to as *deep belief networks*, are very similar to HTM, as has also been pointed out by Hawkins and his team[110] as well as others.[111] Mathematically linking reinforcement learning and deep belief networks is another important area attracting current research interest.

Last but not least, the layered structure and the mixing of bottom-up and top-down reasoning as in the blackboard architectures we described in Chapter 4, appear similar to the hierarchical structure of deep-belief networks as well as that of neocortical models such as HTM. The idea of using predictions from higher layers to direct lower-level reasoning is also a common feature of all these models.

Most importantly, blackboard architectures are examples of *symbolic* reasoning, using logic, classical or otherwise, on 'labelled' concepts. The fact that the symbolic reasoning of blackboard systems and the pattern-matching-based approach of connectionist-neural as well as probabilistic-network models share many similar features, leads us to hope that links between brain-like and symbolic computational models will be made stronger by future research. Progress in this direction should both lead to a better understanding of the brain and enable us to build more intelligent applications.

Network Science

We return now to the web. Do the neuroscientific studies of the brain or neural computational models for prediction have any connection with the size and structure of the web?

How much information is there on the internet? There are at least 75 million servers in the world today, of which a very large fraction are connected to the internet and involved in publishing a part of the web. The amount of data stored in the *indexed* web can be estimated as a few dozen petabytes, where a petabyte is 10^{12}, i.e., 1 with 12 zeros. Google's few million servers index the 50 billion pages or so on the internet. Other studies have shown that the average web page is about half a megabyte.[112] The arithmetic adds up to 25 petabytes. Clearly, while the average web-page size is small, photo and video content are much bigger and growing faster. Further, we have not considered the deep web either, so this is probably a gross underestimate.

Still, we can safely conclude that are at least a few dozen petabytes on the web today. But how much information *could* be stored on the 75 million or so servers in the world? If each server has about a terabyte of data (average PCs have half a terabyte today), this works out to 75,000 petabytes.

As we noted before, the way information is stored and indexed in the web is very different from the brain-motivated techniques discussed earlier. web pages themselves are stored on their respective sites, whose addresses Google inserts into its vast inverted index. The brain, on the other hand, stores information very differently, using mechanisms closer to the sparse-distributed or hierarchical-temporal models suggested by Kanerva and Hawkins. As far as we can tell, there is no equivalent of the Google index for our memories. Instead, information is stored in the synapses that connect the brain's myriad neurons, and retrieved *approximately* when needed in the course of its continuous efforts to predict and respond to external stimuli, at all levels.

There is general agreement that the human brain contains about a hundred billion neurons. Each neuron is connected to other neurons via thousands of synapses, which therefore number in the hundreds of trillions. How much information is stored in these connections? Actually it is quite difficult, if not impossible, to estimate this number. After all, we do not really know how the brain stores information. If Hawkins's HTM is taken as a rational model though, information in the brain is more likely to be comprised of *sequences* of patterns, rather than the static patterns of bits that make up the web pages stored in millions of servers. Sequences, are in principle, infinite, unless we limit their length. Limits on the lengths of sequences that can be stored and retrieved in reasonable time therefore depend on how *fast* the brain operates, which in turn determines how many useful sequences it might be able to store.

Hawkins proposes a 'one-hundred-step rule'. It is known that neurons fire at a rate of 200 Hz, i.e., each firing takes 5 milliseconds or so. Assuming that it takes us around half a second to recognize a face or an object, this is time enough for about a hundred neurons to fire in sequence. In other words, simple memories might well be stored as sequences of a hundred 'firing steps': recognition happens when prediction based on past experience, as embodied in the strengths of synapses, matches such an input sequence as received from the senses.

Of the 100 billion or so neurons, let us imagine only a billion of them as 'inputs', so that each input fires a hundred other neurons 'higher up' in the hierarchical structure postulated by Hawkins. Now, imagine a sparse distributed memory of a billion bits, and on top of that sequences of up to a hundred such patterns. Again, in Hawkins's model these are represented by the equivalent of a Sparse Distributed Memory, but in *time* rather than space. The number of possible hundred-step-long patterns of a billion bits is truly huge. Further, using reasonably straightforward back-of-the-envelope calculations based on the properties of sparse memories, which however do not go into the details, we can conclude that the number of such 1,000-bit, hundred-step memories that a Hawkins-like HTM can store is many orders of magnitude more than could possibly be stored in the web. A few hundred or even thousands of petabytes cannot come anywhere close.

At the same time, and in stark contrast, the 'hardware' in the brain, on the face of it, is far *less* powerful than the collection of computers that power the web. We have already seen that neurons operate at a speed of 200 Hz. The lowest end of PCs available today operate 5 *to* 10 *million* times faster than such a neuron, i.e., a few GHz (gigahertz). Next, each of the 75 million servers in the world today typically has well over a billion transistors. Thus the total number of transistors is in the thousands of quadrillions range. Even assuming we need a few thousand transistors to mimic individual neurons and synapses in 'silicon', the raw hardware capacity of the web today is definitely comparable to that of a human brain. Moreover, it is many millions of times faster.

Clearly the web appears to be a much 'faster' machine than the brain, while the brain is far more copious in memory. So it is indeed paradoxical that the web-intelligence applications of today rely so heavily on storing and retrieving what we think is big data, rather than on exploiting the computational power of millions of computers. Instead, it appears far more likely that the computational prowess of the web could better serve to augment our own relatively limited reasoning speed, rather than our much more voluminous memories. I shall return to such speculations towards the end of the book.

* * *

Now let us consider the network of connections between neurons in the brain, and compare this with the connections that comprise the web. In the case of the web, there are at least two different 'networks' to consider. Most inquiries into the network structure of the web focus on the hyperlinks between web pages; indeed, as we have seen early on, the famous PageRank algorithm of Google indirectly uses this network of links to measure the importance of each web page. However, a different network is also at work in the web, i.e., that of the servers that power the internet and route traffic across its myriad links. Each time you issue a search query, or click a link in your browser, messages travel between servers via routers and fibre-optic communication lines. The same data-communications network also powers email, Facebook, Twitter, and e-commerce transactions.

No single organization owns the network of servers and communication links, which is actually the internet itself. There are many hundreds of internet service providers, or ISPs, that own parts of this massive computer network. ISPs work with each other through a complex, but clearly hierarchical, maze of agreements to route each other's traffic. The network itself is also hierarchical. There are the long-distance fibre-optic lines that move data across continents. Next come the intercontinental and country-specific lines, then metropolitan networks within a city, etc.

As we saw earlier, Hawkins's model of the neocortex also postulated a hierarchical structure. Unfortunately, it is rather difficult to physically verify whether the brain actually has a hierarchical structure of connections; after all, they are not laid out for us to observe like some organizational hierarchy. Further, 'hierarchical' is a very general statement—there can be many different ways to be hierarchical, as we shall see shortly. However, there are some simple properties about network structures that enable us to compare different networks with each other.

* * *

A popular property is the 'degree distribution'. A node in a network that is connected to d other nodes is said to have *degree d*. The fraction of nodes in a network that have degree d is called the degree distribution. For example, in a square mesh, such as a fishing net, every node has three or four connections. There are no nodes with, say, a hundred connections.

However, this is not the case for the network of hyperlinks that comprise the web. Here the degree distribution of the nodes, in this case web-pages, ranges from very small degree nodes, such as those pages that have just a few links pointing to or from them, to those that have literally millions of links, such as wikipedia.org (to which a *very* large fraction of pages link). The degree distribution of this web network is observed to follow a 'power law', i.e., the fraction of pages with d links is inversely proportional to d^r for some r. Through various exercises of mapping the web, r is believed to lie between 1.6 and 2.2; we can take it as 2 for illustration. What this means is that if there are a billion pages that have, say, ten links, i.e., degree 10, then there will be only a hundred thousand that have a thousand links. But the point is that such high-degree pages *will* be there. Further, there will also be pages, albeit only a handful, which have a hundred thousand links.

It turns out that the network structure of the internet itself, i.e., the servers and the links that physically connect them, also follows a power-law degree distribution. However, unlike the web of hyperlinks, this distribution is slightly different, in that very high degree nodes do not exist. This is understandable; after all, there is no physical barrier to hundreds of thousands of pages linking to Wikipedia. However, it is impossible to build a data centre that has a hundred thousand incoming communication links. The data communications network that comprises the internet follows a 'truncated' power-law degree distribution, which is just a normal power-law that stops beyond a certain maximum degree value.

Quite interestingly, studies[113] of neural connections using fMRI* studies appear to indicate that a similar truncated power-law distribution is followed in the brain.

Studying network structures and power-law distributions has become a very popular research topic. Many biological and social, as well as certain technological networks, such as the web and the internet, appear to have such properties. An important property that follows from a power-law distribution is that the network appears to be a 'small world', where any two nodes are connected by a relatively short path. We have all heard of the famous maxim saying that any two people in the world are connected by at most 'six degrees of separation'. It is indeed a small world, in this sense.

Why are small worlds useful? In the case of the internet, it is clearly desirable for a message to be able to get to its destination in the shortest possible number of 'hops'. Perhaps such small-world properties are useful in the brain as well, enabling diverse sensory inputs to rapidly mingle so as to easily form and access invariant representations. After all, the brain is much slower than the internet, and at most a hundred steps of neuronal connections can be traversed in a single instantaneous piece of thought. Small-world properties of the network make this limit a generous one; a hundred steps is more than enough to traverse between any two nodes of the internet, most pairs of web pages, and so possibly also any two neurons in the brain.

---

* *Functional* MRI studies where subjects are given tasks while their brain activity is monitored using MRI scans.

Since power laws and small-world properties have now been commonly found in a variety of biological and natural phenomena, these are today considered to be indicators of systems that can 'adapt' to their environment and behave in surprisingly complex, and yet sometimes predictive, ways.

* * *

What do we think now of 'predicting the future'? Rather than being the domain of soothsayers and astrologers, we find first that there are indeed ways to predict the future based on past experience. Building statistical models and finding efficient ways to store and recall 'memories' does allow us to make predictions. When these predictions are confirmed, they strengthen our models and reinforce stored memories further. Next, the mathematical principles of prediction and brain-inspired neural networks are closely linked, such as Hawkins's memory prediction framework, deep-belief networks and reinforcement learning. Finally, the computational prowess of the internet today rivals and in some ways exceeds that of the brain. Additionally, they are both examples of networks that exhibit a power-law structure with small-world properties that are now believed to be universal features of complex 'adaptive' systems capable of predictive behaviour. Lastly, all indications are that brains *can* not only predict, but that prediction is in fact their *primary* function—a key ingredient that allows us to 'connect the dots', make sense of the world, and, as we shall shortly see, also *control* it.

In principle, therefore, it appears that the internet is capable of making complex predictions. In pockets, and primarily driven by the needs of better online advertising, elements of prediction do show up in the algorithms that power the web. At the same time, the manner in which information is stored in the web is very different from how it is stored and used in the brain. Can the web exploit such radically different organizational principles, such as Hawkins's memory-prediction framework? It certainly has the computational capacity.

The real question is 'why?'. Web applications are driven by practical needs, such as advertising, search, and social networking. To the extent that learning, reasoning, and prediction are needed for these tasks, we certainly find the entire arsenal of artificial intelligence techniques being employed by the Googles of the world. If and when these giants are confronted with needs that challenge their more conventional computational structure, perhaps they will indeed begin to explore other alternatives. Of course, these may or may not end up being anything like the brain-inspired models of Hawkins. More likely, completely new techniques will be found, combining different approaches that are already showing signs of being deeply linked. For example, along the way, we might even find a way to connect higher-level reasoning with neural and statistical models.

As to 'why', we turn now, in Chapter 6, to how learning, reasoning, and prediction can be used to control the external environment. Perhaps the day is not far off when web applications will not only assist us in fulfilling our *information* needs, but also *control* the machines we rely on for our daily lives. In particular, we shall take a closer look at one such unlikely project that is well under way—Google's self-driving car.

6

CORRECT

Running on Autopilot

Last summer I took my family on a driving holiday in the American south-western desert covering many national parks. While driving along some of the long tracts of razor-straight highways, such as between Las Vegas and St George, Utah, I often fought drowsiness, not because of lack of sleep, but from the sheer monotony. A familiar experience for many, no doubt. Hardly any conscious thought is needed during such drives. It must be one's 'System 1', as per Kahneman, which is most certainly doing whatever work is needed. Nevertheless, sleep is not an option. In spite of all the marvellous features embedded in the modern car, the ability to drive itself is, sadly, still missing. The cruise-control button helps a bit, allowing one's feet to relax as the car's speed remains on an even keel. But the eyes and mind must remain awake and alert.

When, if ever, one wonders, will cars with a 'drive' button become as common as those with an automatic transmission? Is driving along a perfectly straight stretch of highway really that difficult? After all, we all know that a modern jetliner can fly on autopilot, allowing even a single pilot to read a novel while 'flying' the aircraft on a long transcontinental flight. In fact, the jetliner would fly itself perfectly even if the pilot dozed off for many minutes or even hours. We insist that at least one pilot be awake and alert only for our own peace of mind, so as to be able to adequately respond to any emergency situation that might arise.

First of all, the ubiquitous autopilot is itself quite a complex piece of equipment. Even to get a plane to fly perfectly straight along a desired heading at a fixed altitude takes a lot of work. The reason, as you must have guessed, is that nature, in the guise of the air on which our jetliner rides, can be quite unpredictable. Wind speeds and directions change continuously, even ever so slightly, requiring constant adjustments to the plane's engine power, ailerons, flaps, and rudder. In the absence of such adjustments, our jetliner would most certainly veer off course, or lose or gain speed, even dangerously enough to trigger a powered dive or a stall.

The unpredictable effects of the environment, which engineers call 'noise', result in almost *immediate* changes to an aircraft's heading, speed, and altitude. The aircraft's 'vital statistics' are continuously and directly being affected by the environment. In contrast, the impact of the natural environment is less immediately felt while driving along a perfectly straight and level, traffic-free highway. Rarely are crosswinds so strong as to cause one's car to stray. Nor are there clouds, rain, or turbulent air pockets. So, shouldn't it be easier to 'auto-drive' a car, once we know how to auto-fly a plane?

Sadly, this is not the case. As it happens, it is the very *immediacy* of the environment's effect on our jetliner that makes it easier to 'control' automatically. The aircraft is equipped with equipment that allows it to continuously sense its heading, speed, and altitude. Such 'sensors' are crucial in making it possible to control the plane and 'correct' for the noise it experiences. A small slowdown caused by increased headwind, and the autopilot immediately reacts by 'stepping on the gas'. A slight drift to the left, and the autopilot 'controller' responds by steering the plane ever so slightly to the right until it regains its desired heading. Hundreds of such minor corrections happen continuously, giving the illusion of perfectly steady and straight flight.

The autopilot's actions are exactly the kind of minute, continuous corrections that each of us performs, all the time, whether it is while riding a bicycle, or even during everyday walking. Our cochlear system, situated in our ears, provides us with our sense of balance, i.e., a continuous estimate of how upright we are, whether cycling or walking. Hardly any conscious thought is required, at least once we have learned to walk or ride. Our unconscious brain automatically issues muscle-control signals so as to keep us upright in response to any perceived deviations from our desired posture.

On the other hand, in the case of a hypothetical self-driving car the situation is not so happy. Suppose the seemingly razor-straight road suddenly curves, even a bit, towards the left. By the time the effects of this 'change in the environment' are 'felt' by the car in a form that can be sensed physically, we might already have driven off the right side of the road. Even if our car veers sharply to the left the minute a few bumps are felt, thereby managing to avert disaster, the experience such a manoeuvre gives the unfortunate passengers is far from desirable.

Human drivers make far greater use of their visual senses, than, say, a pilot of a jetliner in mid-flight. Vision allows the driver to continuously *look* out for and *predict* impending catastrophes, such as a curving road, or oncoming traffic, and avert disaster before it ever comes close to transpiring. Sadly, computer vision, i.e., enabling a machine to 'see' and understand the environment, is one of the most difficult and challenging areas in artificial intelligence. Automatic controllers that need to 'see' are far more challenging to build than, say, those that only need to 'feel'.

However, hope is on the horizon. Sebastian Thrun, formerly a professor of Computer Science at Stanford and now a Google Fellow, has been designing and building self-driving cars for much of the past decade. His latest prototype has now become Google's self-driving car, copies of which have already successfully driven themselves for hundreds of thousands of miles through California traffic.

* * *

Thrun's group at Stanford is not alone. Over the past decade, dozens of research groups across the world have teamed up with leading car manufacturers to compete in a race to build the world's first successful self-driving car. In 2007 DARPA, the US Defense Advanced Research Projects Agency, which funds a large fraction of university research in the US, announced its 'Urban Grand Challenge' competition directed at research groups working on self-driving cars. Previously such competitions, such as DARPA's 2005 event, had challenged self-driving vehicles to negotiate rough off-road terrain. Stanford's 'Stanley' car, also built by Thrun and his group, was the winner of this earlier competition. The urban challenge of 2007 focused on being able to drive in a simulated city environment, while obeying all traffic rules and avoiding other cars, and at the same time completing the course as fast as possible. So, for example, the self-driving cars had to 'decide' which lane to drive in, and when to overtake other cars, all by themselves with no human to direct them.

Of the 11 teams that competed in the final challenge event of November 2007, only six completed the 60-mile course successfully, and of these only three finished within the stipulated six hours. The winning car, from Carnegie Mellon University, took just over four hours. Under a half-hour behind them were the second- and third-placed teams, Sebastian Thrun's team from Stanford, followed by the team from Virgina Tech. Recently Google CEO Eric Schmidt revealed the importance the company places on this project, outlining a vision of driver-less cars and how they could transform the world by, for example, eliminating accidents caused by drunk-driving. But more on these and other possibilities later; first, let us examine exactly how a self-driving car, such as Stanford's 'Junior', the predecessor to Google's self-driving car, actually works.

* * *

Stanford's Junior[114] 'sees' using four lasers mounted on its roof. Each laser is angled downwards to cast its beam across the road ahead and around the car. Just like a radar, these lasers emit narrow pulses of high-intensity light and measure the time taken before the beam reaches an obstacle and gets reflected back, allowing them to determine the distance of the obstructing object. Each laser device emits over a million pulses per second, while rotating hundreds of times a second to provide a 360° view of the world. In addition to laser sensors, Junior is also equipped with a GPS unit, much like those in today's high-end mobile phones. The GPS is, however, a poor cousin to the laser sensors that provide accuracies of a few centimetres, compared to the GPS's rather coarse estimates that are accurate only to a few metres.

Just like any human driver, Junior needs to *look* at the road using its laser-driven eyes, at the same time continuously *listening*, i.e., watching out for any obstacles that might threaten to get in its way, while also *learning* to ignore the occasional leaves and tree branches that pose no threat. Junior's 'brain' must *connect* all the inputs it receives so as to *predict* the immediate future, including the likely paths that nearby moving cars might take. Finally, all these predictions must be processed and converted into directions to the car's steering wheel, accelerator, and brake to continuously *correct* the car's trajectory.

Thus, merely driving a car brings together all the elements from *looking* to *correcting* that I have said are necessary for us to 'connect the dots', make sense of and navigate the world. For example, even while looking and listening with its laser-driven eyes, Junior needs to correct for errors in these measurements using techniques based on probability and Bayes' Rule, just as we did while trying to elicit sentiment from Twitter posts. The movement of other cars needs to be modelled statistically and their future positions predicted, just as future wine prices were predicted by Orley Ashenfelter. Of course, the exact models and techniques used differ considerably, both in nature as well as speed of execution; in fact, Junior needs to perform hundreds of thousands of such calculations every second. Nevertheless, the sum and substance is that using the techniques of looking, listening, learning, connecting, and predicting, Junior is able to accurately determine both its own location and speed with respect to the surrounding road and obstacles, as well as track the motion of nearby moving vehicles.

Feedback Control

Now let's see how Junior *corrects* its own motion so as to go where it wants to. To begin with, what might it take for Junior to simply drive in a reasonably straight line, sticking to its lane on a razor-sharp stretch of empty highway, say in the vast expanses of Utah? What could be easier, especially once equipped with multiple high-accuracy laser-based eyes that can accurately 'see' the lane dividers better than any human eye?

Unfortunately, even driving straight as an arrow needs attention and concentration, as any experienced driver knows. Fall asleep at the wheel, and your car will deviate fairly quickly from its straight and narrow path, even if your hands come nowhere near the wheel. And such deviations are inevitable, while driving a car, controlling an aircraft, or even in the case of our own locomotion. In the latter case, deviations are caused by the 'noise' of gravity itself coupled with the fact that our muscular actions themselves can never be perfectly precise or instantaneous. In the case of a car, the slightest gust of wind, small change in road surface, or even the minutest inaccuracy in the steering system itself, rapidly gets accentuated, causing the vehicle to veer to the left or right.

As a result, the car cannot drive blind, even on a straight road, and needs to use its 'eyes' to monitor and control its inevitable drift. Let us suppose that Junior can 'see' well enough to estimate, with reasonable accuracy, which direction it is moving in. Note that even with its multiple sophisticated laser-sensors, any such an estimate is still prone to errors, so, as mentioned earlier, probabilistic techniques using Bayes' Rule are required. Nevertheless, the best Junior can do is to believe its own estimate of where it is headed; then what?

Clearly, as soon as Junior finds that its front wheels are straying from the straight and narrow, it needs to take corrective action by steering back towards the centre of its lane. But by how much should Junior's steering controller adjust the steering wheel? After all, Junior's brain is merely a computer, and needs to be programmed very precisely to make all such decisions. We might argue that since Junior knows, albeit approximately, how far away from the centre it is, a simple possibility is to correct the steering wheel in *proportion* to this estimated *error*; the larger this error, the harder Junior pulls back on the wheel. Simple, isn't it?

Unfortunately however, this simple 'control strategy' doesn't actually result in as smooth a ride as if you or I were driving. As Junior pulls back on the wheel by an amount proportional to the estimate error, one of two things happen: either the car tends to overshoot the desired orientation, i.e., the correction is too much, or the correction is too little and the car takes forever to return to a straight path. Such phenomena are rife in the the field of *control theory* that concerns itself with such problems.

It turns out that a simple observation allows us to fix the problem of over- or under-correction. The idea is to base the amount by which Junior turns the steering wheel not only on the error it perceives, but also on how *fast* that error changes due to Junior's actions. This is called *feedback control*; the error changes (becomes smaller, one presumes) because of Junior's actions, and this change is itself measured and *fed back* to influence the control strategy itself.

Merely by introducing such a 'differential' element to our simpler 'proportional' control strategy, we are able to compensate for over-corrections and Junior smoothly returns to the desired path. There are further improvements one can make, such as introducing another 'integral' element to the controller so as to also correct for any basic flaws in the steering mechanism itself, such as an inherent 10° bias, which we won't go into in more detail. Putting all three elements together, we get the 'PID', or 'proportional integral differential' controller, which is the basis for all machines that involve controlling moving parts.

While it might appear complicated, the PID control strategy is actually rather simple. All Junior needs to do is estimate three kinds of errors. First, the actual error itself, e.g. how far its front wheels are from the centre line. Second, how much this error estimate has changed since the last time it was measured, i.e., the differential error. Lastly, the total error, which is just the sum of all the errors it has measured so far. Using these three numbers, Junior calculates the steering correction to be used at every instant by a formula such as $p \times \text{error} + d \times \text{differential} + i \times \text{total}$. Now, it might appear that the total error will vary depending on how far off from the centre this process begins. Further, this total will grow continuously and cause the car to drift way off course. In fact, this does happen for most choices of the factor i. Interestingly however, there *are* choices of p, i, and d for which the car does indeed correct itself perfectly, even compensating for any inherent faults in the steering system itself. Of course, this also means that the choice of these parameters must be done very carefully; and we shall return to this question in a short while.

*　*　*

How does feedback control have anything to do with intelligent behaviour, one might ask? After all, it appears to be merely a solution to an engineering problem. Ingenious for sure, and obviously important for building self-driving cars, and presumably many other machines such as aircraft or industrial robots; but intelligent?

It turns out that each of us uses feedback control every day, perhaps even at every instant. To experience this, take a look at the objects in your immediate surroundings, and then close your eyes. Visualize one object at random from those just surveyed, and reach out to pick it up. More than likely, your hand will miss its mark by at least a few inches, which would not have happened if you were looking at the object while reaching out. Your eyes and hand coordinate in a feedback control loop, continuously correcting your movements smoothly. Without this feedback, your reach misses its mark. However, even with your eyes are closed, as soon as you feel the object, feedback control kicks in using your sense of touch instead of sight, and you are immediately able to grasp the object.

The unifying power of feedback control in describing and understanding the world is attributed to Norbert Wiener, who founded the field of *Cybernetics* in the mid-20th century. His 1961 book *Cybernetics: Or Control and Communication in the Animal and the Machine*[115] popularized the field and showed how the ideas of feedback control could be used beyond their obvious engineering applications to explain many aspects of human behaviour and possibly even thought.

During the same period, B. F. Skinner's philosophy of *behaviourism* had come to dominate the field of psychology. Skinner shunned any examination of internal thought processes. 'When what a person does [is] attributed to what is going on inside him, investigation is brought to an end'.[116] According to Skinner, all psychological findings had to be directly measured via the behaviour of people subjected to controlled psychological experiments. Behaviourism in psychology matched and supported the philosophical basis of cybernetics, feeding the belief that intelligent thought should and could be understood *primarily* through how human beings, or even animals, perceive and react to their environment.

Skinner's view that 'what is felt or introspectively observed is not some nonphysical world of consciousness, mind, or mental life but the observer's own body'[116] resonates strongly with Weiner's 'the nervous system and the automatic machine are fundamentally alike in that they are devices, which make decisions on the basis of decisions they made in the past'.[115] Moreover, Wiener's cybernetics was deep and mathematically strong, giving credence to the hope that mathematics would eventually succeed in explaining conscious life as successfully as it served physics in understanding the inanimate.

Even if such hopes have hardly been realized in the half-century since Weiner and Skinner, perhaps we shall indeed learn something about intelligent behaviour by trying to build a self-driving car; so let us press on and return to Junior for a deeper dive.

Making Plans

Clearly, a self-driving car needs to do much more than drive in a straight line. It must perceive and avoid other cars, overtake if required, take turns and exits as needed, and more generally figure out, i.e., *plan*, how to go wherever it needs to. All of us have used Google Maps to plan our road trips; surely Junior could merely do the same to obtain its highest-level driving plan. This time its GPS position sensors would come in handy for navigating across town. But more is needed: when should Junior change lanes or overtake another car, how should it navigate a car park to find space, when must it slow down and when is it safe to speed up?

Multiple levels of *planning* are needed, where planning involves figuring out the 'best' way to achieve some goal. Further, planning is also a key element of intelligent thought. We plan every day, and, for that matter, every instant. Going from one room to another requires a plan, as does deciding what to read or play, and more generally how to plan one's career or retirement. Of course, the latter examples involve conscious, 'System 2' decisions, whereas the former plans for how and where to walk are largely arrived at unconsciously. More on conscious planning later. Let us first see what is involved in Junior's plans, such as, for example, getting from the entrance of a car park to an empty parking slot. We shall even grant Junior a reserved, pre-designated parking area like a company CEO. Junior can focus on just 'getting there' rather than the slightly more difficult task of finding an empty slot.

Imagine that Junior is entering a car park from the north-west corner, and its designated slot is all the way at the other end, i.e., at the south-east corner. The fastest way to get there might be to dart diagonally across the car park, following the shortest path to the opposite corner. Perhaps taking such a path does ignore some driving rules, strictly speaking, but we have all done this at one time or another, so we'll grant Junior this liberty as well. Of course, the car park need not be empty; if the diagonal is blocked by other cars, it no longer remains a 'feasible' path, and Junior needs to find other alternatives, even if they are slightly longer than the diagonal.

Let's see how Junior might figure out the shortest path even in the presence of other cars already parked in the car park. We assume that Junior has some kind of map of the car park itself, including where all the cars are. In the DARPA challenge, each car was indeed given high-resolution satellite maps of the entire course, including car parks. However, in real life Junior would still have to rely on its laser-guided eyes to figure out where other cars were, making life a bit more difficult than we are assuming for the moment.

We assume that what Junior 'sees' is a map such as in Figure 6, which has been divided into small squares (rectangles in the figure) such as on a chessboard. Junior is at the top left (i.e., north-west) corner, and needs to get to the bottom right, south-east, end as quickly as possible. We assume for simplicity that Junior cannot move diagonally, i.e., it can move south, east, north, or west at each move of its eventual path across the car park. Here is one way Junior might proceed to

O	B	F		🚗		🚗		
C	A	🚗		🚗		🚗		🚗
D	E	🚗		🚗		N	P	
🚗		🚗		🚗		J	M	🚗
		🚗				K	L	Q	G

FIGURE 6 Navigating a car park

'think' while going about trying to find the shortest path to the other corner.

Like most algorithms, this one also proceeds as a number of steps. At each step Junior 'expands' a particular square by examining all squares that could be reached from that square in one move, i.e., at most the square's four neighbours. For each neighbouring square Junior calculates a 'cost' indicating how many moves away the square is from the north-west corner (called the 'origin', 'O', in the figure). This cost is calculated by simply adding 1 to the number of moves required to get to the square currently being expanded, which, presumably, has been computed in previous steps of the algorithm.* Each such neighbour, along with its cost, is entered into a 'ready list' of positions that remain to be expanded, as well as marked on the map as 'considered' so that it is not inadvertently added to the ready list in the future. Next Junior chooses one of the lowest-cost squares on its ready list as its next target for expansion and removes it from the ready list. (So the ready-list keeps growing and shrinking from step to step.)

Let's follow Junior's 'thoughts' as it plans how to get to its designation using this algorithm. Junior begins by 'expanding' its starting position, i.e., the origin O, and examining its two neighbours B and C to the east and south. Junior counts the number of moves required to get to each of these squares from the origin. In the beginning, it takes

* We use 'step' to mean step of the algorithm and 'move' to indicate units of movement on the map of squares representing the parking lot.

o moves to get to O, so each of the squares B and C is added to the ready list with a 'cost' of 1, since it would take Junior one move to get to each of them from the origin O. Additionally, Junior also marks each of these squares on its map as 'considered', so that it does not inadvertently consider them again as a candidate to put on the ready list.*

Next Junior can choose to expand another square on its ready list that has the lowest cost, which is now one of the squares B or C, since each of them have an equal 'cost' of 1. Let us say Junior chooses to expand square C, which is dutifully removed from the ready list, leaving just B for the present.

Junior now looks at the neighbours of square C on its map, omitting the square O which it has already 'considered'. This leaves squares A and D to be put on the ready list as well as simultaneously marked as 'considered' on the map. Only now these squares carry a cost of 2, since it would take two moves to reach them from the origin (one, the cost of getting to C itself, plus one more). The ready list now has three squares: [B(1), A(2), and D(2)], i.e., B with a cost of 1, A and D with a cost of 2 each. Additionally, squares O, A, B, C, and D all stand marked as 'considered' on the map.

In step three, Junior once again looks at its ready list to find a square to expand next, and chooses B instead of A or D, since the former has a lower cost. So square B is chosen for expansion, and of course, simultaneously removed from the ready list. The set of possible neighbours of B now includes A, which has already been considered, and square F, which is therefore put on the ready list and marked with a cost of 2, i.e., one more than the cost of B, which Junior remembers as being 1.

The next step will be to expand square A, at which point only E is added to the ready list with a cost of 3, since the square with an already parked car has to be ignored, and its other neighbours B and C have

* Needless to say, the origin O is also marked as 'considered', an exception to the rule since it was never itself placed on the ready list.

already been marked as 'considered'. At this point the ready list will be [E(3), D(2), F(2)], i.e., E with a cost of 3, and D and F costing 2. One of the latter two squares is chosen at random for the next expansion, and so on.

As the procedure continues in this manner Junior eventually 'reaches' (albeit logically, i.e., in order to 'expand') the goal position G, its designated parking spot in the south-east corner. At this point the process of examining new squares can stop, since Junior has by this time found a path to the goal, albeit after having taken many diversions along the way. Further, the number of moves, or cost, which Junior has calculated for the goal square must be the length of the shortest path. To see why this must be the case, recall that at each step the square chosen from the ready list is the one with the least cost in terms of number of moves away from the origin. Consequently, as each of its neighbours are examined, their costs as calculated by the algorithm also represent the length of the shortest path from O, and so on.

All that remains now is to retrace the actual shortest path, which Junior is able to do as follows, provided it had managed to also keep a record of the direction, i.e., north, south, east, or west, from which it was examining each square as it was put on the ready list. In other words, Junior remembers which square was being expanded for every addition to the ready list. So, starting from the goal G, Junior remembers that Q was being expanded when G was put on the ready list. At Q it remembers that L was being expanded when Q was added to the ready list. At L it remembers that K was being expanded when L was added to the ready list, and so on. To see why, note that the cost (i.e., distance from O) of M is higher than K, hence K would have been expanded before M, and L added to the ready list during K's expansion rather than M. Backtracking in this manner, Junior can reconstruct the shortest path to G, and then actually start its engines and get moving.

* * *

The algorithm just described is commonly referred to as 'Dijkstra's shortest path', or DSP, after the famous computer scientist Edsger Dijkstra.[117] An important variant of DSP is called the A* algorithm invented by Nils Nillson of Stanford University in 1968.[118] This modified planning algorithm has become widely used for a variety of planning tasks, especially in artificial intelligence, and especially in programming computers to play games such as chess. A* adds the following very important modification to DSP that also serves to explain its use in diverse planning scenarios.

Suppose Junior reaches square K for expansion during the DSP procedure. Since the algorithm chooses a square at random from amongst equal-cost squares on the ready list, it is quite possible that it expands J before L, and thereby ends up considering N in addition to M. On the other hand, if it happens to choose L first, thereby putting Q on the ready list along with M, and thereafter also chooses to expand Q before M, it could complete its task sooner. The question is, of course, how does it know which square to choose from amongst those with equal cost?

The idea that comes to our rescue is that of a 'heuristic' cost. Even though Junior has no idea what the length of the actual shortest path is, given that there are cars blocking the simple diagonal path, it is safe to say that the shortest path cannot be shorter than the diagonal. In the situation just discussed, for example, in the absence of any parked cars, the square J is clearly further from G than L, so given a choice between J and L, the algorithm *should* prefer to expand L first if possible. By using such heuristic pre-knowledge A* avoids fruitless explorations and so ends up being far more efficient than simply DSP.

As already mentioned, algorithms such as A* can be used even for planning tasks that have nothing to do with navigating in physical space. For example, A*-like techniques have been used in programming chess-playing computers. Instead of physical locations along which to plan a path, in the case of chess the options to be explored are the possible sequences of moves to be played. The process of examining which sequence of moves is better than another requires some way to measure the cost at each step, which is provided by a heuristic formula that can evaluate any particular board position based on data from previously played games. Such programs evaluate not only the board position resulting from a single move, but usually many steps into the future, which is where A* comes in handy. Instead of having to reach a particular final position, the goal becomes to reach a position having the highest possible score, given the requirement that one does in fact have to move in order to play the game.

Chess-playing programs look many moves ahead to evaluate the best next move to make; and while doing so they assume that at each step their opponent's move is also the best estimate that can be computed within the time available to 'make the move'—a bit like Watson trying to figure out the best possible answer to a *Jeopardy!* question, at least the sense that in both cases computational power is the limiting factor. Evaluating all possible chess moves is not an option, there are just too many; similarly, searching all possible answers is just as impractical for Watson.

Returning to Junior once more, A* planning is used not only for deciding which physical path to follow, but also in making decisions such as whether or not to overtake another car. To make such decisions Junior needs to estimate not only where the other car is but also how fast it is going, as well as how fast cars in the neighbouring lane are travelling. Again, while the planning tasks are are more complex, A* still works. Of course, there is the added complication that unlike in our example, Junior does not know all the obstacles present in its environment beyond what it can see. Thus, Junior's A* is a highly 'local' version that only knows about objects in the line of sight, and so Junior needs to continuously rerun its A* planner as new objects come into view.

* * *

CORRECT

The A* procedure is an example of an *optimization* algorithm, since it constructs an 'optimum' path from start to goal. In general, optimization deals with maximizing or minimizing some 'cost', which in this case was path length. In other situations, there might be different costs to be minimized or maximized, such as board scores in chess.

In fact, we have seen optimization at work in Chapter 5 as well, while trying to find a model to describe wine prices like Orley Ashenfelter. The problem there was to find the best model parameters a, b, c, and d that would minimize the 'cost' defined by the error between the wine price as predicted by the model versus actual historical data.

Recall the PID controller that Junior uses to steer itself. We found that the choice of the 'control parameters' p, i, and d was crucial. In fact, not only do different choices work better than others by correcting Junior's orientation faster, there are also many dangerous combinations that could throw the car violently off course. Once more, this is an example of an optimization problem, where we need to find a combination that not only works, but works well, i.e., brings Junior back on track as fast as possible.

In Chapter 5 we saw how to find an optimum choice for the parameters a, b, and c in the wine-prices model by making many small changes to some initial guess for a, b, and c. Once we find a combination that cannot be improved further in this manner, we declare it to be our best guess. There is a catch though: while starting from a random guess works for the 'linear' wine-prices model, such a choice need not always work. For example, in the case of finding optimal PID control parameters, it is more than likely that a random initial guess for p, i, and d will send Junior wildly off course. In such a case, any minor adjustments to the control parameters would be just as bad, and we would be stuck. So in general we need to assume that the initial solution that we start out with is 'close enough' to the optimum solution that we seek. Unfortunately, there is often no way to make such a good guess with certainty.

Moreover, what gives us the confidence that just because we find some solution, either for the wine model or PID parameters, which cannot be improved by small modifications, it is indeed the *best* possible solution? Might it not be the case that there are better solutions that can be arrived at only by starting from other initial guesses? As it happens, this is not a problem for the wine-prices model, again because its equation is *linear*. For more general *non-linear* problems, such as controlling Junior, there is *no* guarantee that a solution that cannot be improved 'locally' via small adjustments is also a 'global' optimum solution.

* * *

Reflect for a moment on how a baby figures out how to control its limbs. Initially it is unable to reach out and grasp objects; it makes mistakes, and often knocks things over. Such mistakes, even gross ones, are used to learn better and better ranges for its own control parameters. Eventually, they are fine-tuned enough so that movement, grasping, crawling, and eventually walking become unconscious skills.

Obviously we cannot allow such destructive experimentation at high speeds with a real-life Junior. However, there is merit in taking some clues from real life even here. As any child familiar with computer games knows, one doesn't have to actually build a self-driving car to test-drive it. We could merely simulate Junior in a very realistic computer game. In fact, that is effectively what is done while designing not only self-driving cars, but all kinds of control systems, including aircraft to industrial robots. Of course, the simulations no longer remain game-like, but the principle is the same; trial and error is often the only way to tackle optimization problems efficiently.

Stepping back for a moment now, let us ask once more whether control, planning, and optimization necessarily require intelligent thought at all. The natural world provides many interesting insights in this regard; in particular the behaviour of swarms of bees, flocks of birds, and ant colonies appear to magically solve optimization problems that leave both humans and computers far behind.

Flocks and Swarms

Think of a large flock of birds flying in unison. Often dozens of birds are able to synchronize their movements with ease, executing complex manoeuvres that would challenge the best of fighter pilots. Notice how a flock of pigeons simultaneously gather near a park bench where someone is distributing birdseed. There is no apparent leader in such a flock. Moreover, in many cases the flock is so dense that each bird can hardly see beyond its immediate neighbours. Are these birds communicating somehow; a form of telepathy perhaps? Indeed, this is the only explanation that early observers of nature, such as Edmond Selous,[119] were able to find: 'it seems to me that they must think collectively ... the imperfect calling back of something which we have lost', he wrote in 1931.

In the past few decades, zoologists such as Frank Heppener and even physicists such Andrea Cavagna have used high-speed photography to conduct careful studies of exactly how birds flock together.[120] What they found was that far from telepathy, or even any form of cognitive communication, birds appear to follow very simple rules. On the one hand, in the absence of any other stimuli, they merely mimic six or seven of their nearest neighbours. On the other hand, birds that are able to sight food or sense a predator's approach obviously react to such opportunities or threats. Most importantly, the behaviour of each individual bird is a *combination* of both kinds of inputs.

By incorporating similar simple rules of interaction in large numbers of 'artificial' birds through a computer simulation and displaying the resulting behaviour using high-resolution computer graphics, the computer scientist Craig Reynolds was able to reproduce highly realistic flocking behaviour indistinguishable from that of natural flocks.[120]

Subsequent to Reynolds's work in the 1980s, flocking behaviour using simple rules has been used in programming vivid realism into computer games as well as highly realistic hordes of animals, armies, and other 'flocks' while making animation movies.

But let us now return to our original goal. What might flocking have to do with optimization and path planning, such as finding the best set of PID control parameters, or the shortest path to a goal? In 1995 James Kennedy and Russell Eberhart described a new algorithm called 'particle swarm optimization', or PSO, inspired by exactly such flocking behaviour in nature.[121] Kennedy and Eberhart's approach was to find an optimal solution, not through trial and error, but by simulating many artificial 'particles' that would behave in a manner mimicking a flock of birds They argued that just as flocks of birds all manage to converge onto the *most likely* source of food, or for that matter almost *optimally* evade a dangerous predator or treacherous path, the particles could similarly arrive at the optimal solution for any optimization problem.

Inspired by Heppener's careful photographic studies of flocking and the apparent success of simple rules as demonstrated by Reynolds's computer graphics, Kennedy and Eberhart's particles also *combine* the influence of neighbouring particles along with measurements of how good a solution each particle has managed to stumble upon.

As an example, let's see how we might simulate a particle swarm to find optimal PID parameters p, i, and d for a control problem, such as steering Junior. We can imagine dozens or even hundreds of particles floating in normal three-dimensional space, each representing different random choices of control parameters.

In other words, we use the control parameters p, i, and d as the coordinate positions of particles. Each particle runs its own independent simulation of a PID controller, using its own particular combination of control parameters, and measures how long it takes for the controller to reach a common goal: for example, the goal might be to correct a small deviation from the centre line of the road in the case of our self-driving car, Junior. In other words, each particle measures the *quality* of its current best guess for the 'solution' to the PID optimization problem. Next, the particle figures out which of its neighbouring particles has the best-quality solution. Additionally, each particle also remembers its own 'personal best' solution.

Each particle behaves as if it is actually moving in a certain direction with some *velocity*, as part of a swarm, and continuously changes its 'position', and thereby its guess of the solution. However, rather than moving only in a straight line, it also adjusts its velocity continuously by combining two factors, mimicking birds flying in a flock: first, how far it is from its own personal best solution, and second, how far it is from the best solution of its current set of seven or eight neighbours. As a result the particle changes its velocity by an amount proportional to this combination, and in a direction that averages these two factors.

The PSO algorithm simulates many dozens or even hundreds of particles in this manner. At each step every particle computes the quality of its solution, adjusts its velocity by combining two factors as just described, and then moves to a new position based on whatever velocity it happens to arrive at. When one observes such a particle swarm in its search for a solution, we truly find it behaving very much like a natural flock of birds or swarm of insects. Moreover, the swarm rapidly arrives at the best possible solution. Further, if there are many almost equally good solutions, it manages to find most of them rather than only one.

Apart from giving us a novel optimization technique, the fact that particle swarms are able to find optimal solutions, both as an algorithm as well as in nature, might lead us to doubt whether control, such as driving steadily on straight and narrow path, actually requires any intelligent thought at all.

Tasks such as picking up objects, walking, and even driving are all control and planning tasks that we accomplish with ease and without much conscious attention. The 'unconscious' but optimal behaviour of particle swarms indeed provides an interesting rational model for such unconscious 'System 1' behaviour in our own lives. Are there simulated 'swarms' of some kind continuously finding optimal control solutions amongst the billions of neurons in our brains, and these too, as unconsciously as flocks of birds and swarms of bees? Perhaps; we have no way of knowing for sure.

Problem Solving

Now let us take another look at the A* algorithm. Techniques such as swarm optimization rely on 'neighbourhood' exploration, or 'local' search, to explore many different initial guesses in the hope that some of them are close enough to an optimal solution, so that the swarm as a whole can find its way there. In contrast, A* actually does *construct*, from scratch, the best solution, i.e., the shortest possible path to the goal. It does *not* need to start with a good initial guess, which in its case would be some path to the goal, and iteratively improve it. Instead, A* constructs the optimum path from scratch. In fact it explores many alternative ways to construct a path, tracing back its tracks as required in order to explore alternative choices.

Another important difference between planning, e.g., finding shortest paths and, say, minimizing the control error, is that the latter is an example of *continuous* optimization. On the other hand, a planning task, such as finding the shortest path on a grid of squares, is a *discrete* optimization problem. To understand what this means, notice that the control parameters, p, i, and d, are real numbers, and therefore in principle there is a 'continuum' of infinite possible values to choose from. In contrast, since the number of squares in the grid is discrete

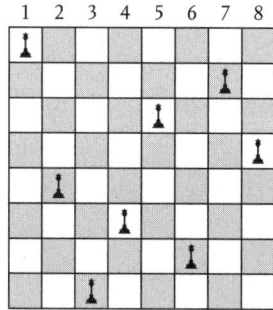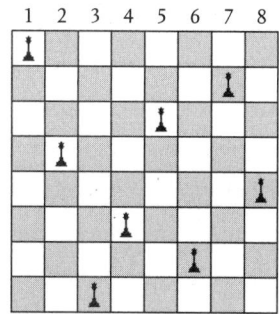

FIGURE 7 Eight queens puzzle

and finite, so are the number of possible paths from start to goal, of which one or more are the shortest in length.

At first glance it might appear that discrete problems with a finite number of options to be explored should be easier than continuous ones that have infinite possibilities. Unfortunately this is not the case.

* * *

The eight-queens problem is a popular chess puzzle in which the task is to place eight queens on a chessboard so that no two queens threaten each other. Figure 7 illustrates this puzzle. While the arrangement on the left is a valid solution, the one on the right is not, since two pairs of queens, i.e., in columns 2 and 4, as well as 6 and 8, are threatening each other.

For small chessboards, such as a 4×4 board, the puzzle is trivial to solve. It gets more difficult for larger sizes, including the standard 8×8 board. Even in the 8×8 case, of the over 4 billion possible arrangements of eight queens, only 92 are correct solutions to the puzzle. Now, could a computer solve this puzzle, not only for 8×8 boards, but for n queens on an $n \times n$ board? The puzzle clearly requires some kind of reasoning, at least for humans. Even for a machine, the brute force approach, i.e., enumerating all possible solutions and ruling out those that do not work, will also fail miserably for larger values of n.

For example, with a 20 × 20 board, there are over 10^{18} possibilities,* which is far more than the fastest of computers can explore in a human lifetime. So, even a finite number of possibilities can still be so large as to be effectively infinite for all practical purposes.

Nevertheless, it turns out that A*-style reasoning can indeed solve the eight-queens problem; let's see how. For simplicity we'll use a board of size four to illustrate the A*-like heuristic search procedure that constructs a solution. First, let us consider what needs to be constructed. Clearly we need to choose the positions of four queens on the board. With just a little thought we might realize that two queens cannot be in the same row or column, so we may as well name the queens by the row they lie in, since there can be at most one per row. Now we merely need to find four numbers, the position of the row-1 queen, the row-2 queen, and so on, in such a manner that the *constraints* of the problem are satisfied, i.e., no two queens threaten each other.

Let's start by enumerating the choices for the row-1 queen, such as 1-1, and 1-2, with the second number representing which square in row 1 it occupies. Since the board is symmetric, we don't need to bother with 1-3 or 1-4, since any solutions with these choices will be mirror images of those with 1-1 or 1-2. As we did while constructing a shortest path using A*, we keep track of these two choices by adding them to a 'ready list', and then proceed to 'expand' each one in turn. Let us first expand 1-1, i.e., we assume the row 1 queen is in position 1, and then proceed to examine possible choices for the row-2 queen. We rule out 2-1 and 2-2 since these will be in the line of fire of queen one, leaving us with 2-3 and 2-4; these are duly added to the ready list as partial solutions (1-1, 2-3) and (1-1, 2-4) respectively.

You may recall that in A* we sorted the ready list based on the length of the path each choice represented, since we wanted to find the

---

* A billion billion, or 1 with 18 zeros.

shortest path. In contrast, for the queens puzzle we are more interested in finding *a* solution, as fast as possible. So instead we sort the ready list by the completeness of the solution. Thus (1-1, 2-3) comes before (1-2), since the former is more complete than the latter. As in A*, we continue picking up the partial solutions from the ready list and expanding them further. Feasible solutions, i.e., those that do not involve a pair of mutually threatening queens, are added to the ready list, unfeasible ones are ruled out.

* * *

Technically speaking, the n-queens puzzle is actually not an optimization problem; there is nothing being maximized or minimized. Instead, the task is to find *a* feasible solution given a set of constraints. Such problems are called, not surprisingly, *constraint satisfaction problems*, or CSPs. Planning techniques based on A* apply equally to CSPs as well as discrete optimization problems such as finding shortest paths. Moreover, most real-world problems are almost always a combination of constraint satisfaction and optimization.

For example, suppose a self-driving delivery van based on the Junior model was asked to deliver supplies to a *number* of locations across the city, rather than merely travel from one end of a car park to the other. As in any reasonably large city, it is possible to drive from any one location directly to any other. At the same time, some locations will be near each other, while other pairs might be at opposite ends of the city. All that we want Junior to figure out is the *sequence* in which to visit its designated destination locations. Ideally Junior should find the sequence that takes the least overall time, i.e., the shortest total path.

Just as in the case of the queens puzzle, if the number of locations Junior needs to visit is small, say four or five, it is easy to check all possible sequences and find the shortest path. However, as soon as the number of locations becomes even moderately large, the task rapidly becomes intractable: with just 15 locations, Junior is faced with over 43 billion combinations to check.

In fact, this task is called the *travelling salesman problem* with n locations (or TSP for short), and is closely related to other intractable problems such as the *satisfiability* problem (or SAT) that we discussed in Chapter 4. We encountered SAT while trying to figure out how difficult it would be to prove or disprove any logical statement with n unknown 'facts', each having but two possible values, true or false. Both SAT and TSP are examples of NP-Complete problems as defined by Steven Cook in 1971, which have *no* known efficient solution for large n. Soon thereafter, in 1972, a whole host of related problems, including TSP, was shown to be in the same 'intractable' league by Richard Karp.[122]

Even though TSP is really hard to solve, planning techniques such as A* can be used to attempt finding reasonable solutions, even if not the shortest one. Just as in our earlier path-planning example, we start from some location and expand alternative paths from there, choosing a new location that produces a new partial path of the shortest length amongst the alternatives yet to be tried. As before, A* maintains a ready list of paths to be further expanded, from which the shortest path is chosen to expand further. As soon as at least some number of complete paths appear on the ready list, we choose the smallest among them and declare it as the best we can find. Unfortunately, the path so found will almost never be the shortest one; after all, the problem is really hard and we would be incredibly lucky to find the shortest path. Still, A* does reasonably well, and can do even better using more sophisticated heuristics that we won't get into here.

* * *

The A* algorithm for path-planning is an example of a more general category of planning techniques called heuristic search planners, or HSP for short. The idea of searching through alternatives for constructing a solution by systematically exploring different alternatives is a powerful idea that goes way back to a 1959 proposal by Newell,

Shaw, and Simon called the 'general problem solver', or GPS. In fact, Newell and Simon's paper[123] was entitled 'GPS: A Program that Simulates Human Thought'.

As we have mentioned earlier, heuristic search has been used in chess-playing computers, including IBM's Deep Blue that beat world chess champion Garry Kasparov in 1997. Did Deep Blue indeed mimic human thought? The consensus so far is clearly the negative. In spite of the heuristics used to limit its search, Deep Blue examined as many as 200 million chess positions per second. In comparison, it was estimated that Kasparov examined at most three positions per second. Deep Blue still appeared to be a brute force approach; brawn vs brain, rather than anything close to intelligent thought. Still, a few, including Nils Nilsson himself, think differently:

> Although Deep Blue relied mainly on brute-force methods rather than on reasoning (for example), it did use heuristic search, one of AI's foundational techniques. The differences between Kasparov and Deep Blue simply indicate how much better chess programs would fare if they employed human-chess-playing knowledge … and machine learning.[2]

Since 1997, chess-playing programs have become cheaper, due in some part to Moore's Law and the rapidly decreasing cost of raw computing power, but also by being able to learn better heuristics from vast amounts of data via machine learning.

Puzzles such as the eight-queens problem certainly do tax our brains. Others such as TSP tax even the fastest of computers. Moreover, planning techniques such as A* use *heuristics* to limit their search, much as we rely on 'gut feeling' derived from years of experience. Certainly very different from the random trial-and-error of swarms of bees and flocks of birds. So, in spite of the differences between Garry Kasparov and Deep Blue, it surely appears that techniques for discrete optimization might indeed provide a 'rational model' for some aspects of the computations that underlie intelligent thought as we plan our lives and actions.

Even if that is the case, the natural world has further surprises yet; examples of complex 'discrete' planning also abound in natural systems, just as we found swarms and flocks to be inspirations for continuous optimization. To find such examples, we need to turn from flying birds and bees to the surprisingly efficient behaviour of the lowly ant and, more importantly, *ant colonies*.

Ants at Work

If you have ever observed an anthill 'at work' in any detail, it might certainly appear that ants are quite dumb; you might see some of them going around in circles, others repeating and then undoing their own actions, and even destroying the work of other ants. Still, when viewed over a span of hours at a macro-level, the ant colony as a whole miraculously appears to achieve a lot of useful work. The colony is able to find food sources and focus on the most promising ones, from which it rapidly transports goods as efficiently as a Walmart does from its suppliers. The colony senses predators and reacts appropriately, like a modern army with sophisticated communications; and when damaged it rebuilds its ramparts with remarkable alacrity. The ant colony indeed appears to be smart, even if ants themselves are not.

Still, there is no centralized brain behind the ant colony. Contrary to popular renditions, the queen ant is just as dumb as the rest. There is no strategy being formulated or debated, nor are orders being transmitted 'down the chain' as in a human organization. Yet, the colony's 'emergent' behaviour appears surprisingly efficient, and bordering on the intelligent.

Since the late 1980s, researchers such as Jean-Louis Deneubourg[120] have studied the behaviour of ants to figure out how they manage to produce such efficient, and almost intelligent, emergent behaviour. One of the mechanisms ants use to communicate is by judiciously releasing small amounts of chemicals called 'pheromones' along the paths they take. For example, forager ants will drop pheromone along their path when returning to the colony laden with food supplies, thereby directing other foragers to follow in their footsteps to get more food.

Interestingly, the very simple mechanism of 'following the pheromone' allows the colony as a whole to find the *shortest* path to a food source. Longer paths to a food source accumulate pheromone at their source slower than shorter ones, simply because ants take more time to return with food from faraway sources or along longer paths to the same source. As a result, foragers setting out on their journey naturally follow shorter paths to the nearest sources, simply because these are the ones with higher concentrations of pheromone.

Inspired by Deneubourg's and other studies of how ants manage to find shortest paths using pheromones, Marco Dorigo, in his 1992 thesis, suggested using 'virtual' ants to solve more general optimization problems, such as the travelling salesman problem. Dorigo's seminal work spawned a whole new class of techniques that now go by the name *ant-colony optimization*, or ACO.[124]

* * *

Let's see how ACO can be used to find good solutions for the travelling salesman problem. Recall that the travelling salesman problem involves finding the shortest path that visits a set of prescribed locations. A number of virtual ants are simulated, one by one. Each ant starts from a random location and greedily constructs a path that includes all other locations by choosing, at each step, the closest location amongst those remaining to be covered. As an ant travels from location to location, it leaves behind some 'virtual pheromone' on the connection (or 'edge') between every consecutive pair of locations that ends up being included in its final path. At the same time, mimicking real life, pheromone evaporates over time, so the pheromone finally left behind by ants that end up with very long paths largely evaporates by the time the ant is done. As a result, once all ants have found their first path, the pheromone trails remaining reflect those pairs of locations that ended up being used in shorter paths; i.e., an edge (connecting a pair of locations) that has a large pheromone residue participated in more and shorter paths than other edges with less pheromone residue.

Next, the ants repeat the procedure again. However, this time they favour paths that already have larger pheromone residue, in addition to taking into account which location is the nearest. As a result, after the second round of path-finding, many ants succeed in bettering their earlier performance and find shorter paths than before. As before, they leave pheromone during this second round as in the first, even as the residues left behind earlier continue to evaporate. When the process of letting loose virtual ants is repeated a number of times, we find that fairly good TSP solutions, i.e., reasonably short paths, are found by many ants.

Well, maybe finding shortest paths is what ants do well anyway, so perhaps the fact that ACO can be used for problems such as TSP is not surprising. More interestingly though, ACO techniques work equally well on many other problems, including the eight-queens puzzle, which appears to have little to do with finding shortest paths of any kind.

Here is how the queens puzzle can be solved using ACO. As before, the algorithm simulates many ants each exploring solutions independently, only communicating via the pheromone trails they lay. An ant starts from some row-position, i.e., by placing a queen at a random position in some random row. Next, the ant chooses another row and position at random, except for avoiding obviously incorrect choices such as choosing a column already chosen earlier. Once an ant finishes, i.e., assigns positions to all n queens, it calculates how bad its solution is in terms of the number of queens that are in fact threatening each other. Finally, the ant lays pheromone trails along the 'path' of choice-pairs it made while constructing its solution. For example, an ant that chooses position (2,4) after (1,1) lays pheromone on the (1,1) → (2,4) pair, or 'edge'. Ants that happen to stumble upon reasonably good assignments release more pheromone than those whose solutions were poorer. So the total pheromone deposited on the (1,1) → (2,4) edge will be proportional to how many good solutions actually included this particular choice during their construction.

In subsequent iterations ants tend to favour solutions constructed using edges with higher pheromone levels rather than completely random ones. The procedure is repeated many times, with pheromone evaporating continuously. In the end, hopefully, we will find some ants that have found the solution. In practice, ACO is in fact able to solve the n-queens problem fairly well.[125]

If it hasn't already occurred to you, ant colony techniques are also related to A* planning in some respects. The hard work of other ants in previous rounds of ACO, as reflected in the pheromone levels, acts as heuristics do in A*, ensuring that steps that are likely to be poor are moved to the end of the queue in future rounds of ant-led exploration.

Darwin's Ghost

All the techniques for planning and optimization we have seen so far, including A* as well as particle swarm and ant-colony optimization, perform trial-and-error exploration of a large number of possible solutions, with some element of randomness in the way solutions are constructed. Of course, PSO and ACO rely on random choices to a larger extent as compared to A*.

Even random explorations need to be controlled in some manner; by neighbourhoods in the case of PSO and via pheromone levels in ACO. Somehow, it appears that random exploration using simple rules can often perform just as well as the careful, logical steps followed in A*. We might conclude from these discussions that sophisticated behaviour need not be the sole prerogative of intelligent thought. Rather, we may just as well begin to suspect that random exploration has much more to teach us about what is involved in conscious thought and intelligent reasoning than any 'hard' logic. Is the latter merely a by-product of, rather than the basis for, intelligence?

And speaking of trial and error, is not Darwinian evolution itself a trial-and-error phenomenon that has resulted in, among other things, neurons and brains that appear to be the seat of intelligent thought itself?

In fact, the origin of diversity in nature via natural selection has indeed been the inspiration for a class of optimization algorithms called *genetic algorithms*, invented in the 1970s by John Holland.[126] The key idea of a genetic algorithm is that two reasonably good solutions obtained by random exploration can be *combined* with each other in much the same manner as chromosomes from two parents are combined to form a child's genetic blueprint.

To solve an optimization problem using a genetic algorithm, we first need to encode candidate solutions in some manner so that they can be represented as a mere sequence of symbols. The idea is that such a representation of candidate solutions is analogous to how a bunch of chromosomes represents all the genetic properties that define a complete organism in the natural world.

For example, a candidate solution to the travelling salesman problem is comprised of n locations arranged in a sequence, which can serve as its chromosome coding. In the case of the n-queens puzzle, a candidate solution might be represented by a sequence of n numbers giving the position to place a queen in each of the n rows on the board.

A genetic algorithm begins by *randomly* producing a large number of candidate solutions, each represented by a chromosome coding such as the ones just described. Next, the *fitness* of each solution is calculated. In the case of TSP, fitness would mean the total distance covered by a path; for the n-queens puzzle, fitness might be the number of mutually threatening pairs in an arrangement of queens. The large set of candidate solutions is filtered to weed out the poorer ones, according to their fitness, much as happens in true Darwinian selection in the natural world.

Finally, random pairs are chosen from the remaining 'fit enough' candidates and combined, or 'mated'. For example, suppose we have two 'parent' chromosomes, (2, 3, 5, 8, 9, 7, 1, 4, 0, 6) and (0, 5, 6, 2, 9, 8, 7, 1, 3, 4), each representing candidate solutions for a 10-location TSP. Combining, or mating, these chromosomes takes place in a manner that mimics real life, by cutting both the parents at some 'crossover' point and then swapping corresponding segments of each parent chromosome with each other. In this example the crossover procedure might involve cutting each parent at, say its third position, and swapping segments, yielding the two child sequences (2, 3, 5, 2, 9, 8, 7, 1, 3, 4) and (0, 5, 6, 8, 9, 7, 1, 4, 0, 6).

Unfortunately, though, we now find that locations are repeated, such as 2 and 3 in the first child, and 0 and 6 in the second. Since valid TSP solutions need to visit each of the 10 locations, these errors need to be repaired somehow. Fortunately, repair is simply accomplished by allowing one of the duplicates, say the first, to be replaced randomly by any of the locations missing in the child. So, by replacing the first 2 by 0 and the first 3 by 6, we get as the repaired first child (0, 6, 5, 2, 9, 8, 7, 1, 3, 4), which is a valid candidate solution for TSP. Similar repair yields (3, 5, 2, 8, 9, 7, 1, 4, 0, 6) by replacing the first 0 with 3 and the first 6 with 2, again yielding a valid new candidate TSP solution.

The new population of candidate solutions is comprised of all the earlier deemed fit parents along with all their children. Note that in order to produce enough members in this next stage, many pairs may need to be mated from amongst those selected as fit after the first round; polygamy and bigamy is not only desirable here, but encouraged! Once a new population is produced, it too is weeded of poor candidates and the process continues until sufficiently fit solutions are found.

Genetic algorithms rapidly find good solutions to many difficult problems. Further, they are notoriously easy to apply. For example, notice that *exactly* the same crossover procedure can work equally well for the n-queens puzzle to combine, or 'mate', two candidate solutions. The genetic analogy certainly seems as pervasively applicable in algorithm design, as the common genetic basis is prevalent in all life forms known to us.

Intelligent Systems

Let's take a few steps back and see where we have arrived. Programming a self-driving car was our first example where we explored how predictions need to lead to corrections, in order to make any difference in the real world. Smooth and stable corrections, either to Junior's steering wheel, or even to our own limbs, require control algorithms. Next, arriving at good control strategies was itself found to be an example of a more general optimization problem: in control we seek to continuously navigate in a manner that minimizes the error from our desired goal. Optimization and planning allows us to find the 'best' strategy to control a self-driving car, or, for that matter, the best path across a parking lot, or even complex tours across town while delivering supplies to many customers.

Optimization techniques themselves range from the shortest-path and A* planning techniques, to the naturally inspired particle swarm, ant colony, and genetic algorithms. Moreover, these techniques go well beyond mere planning shortest paths; they can be used to find good solutions to a variety of difficult problems, including puzzles such as the n-queens problem that clearly tax our mental faculties.

Many real-life systems rely on optimization techniques every day. When you book a rental car, purchase an airline ticket, shop online, or even walk around in a real physical store shopping for almost anything, the prices that you see and the products you find, even the shelves they lie on—all these are but the final results of continuous optimizations designed to not only give you a good price, but also take into account many factors that help the provider. The locations where cars are likely to be available; the expected load on the flight sector you are looking for; even the inventory levels, production plans, and competitive positioning of the products you are browsing—all these factors and many more are taken into consideration, either as constraints or as part of a cost that needs to be minimized or a profit to be maximized.

Behind the scenes also, manufacturing companies are continuously forecasting, i.e., predicting demand based on past sales, consumer sentiment, and even weather. Demand predictions are fed into complex optimizations to calculate exactly how much of which product to produce, and where. Further optimizations decide how to best ship components to where they need to reach, and that too just in time to avoid building up costly inventory in warehouses.

Moreover, real-life optimizations are not limited to the commercial world alone. Public utilities that each of us rely on in everyday life are equally complex to manage. The way power is distributed across a national electric grid is rife with optimization problems. In many countries power is traded between provinces or states, with prices being determined by complex calculations that take into account predicted surpluses and deficits, which are continuously corrected by actual demand and supply. In the future, as many writers including Thomas Friedman have predicted,[127] flexible energy pricing will also include the *source* of the power, with greener sources, such as wind or solar power, costing less than those more harmful to the environment, such as coal-fired sources. A windy or sunny day may see energy prices dipping sharply as windmills and solar panels produce more surplus power.

Last but not least, water scarcity looms large in many parts of the world. Increasing sophistication in how best to store, distribute, and price water is likely to become the basis of next big public utility, almost as important as the pervasive electricity grid. Once more, complex optimizations will be needed to find good solutions.

Finally, as complicated as all these above real-life examples might appear, they can all be understood in exactly the same manner as the simple optimization and control problems we have described earlier. Predict the future, be it demand, supply, or the environment. Use these predictions to find optimal solutions, and then navigate (i.e., correct) one's organization or public utility towards an optimal state. Complex systems, from self-driving cars to massive industries, all share many similarities with each other as well as perhaps with the most complex systems of all, human beings themselves.

* * *

While describing a future filled with self-driving cars, Eric Schmidt imagined that each car would have a 'drive' button. Presumably one would first tell the car *where* to drive to, somehow; perhaps even via one's voice-recognition-enabled mobile phone.

Underlying such a drive button lie many *layers* of control and optimization. At the lowest level is that of Junior trying to drive in a straight line. At the next level comes planning how to take a turn, overtake another car, or change lanes. The output of this layer is the path to be followed by the earlier, lower layer. At the same time, a still higher layer needs to decide *whether or not* to overtake the next car, change lanes, or take a turn. These decisions could be based on local conditions such as the speed of neighbouring cars and the relative emptiness of other lanes. Alternatively, instructions may arrive from even higher layers as to whether an exit to be taken is imminent, or the next left turn just needs to be taken, full stop. At the very topmost level there might even be a complex TSP-like planner that computes the best path to your final destination taking into account knowledge about expected traffic conditions, roadblocks, and even the collective intentions of *all* users of self-driving cars. In a recent talk,[128] Vint Cerf, a Google Fellow, who incidentally, is also credited with the invention of the internet itself, remarked that the day is not far of when four self-driving cars arriving at a four-way stop sign would actually wirelessly communicate with each other to decide which of them should go first. 'Fender benders' arising from the all-too-familiar misunderstandings that often occur at such junctions would be a thing of the past!

Now, a hierarchical control structure such as that just described is actually quite common. Think of the aeroplane autopilot systems used today. Planes already have a 'fly' button, even if we are yet to experience Google's drive-button-enabled cars. At the highest level, all the pilot needs to feed in is the desired destination and a few markers along the way indicating which route to take. Then he can sit back and relax. On the other hand, at the lowest level, each aileron, flap, and rudder needs to be adjusted continuously in response to minute changes in wind speed and direction. This lowest level is given its goals, e.g., fly straight and level, or bank gently and turn 30° to the left, by the next higher level of control. Whether to fly straight or turn is decided at the intermediate level taking into account local navigational needs, such as having to avoid a patch of rain, along with the longer-term goals set by higher levels of path planning. At the same time, each level uses control concepts to continuously monitor and correct itself to stay on course and achieve its own individual goals.

* * *

When Norbert Wiener suggested that the concept of feedback control systems could serve as a useful model for describing human thoughts and actions, he also had a hierarchical structure in mind. At the lowest levels, our brain unconsciously monitors and controls many hundreds of vital functions, from our heart and lungs to the numerous chemical levels that must be maintained within a comfortable range. At the next level, also largely unconsciously, come individual muscular movements that are executed in close coordination so as to achieve fluid gestures such as raising one's hand, or grasping an object. As designers of industrial robots know only too well, replicating the simplest of human gestures by a mechanical robot requires tremendously complex planning and optimization.

Even if we consider the arena of conscious volition, individual gestures and movements are themselves only the lowest levels of conscious planning and control. Ever higher levels include deciding, planning, and executing a walk across the room, one's commute to work, the dozens of carefully thought-out decisions and actions we perform daily, and so on to the highest levels of planning a career, or an entire life.

What kinds of predict–correct cycle allow us to plan and control our actions at higher levels of thought? Surely there must be some stage at which logical, *symbolic* thought emerges miraculously from lower-level feedback loops. We have encountered this dilemma earlier, while discussing Hawkins's hierarchical temporal memory and his memory-prediction model of intelligent thought. As we have seen in this chapter, planning and optimization tasks can indeed be achieved by far dumber entities, such as ants and birds, albeit operating in large numbers. Do these shed any light on the open question of how to connect lower levels of largely statistical processing to higher symbolic forms of reasoning? We just don't know, yet.

Moreover, it has also been argued that it is precisely our symbolic abilities, however they might actually arise, that distinguish humans the most from other animals, including other primates, and perhaps also natural systems such as swarms or ant colonies. Patrick Winston, one of the stalwarts of artificial intelligence research from its beginnings, makes this point.[129] He quotes the anthropological studies of Ian Tattersall[130] that suggest that not only do other animals, primates included, lack symbolic abilities, but that symbolic thought emerged rather suddenly in our ancestors with the advent of Cro-Magnon man, only around 50,000–70,000 years ago. Winston also quotes the linguist Noam Chomsky's interpretation of Tattersall's findings, i.e., that it is specifically the ability to *connect* two symbolic concepts to make a third that brings us powers of reasoning, which in turn leads to the development of language. Indeed, I have submitted a similar thesis in this book as well, specifically in Chapter 4, 'Connect', but also by emphasizing that 'connecting the dots' is the key to how we make sense of and navigate the world.

With language comes the ability to tell and understand *stories*, which leads to Winston's 'strong story hypothesis', i.e., that this is the key to how we differ from all other animals. Added to this is our ability to *imagine* stories that may not even have occurred, which in turn comes from the 'directed perception hypothesis', i.e., being able to direct our neurological apparatus for perception, mainly visual, but also auditory, towards imagined events.[129]

> Storytelling helps us control the future … if this drug is used then that will happen … our experience, recalled through *stories*, is the way we imagine and control the future[3]

says Winston. As a result, we can literally 'see' what might happen in the future, however immediate or remote. Further, we can also imagine what is *likely* to be the consequence of our actions, and others' reactions, thereby 'seeing' even further into the future. Imagining the future is exactly what chess champion Garry Kasparov does. So does the computer Deep Blue while executing symbolic A*-like search. It is just that Garry adds an extra ton of 'gut feeling', which Deep Blue's heuristic optimizations cannot match.

Moreover, we can imagine similar algorithmic techniques—coming up with predictions using reasoning, coupled with statistical learning to improve heuristics, followed by optimal planning—as being able to explain, to a certain extent, how we plan our day, or week, or career. First, by simply imagining the possibilities, symbolically. We then explore many alternatives, pruning them using previously learned 'gut feeling'. Our navigations are at first hypothetical and imagined, sometimes even unconsciously. Finally they become real when we execute conscious actions, in which control is exercised to ensure we stay on our predetermined course. Last but not least, all these explorations and executions are continually taking place at many levels, hierarchically, as well as at many different timescales, from moments and hours to days and years.

In contrast, even though the natural world of ants and bees is full of optimization and planning, their brains, along with those of other animals, appear to lack *constructive* symbolic abilities. From constructive imagination in the symbolic universe we are able to explore a far wider range of possibilities, and further into the future than other animals. It is this evolutionary accident that we call intelligence.

* * *

Look and *listen* to *learn* from past, *connect* to imagine and then *predict* the future, and finally *correct* one's actions. We have come full circle, even though we might not fully understand the origins of symbolic thought. Further, as we have seen, we can indeed program many capabilities that closely resemble those arising from 'true' intelligence into the large-scale, web-based systems that are likely to increasingly permeate our societies: search engines, social platforms, smart energy grids, self-driving cars, as well as a myriad other practical applications. All of these will increasingly share many features of our own intelligence, even if lacking a few 'secret sauces' that might remain to be understood.

Epilogue

PURPOSE

As I have argued in the previous chapters, intelligent behaviour, be it human or as exhibited by an appropriate web-intelligence application, is comprised of six elements: *looking, listening, learning, connecting, predicting*, and finally *correcting*. In the end, the final element, *correct*, serves to control our journey and guide us closer to our *goals*.

In the case of online advertising, the goal was to target advertisements better. In the case of the self-driving car, the goal should be a safer ride for each car, and less congested roads at a higher level. Similarly, the smart grid might aim to regulate energy usage and reduce the societal carbon footprint.

Even if by looking, listening, learning, connecting, predicting, and correcting, web-intelligence systems are able to mimic intelligent behaviour in the pursuit of such goals, we should also ask where these goals come from. Obviously the answer is 'from us'. The web-intelligence systems themselves do not generate their overarching goals; these are built in, by their creators, i.e., us.

We are, of course 'different'; we have, or at any rate, appear to have 'free will', and decide our own goals. So whatever web intelligence, AI, or any other concoction of computing techniques might achieve, we will still be different, of course. Sure? To make certain, we must also try to understand where our own goals come from. At times the discussion that follows will tend to stray into the philosophical, but bear with me; there is something at the end.

* * *

For inspiration we turn to the neuroscientist Antonio Damasio's exploration of just this subject in his recent book *Self Comes to Mind*.[75] Damasio argues first that the *mind*'s primary function is to map, or represent, the world. In the process of such mapping, first the body, then the external world around us, and finally our experiences, are all mapped and represented in some form. This is much as we have argued from a computer science perspective as well. *Learning* is all about arriving at representations, or models, of the world, while *connecting* and *predicting* exercise these models to reason and make predictions about the world.

The *self*, on the other hand, is different from the mind, according to Damasio. As the mind maps the external world, the self maps the mind, or rather, its historical, autobiographical experience. The self is the capability to reflect on previous states of mind, which in turn are representations of the body and external world.

Of course, the mind or self, however Damasio might differentiate between them, are in the end comprised of mental states arising from neuronal firing patterns. So, if our reductionist arguments are valid, these too must be governed by logic and mathematics at some level. Here we can find some comfort in that we have seen that mathematical structures, such as Gödel's construction, do indeed possess the capability for self-reference and therefore possibly also self-representation, a point which has also been argued extensively by others such as Hofstadter.[74] So perhaps we can indeed believe Damasio's self–mind dichotomy even while wearing lenses of computer science and mathematics.

* * *

Purpose, according to Damasio, stems from *homeostasis*, which is nothing but the need to maintain various parameters of one's body and environment in a range that is best suited for *survival*. The job of the self, as opposed to the mind, is to reflect on one's current situation and compare it with possibly better states of 'well-being'. The self is aided in this endeavour at the lowest level by chemical monitors of well-being, such as dopamine. At higher levels it is the *mind* that comes to its aid, via imagination, which is nothing but the *prediction* of possible future states of well-being along with analyses of the the means to achieve them, by reasoning, i.e., by *connecting the dots*.

Homeostasis defines *biological value*, from which in turn follow *all* value systems that permeate our existence and bring purpose into our lives. These range from the personal, e.g., the value of a full stomach, to the sociocultural, e.g., the benefits of protecting our families, and eventually the value of a just society: 'The conscious minds of humans, armed with such complex selves and supported by even greater capabilities of memory reasoning and language, engender the instruments of culture and open the way into a new means of homeostasis at the level of societies and culture'[75] argues Damasio, going on to say: 'Justice systems, economic and political organisations, the arts, medicine, and *technology** are examples of the new devices of regulation'.

* * *

Complex web-intelligence systems are just beginning to emerge out of the past decade of progress in large-scale AI, driven initially by online advertising. Self-driving cars and smart energy grids are the forerunners of even more complex systems that will eventually power and intelligently control our world and lives.

In the language of Damasio we might well view the web-intelligence systems that we shall inexorably weave into the fabric of our society as an evolution of our *minds*. At the same time, the societal changes brought about by these very systems, such as the social networks that are already changing the way we relate to each other, could be viewed as the evolution of our collective self, again in Damasio's terms of extended homeostasis.

---

* Emphasis added.

Today, in spite of all their achievements, our web-intelligence systems remain rather rudimentary implementations of the elements of looking, learning, connecting, predicting, and correcting, at least as compared to the human brain. Moreover, the linkages between these elements, while present, are far from the level of integration that the human brain achieves. How far can we go by continuing to engineer these elements and the linkages between them to make them even stronger? Is it just a matter of more engineering and better techniques that can bring about a fundamental evolution of our collective self synergistically with ever more powerful web-intelligence minds?

* * *

Perhaps the key missing ingredient is *purpose*, or rather how it is engineered. Not that web-intelligence systems need to have purpose; that will always come from our collective self, as argued earlier. However, today we engineer purpose into our creations at a micro-level. We decide exactly *how* better targeted advertising should be achieved, and build in the required machine-learning and prediction code. We decide the route-mapping algorithms, control systems, as well as higher-level planning techniques to use when building a self-driving car or even a future network of such vehicles. We define the pricing policies for each type of energy source based on our current understanding of carbon footprint and our estimate of its value vis à vis economic considerations. In each case, we 'hard-code' our goals into these systems, at a fairly low level.

Suppose we were able to pass on purposes to our systems slightly differently: we decide the homeostatic parameters for both safe driving and traffic congestion. Similarly, we might define the goals of a pollution-free, carbon-neutral, yet cost-efficient energy economy. Last but not least, maximizing an online advertising network's net market worth might well serve as its 'purpose'.

Could our web-intelligence systems, be they for online advertising, traffic management, or smart energy, do all the rest? In other words, could they reason about possible advertising strategies, traffic-control policies, or grid-management models, try them out, measure the results, and take decisions, even if suboptimal? Could they then continue the process iteratively, much as we do? And last but not least, would they ever appear to be *creative* in their endeavours?

The question of whether machines can even appear to be creative is as hotly debated as the core philosophical question of strong AI itself. Computational creativity has recently been carefully analysed by Margaret Boden.[131] She identifies three types of creativity: combinational, exploratory, and transformational. As she demonstrates by citing various AI projects, each type of creative behaviour can be computationally achieved using many of the techniques we have discussed in this book: analogical reasoning, heuristic search, and genetic algorithms in particular. In conclusion she remarks that

> thanks in part to AI, we have already begun to understand *what sort of phenomenon* creativity is. Still something of a mystery, perhaps. And certainly a marvel. But not—repeat—not—a miracle.[131]

So what seems to be clear from our discussions so far is that to achieve even a glimmer of the reflection, complex reasoning, and even creativity needed for a higher-level programming of purpose, a true integration across all the elements of look, listen, learn, connect, predict, and correct is needed.

If indeed we could articulate purposes at such high levels and achieve such an integration of elements, our web-intelligence 'minds' might well serve our collective, societal selves much more in the manner in which our own individual selves are served by their respective minds. This, if at all, is possibly where AI, in the form of web intelligence, might be headed. Not the 'strong AI' of lore with its independent, 'intelligent machine' that can merely fool a human observer. Instead, a synergy between the collective selves of a networked society and multiple web intelligence minds adding the power to connect the dots, at web scale, as never before. Utopian? Perhaps, but possibly also merely a different way to think about programming our web intelligences, and a different level to which we might entrust technology with our collective 'biological value'.

* * *

We began our journey by articulating the potential that web-scale AI offers to mimic our abilities to 'connect the dots' and make sense of the world. Along the way we studied each of the elements that enable us to do so: *look, listen, learn, connect, predict,* and *correct.* In each case we began virtually from scratch, arguing from fundamentals and elucidating the basic principles of large parts of computer science and AI in the process. Yet, even while doing so we tried not to lose sight of the big picture of how these elements are all integrated within our own minds. At the same time, the 'hidden agenda' was always the position articulated earlier, albeit at the end of our journey: contrary to both the over-idealistic goals of 'strong AI' as well as the perhaps far-too-pedestrian goals of weak AI, web-intelligence technology just might have the potential to become a *mind,* while continuing to derive *purpose* from our collective societal *selves.*

Finally, I want to conclude by asking, is this next step a simple one? While optimism is good, there is also ample reason to be cautious. As we have witnessed in this book already, there are two distinct flavours of AI, both the science and the technology: statistical, connection-oriented, or 'low-level' techniques on the one hand, dealing with perception and learning from vast volumes of data, at a higher level we have the symbolic approach; reasoning, logic, knowledge representations, etc. And as of today the twain do not meet: 'Not enough people are working at the interface, . . . both how the symbolic arises from as well as *influences* the perceptual side',[3] says Pat Winston.

Further, even on the symbolic side, we are far from understanding what our inner representation is:

> The focus is wrong, it's Turing's fault actually, . . . as if reasoning is the centre of intelligence, . . . reasoning is just the shadow on the wall, logic is only

a special case of very precise story telling...If I thought this is where we would be 50 years ago, I probably would have hung myself!

says Winston,[3] disappointingly. We have, he concludes, 'made tremendous contributions on the engineering side, but not enough on the science'.

For the web-intelligence systems of today to cross the chasm, integrate the six different elements, and become a mind, I believe the link between perceptual and symbolic needs to be understood properly. So, it certainly appears that there is much science remaining to be done. Hopefully, though, I have convinced you of both the *potential* as well as the *purpose* of such an effort.

* * *

REFERENCES

PROLOGUE

1. Alan M. Turing, 'Computing Machinery and Intelligence', *Mind*, 59 (1950), 433–60.
2. Nils Nilsson, *The Quest for Artificial Intelligence* (Cambridge: Cambridge University Press, 2010).
3. Patrick H. Winston, private conversation, May 2012.
4. John McCarthy, Marvin L. Minsky, Nathaniel Rochester, and Claude E. Shannon, 'A Proposal for the Dartmouth Summer Research Project on Artificial Intelligence', *AI Magazine*, 27/4 (2006).
5. Margaret A. Boden, *Mind as Machine: A History of Cognitive Science* (Oxford: Oxford University Press, 2006).

CHAPTER 1

6. Sir Arthur Conan Doyle, 'A Scandal in Bohemia', *The Strand Magazine* 2/7 (July 1891).
7. Sir Arthur Conan Doyle, 'The Adventure of the Copper Beeches', *The Strand Magazine* (June 1892) (part of a collection entitled *The Adventures of Sherlock Homes*).
8. Vannevar Bush, 'As We May Think', *Atlantic Monthly* (July 1945).
9. As related to vo.co.uk by a Google spokesperson, April 2011.
10. Nicholas Carr, *The Shallows: What the internet is Doing to Our Brains* (New York and London: W. W. Norton, 2010).
11. Nicholas Carr, 'Is Google Making Us Stupid?', *The Atlantic* (July–Aug. 2008).
12. Sergey Brin and Lawrence Page, 'The Anatomy of a Large-Scale Hypertextual Web Search Engine', *Computer Networks and ISDN Systems*, 30/1 (1998), 107–17.
13. Tim Berners-Lee, 'World-Wide Web: The Information Universe', *Electronic Net-working*, 2/1 (1992), 52–8.
14. Thomas L. Griffiths, Mark Steyvers, and Alana Firl, 'Google and the Mind', *Psychological Review*, 18/12 (2007), 1069–76.
15. Daniel L. Schacter, *Searching for Memory: The Brain, the Mind, and the Past* (New York: Basic Books, 1997).
16. Pentti Kanerva, *Sparse Distributed Memory* (Cambridge, Mass.: A Bradford Book, 1990).

17. Piotr Indyk and Rajeev Motwani, 'Approximate Nearest Neighbors: Towards Removing the Curse of Dimensionality', *STOC '98: Proceedings of the 30th Annual ACM Symposium on Theory of Computing* (New York: ACM, 1998), 604–13.

18. Jayant Madhavan et al., 'Web-Scale Data Integration: You Can Only Afford to Pay as You Go', *Proceedings of CIDR* (2007).

19. Jayant Madhavan, David Ko, Lucja Kot, Vignesh Ganapathy, Alex Rasmussen, and Alon Halevy, 'Google's Deep Web Crawl', *Proceedings of the VLDB Endowment* (2010).

20. Anand Rajaraman, 'Kosmix: High-Performance Topic Exploration Using the Deep Web', *Proceedings of the VLDB Endowment*, 2/2 (Aug. 2009), 1524–9.

21. Meghan E. Irons, 'Caught in a Dragnet', *Boston Globe*, 17 July 2011.

22. Ronald Kessler, *The Terrorist Watch* (New York: Three Rivers Press, 2007).

23. V. S. Subrahmanian, Aarron Mannes, Amy Sliva, Jana Shakarian, and John P. Dickerson, *Computational Analysis of Terrorist Groups: Lashkar-e-Taiba* (New York: Springer, 2013).

24. 'Home Minister Proposes Radical Restructuring of Security Architecture', *Press Information Bureau*, Government of India, 24 December 2009.

25. V. Balachandran, 'NATGRID Will Prove to Be a Security Nightmare', *Sunday Guardian*, 19 Aug. 2012.

CHAPTER 2

26. Claude E. Shannon, 'A Mathematical Theory of Communication', *Bell System Technical Journal*, 27 (July and Oct. 1948), 379–423, 623–56.

27. Karen Spaärck Jones, 'A Statistical Interpretation of Term Specificity and Its Application in Retrieval', *Journal of Documentation*, 28/1 (1972), 11–21.

28. Akiko Aizawa, 'An Information-Theoretic Perspective of TF-IDF Measures', *Journal of Information Processing and Management*, 39/1 (2003), 45–65.

29. Scott Deerwester, Susan T. Dumais, George W. Furnas, Thomas K. Landauer, and Richard Harshman, 'Indexing by Latent Semantic Analysis', *Journal of the American Society for Information Science* 41/6 (1990), 391–407.

30. András Csomai and Rada Mihalcea, 'Investigations in Unsupervised Back-of-the-Book Indexing', *Proceedings of the Florida Artificial Intelligence Research Society* (2007), 211–16.

31. Arun Kumar, Sheetal Aggarwal, and Priyanka Manwani, 'The Spoken Web Application Framework: User Generated Content and Service Creation through Low-End Mobiles', *Proceedings of the 2010 International Cross Disciplinary Conference on Web Accessibility* (2010).

32. James Gleick, *The Information: A History, a Theory, a Flood* (New York: Pantheon Books, 2011).

33. A. Frank and T. F. Jaeger, 'Speaking Rationally: Uniform Information Density as an Optimal Strategy for Language Production', *30th Annual Meeting of the Cognitive Science Society (CogSci08)* (2008), 933–8.

34. Van Deemter, *Not Exactly: In Praise of Vagueness* (Oxford: Oxford University Press, 2010).

35. Noam Chomsky, *Syntactic Structures* (The Hague: Mouton Books, 1957).

36. Alexis Madrigal, 'How You Google: Insights From Our Atlantic Reader Survey', *The Atlantic* (online), 19 Aug. 2011.

37. Graham Rawlinson, 'The Significance of Letter Position in Word Recognition', PhD Thesis, Nottingham University, 1976.

38. <http://www.feeltiptop.com>.

39. John Battelle, *The Search: How Google and Its Rivals Rewrote the Rules of Business and Transformed Our Culture* (New York: Portfolio Books, 2005).

40. Marshall McLuhan, *Understanding Media: The Extensions of Man* (New York: McGraw Hill, 1965).

CHAPTER 3

41. D. A. Ferrucci, 'Introduction to "This is Watson"', *IBM Journal of Research and Development* 56/3–4 (2012).

42. Sharon Bertsch McGrayne, *The Theory that Would Not Die: How Bayes' Rule Cracked the Enigma Code, Hunted Down Russian Submarines, and Emerged Triumphant from Two Centuries of Controversy* (New Haven: Yale University Press, 2011).

43. E. M. Gold, 'Language Identification in the Limit', *Information and Control*, 10/5 (1967), 447–74.

44. D. Haussler, M. Kearns, and R. Schapire, 'Bounds on the Sample Complexity of Bayesian Learning Using Information Theory and the VC Dimension', *Machine Learning: Special Issue on Computational Learning Theory*, 14/1 (January 1994).

45. L. Valiant, 'A Theory of the Learnable', *Communications of the ACM*, 27 (1984), 1134–42; L. Valiant, *Probably Approximately Correct* (New York: Basic Books, 2013).

46. Rakesh Agrawal and Ramakrishnan Srikant, 'Fast Algorithms for Mining Association Rules in Large Databases', *Proceedings of the 20th International Conference on Very Large Data Bases, VLDB Endowment, Santiago, Chile* (Sept. 1994), 487–99.

47. Paulo Shakarian and V. S. Subrahmanian, *Geospatial Abduction* (New York: Springer, 2012).

48. Robert M. Bell, Yehuda Koren, and Chris Volinsky, 'All Together Now: A Perspective on the Netflix Prize', *Chance* 23/1 (2010), 24–9.

49. David M. Blei, Andrew Y. Ng, and Michael I. Jordan, 'Latent Dirichlet allocation', *Journal of Machine Learning Research*, 3/45 (Jan. 2003), 993–1022.

50. D. Blei, 'Introduction to Probabilistic Topic Models', *Communications of the ACM* (2011), 1–16.

51. L. M. Oakes, J. S. Horst, K. A. Kovack-Lesh, and S. Perone, 'How Infants Learn Categories', in *Learning and the Infant Mind* (New York: Oxford University Press, 2008), 144–71.

52. George Lakoff and Rafael E. Nunez, *Where Mathematics Comes From* (New York: Basic Books, 2000).

53. Andy Clark, *Natural-Born Cyborgs: Minds, Technologies and the Future of Human Intelligence* (New York: Oxford University Press, 2003).
54. Leslie Marsh, *Cognitive Systems Research*, 6 (2005), 405–9.
55. Richard Dawkins, *The Selfish Gene* (Oxford: Oxford University Press, 1976).
56. Oren Etzioni, Anthony Fader, Janara Christensen, Stephen Soderland, and Mausam, 'Open Information Extraction: The Second Generation', *International Joint Conference on Artificial Intelligence* (2011).
57. Oren Etzioni, Michele Banko, Stephen Soderland, and Daniel S. Weld, 'Open Information Extraction from the Web', *Communications of the ACM* (2008), 68–74.
58. John Searle, 'Minds, Brains and Programs', *Behavioral and Brain Sciences*, 3/3 (1980), 417–57.
59. Douglas R. Hofstadter and Daniel C. Dennett, *The Mind's I: Fantasies and Reflections on Self and Soul* (New York: Basic Books, 1980).
60. P. Guha and A. Mukerjee, 'Baby's Day Out: Attentive Vision for Pre-Linguistic Concepts and Language Acquisition', *Proceedings of 4th Workshop on Attention in Cognitive Systems WAPCV-2007* (Hyderabad: Springer, 2007), 81–94.

CHAPTER 4

61. *Horrible Bosses*, directed by Seth Gordon, released June 2011 by New Line Cinema.
62. Sir Arthur Conan Doyle, *A Study in Scarlet* (London: Ward, Lock & Co., 1888).
63. Robin Smith, *Aristotle: Prior Analytics* (Indianapolis: Hackett, 1989).
64. Bill MacCartney and Christopher D. Manning, 'Natural Logic for Textual Inference', *RTE '07, Proceedings of the ACL-PASCAL Workshop on Textual Entailment and Paraphrasing* (2007), 193–200.
65. Karen Myers, Pauline Berry, Jim Blythe, Ken Conley, Melinda Gervasio, Deborah L. McGuinness, David Morley, Avi Pfeffer, Martha Pollack, and Milind Tambe, 'An Intelligent Personal Assistant for Task and Time Management', *AI Magazine*, 28/2 (2007), 47–61.
66. J. Weizenbaum, 'ELIZA: A Computer Program for the Study of Natural Language Communication between Man and Machine', *Communications of the ACM*, 9/1 (1966), 36–45.
67. R. Brachman, 'What's in a Concept: Structural Foundations for Semantic Networks', *International Journal of Man-Machine Studies*, 9 (1977), 127–52.
68. R. Brachman and H. Levesque, 'Expressiveness and Tractability in Knowledge Representation and Reasoning', *Computer Intelligence*, 3 (1987), 78–93.
69. Tim Berners-Lee and Mark Fischetti, *Weaving the Web: The Original Design and Ultimate Destiny of the World Wide Web by Its Inventor* (London: Orion Business Books, 1999).
70. <http://www.cyc.com>.
71. <http://www.mpi-inf.mpg.de/yago-naga/yago>.
72. <http://www.wolframaplha.com>.

73. E. Nagel and J. R. Newman, *Gödel's Proof* (New York: New York University Press, 1958).

74. Douglas R. Hofstadter, *I Am a Strange Loop* (New York: Basic Books, 2007).

75. Antonio Damasio, *Self Comes to Mind: Constructing the Conscious Brain* (New York: Vintage Books, 2012).

76. Stephen A. Cook, 'The Complexity of Theorem-Proving Procedures', *STOC '71: Proceedings of the Third Annual ACM Symposium on Theory of Computing* (1971), 151–8.

77. Charles L. Forgy, 'Rete: A Fast Algorithm for the Many Pattern/Many Object Pattern Match Problem', *Artificial Intelligence*, 19/1 (1982), 17–37.

78. Haroon Siddique, 'Timeline: Transatlantic Airline Bomb Plot', *The Guardian*, Tuesday, 8 Sept. 2009.

79. Colin Reimer Dawson, 'Explaining-Away Effects in Rule-Learning: Evidence for Generative Probabilistic Inference in Infants and Adults', doct. diss., University of Arizona, 2011.

80. Judea Pearl, *Probabilistic Reasoning in Intelligent Systems: Networks of Plausible Inference* (San Francisco: Morgan Kaufmann, 1988).

81. David C. Knill and Alexandre Pouget, 'The Bayesian Brain: The Role of Uncertainty in Neural Coding and Computation', *Trends in Neurosciences*, 27/12 (2004), 712–19.

82. Stephen Baker, *The Numerati* (Boston: Houghton Mifflin Books, 2008).

83. 'The 9–11 Commission Report: Final Report of the National Commission on Terrorist Attacks Upon the United States', <http://www.fas.org/irp/offdocs/911comm.html>.

84. Paulo C. G. Costa, Kuo-Chu Chang, Kathryn Laskey, Tod Levitt, and Wei Sun, 'High-Level Fusion: Issues in Developing a Formal Theory', *International Conference on Information Fusion* (2010).

85. Oliver Selfridge, 'Pandemonium: A Paradigm for Learning in Mechanisation of Thought Processes', *Proceedings of a Symposium Held at the National Physical Laboratory* (Nov. 1958).

86. Pamela McCorduck, *Machines Who Think: 25th Anniversary Edition* (Natick, Mass.: A K Peters, Ltd., 2004).

87. Victor Lessor, Richard Fennel, Lee Erman, and Raj Reddy, 'Organization of the Hearsay II Speech Understanding System', *IEEE Transactions on Acoustics, Speech and Signal Processing* (1975).

88. H. Penny Nii, 'Blackboard Systems', in Avron Barr, Paul R. Cohen, and Edward A. Feigenbaum (eds.), *The Handbook of Artificial Intelligence*, vol. iv (Reading, Mass.: Addison-Wesley, 1989), 182.

89. Douglas R. Hofstadter, *The Copycat Project: An Experiment in Nondeterminism and Creative Analogies* (Cambridge, Mass.: MIT CSAIL Publications, 1984).

90. Melanie Mitchell and Douglas R. Hofstadter, 'The Emergence of Understanding in a Computer Model of Concepts and Analogy-Making', *Physica D*, 42 (1990), 322–34.

91. Gautam Shroff, Saurabh Sharma, Puneet Agarwal, and Shefali Bhat, 'A Blackboard Architecture for Data-Intensive Information Fusion using Locality-Sensitive Hashing', *Proceedings of the 14th International Conference on Information Fusion* (2011).

CHAPTER 5

92. 'Pawan Sinha on how brains learn to see', TED Talk by Pawan Sinha, MIT, 25 Feb. 2010.

93. Jeremy Ginsberg, Matthew H. Mohebbi, Rajan S. Patel, Lynnette Brammer, Mark S. Smolinski, and Larry Brilliant, 'Detecting Influenza Epidemics Using Search Engine Query Data', *Nature* 457 (19 Feb. 2009), 1012–14.

94. Vivek Ranadive and Kevin Maney, *The Two-Second Advantage* (New York: Random House 2011).

95. Gautam Shroff, Puneet Agarwal, and Lipika Dey, 'Enterprise Information Fusion', *Proceedings of the 14th International Conference on Information Fusion* (2011).

96. Kashmir Hill, 'How Target Figured Out a Teen Girl Was Pregnant Before Her Father Did', *Forbes* (Feb. 2012).

97. Ian Ayres, *Super Crunchers: Why Thinking by Numbers is the New Way to Be Smart* (New York: Random House, 2007).

98. Paul J. Werbos, 'Beyond Regression: New Tools for Prediction and Analysis in the Behavioural Sciences', PhD thesis, Harvard University, 1974.

99. David E. Rumelhart, Geoffrey E. Hinton, and Ronald J. Williams, 'Learning Representations by Back-Propagating Errors', *Nature* 323 (8 Oct. 1986), 533–6.

100. M. Schmidt and H. Lipson, 'Distilling Free-Form Natural Laws from Experimental Data', *Science*, 324 (2009), 81–5.

101. Malcolm Gladwell, *Outliers* (New York: Little, Brown & Co. 2008).

102. Daniel Kahneman, *Thinking, Fast and Slow* (New York: Farrar, Straus and Giroux, 2011).

103. Rajesh Rao and Olac Fuentes, 'Learning Navigational Behaviours Using a Predictive Sparse Distributed Memory', *4th International Conference on Simulation of Adaptive Behavior* (1996).

104. Miao Wan, Arne Jönsson, Cong Wang, Lixiang Li, and Yixian Yang, 'A Random Indexing Approach for Web User Clustering and Web Prefetching', *Asia Pacific Conference on Knowledge Discovery from Data (PAKDD)* (2011).

105. Itamar Arel, C. Rose, Thomas P. Karnowski, 'Deep Machine Learning: A New Frontier in Artificial Intelligence Research', *IEEE Computational Intelligence Magazine* (Nov. 2010).

106. Jeff Hawkins, *On Intelligence* (New York: Times Books, 2004).

107. Vernon B. Mountcastle, 'An Organizing Principle for Cerebral Function: The Unit Model and the Distributed System', in Gerald M. Edelman and Vernon B. Mountcastle (eds.), *The Mindful Brain* (Cambridge, Mass.: MIT Press, 1978).

108. As related by John Locke, in *An Essay Concerning Human Understanding* (1690).

109. R. Held, Y. Ostrovsky, B. Degelder, T. Gandhi, S. Ganesh, U. Mathur, and P. Sinha, 'The Newly Sighted Fail to Match Seen with Felt', *Nature Neuroscience* 14/5 (2011), 551–3.

110. Dileep George and Jeff Hawkins, 'Towards a Mathematical Theory of Cortical Micro-Circuits', *Computational Biology* 5/10 (2009).

111. Honglak Lee, Roger Grosse, Rajesh Ranganath, and Andrew Y. Ng, 'Unsupervised Learning of Hierarchical Representations with Convolutional Deep Belief Networks', *Communications of the ACM* 54/10 (Nov. 2011).

112. <https://developers.google.com/speed/articles/web-metrics>.

113. Ed Bullmore and Olaf Sporns, 'Complex Brain Networks: Graph Theoretical Analysis of Structural and Functional Systems', *Nature Reviews of Neuroscience* 10 (Mar. 2009), 186–98.

CHAPTER 6

114. M. Montemerlo et al., 'Junior: The Stanford Entry in the Urban Challenge', *Journal of Field Robotics*, 25/9 (2008), 569–97.

115. Norbert Wiener, *Cybernetics: Or Control and Communication in the Animal and the Machine* (Cambridge, Mass: MIT Press 1961).

116. B. F. Skinner, *About Behaviourism* (New York: Vintage Books, 1974).

117. E. W. Dijkstra, 'A Note on Two Problems in Connexion with Graphs', *Numerische Mathematik* 1 (1959), 269–71.

118. P. E. Hart, N. J. Nilsson, and B. Raphael, 'A Formal Basis for the Heuristic Determination of Minimum Cost Paths', *IEEE Transactions on Systems Science and Cybernetics SSC* 4/2 (1968).

119. Edmond Selous, *Thought-Transference (or What?) in Birds* (London: Constable & Co, 1931).

120. Peter Miller, *Smart Swarm* (London: Collins Books 2010).

121. J. Kennedy and R. Eberhart, 'Particle Swarm Optimisation', *Proceedings of IEEE International Conference on Neural Networks* (1995).

122. Richard M. Karp, 'Reducibility Among Combinatorial Problems', in R. E. Miller and J. W. Thatcher (eds.), *Complexity of Computer Computations* (New York: Plenum, 1972), 85–103.

123. A. Newell and H. A. Simon, 'GPS: A Program that Simulates Human Thought', Defense Technical Information Center, 1961.

124. M. Dorigo, 'Optimisation, Learning and Natural Algorithms', PhD Thesis, Politecnico di Milano, Italy, 1992.

125. Christine Solomon, 'Ants Can Solve Constraint Satisfaction Problems', *IEEE Transactions on Evolutionary Computation*, 6/4 (2002).

126. John H. Holland, *Adaptation in Natural and Artificial Systems* (Ann Arbor: University of Michigan Press, 1975).

127. T. L. Friedman, *Hot, Flat, and Crowded: Why We Need a Green Revolution–and How it Can Renew America* (New York: Farrar Straus & Giroux, 2008).

128. Vint Cerf, 'Computer Science in the 21st Century', keynote lecture at the ACM-India meeting, Chennai, India, 25 Jan. 2013.

129. P. H. Winston, 'The Strong Story Hypothesis and the Directed Perception Hypothesis', *AAAI Fall Symposium Series* (2011).

130. I. Tattersall, *Becoming Human: Evolution and Human Uniqueness* (New York: Mariner Books, 1999).

EPILOGUE

131. Margaret A. Boden, 'Computer Models of Creativity', *AI Magazine*, 30/3 (Fall 2009), 23–34.

INDEX